"CUIDICH 'N RIGH"

A
HISTORY
OF THE

Queen's Own Highlanders
(Seaforth and Camerons)

by
Lieutenant Colonel Angus Fairrie

Introduction

This booklet has been prepared at Regimental Headquarters of the Queen's Own Highlanders, Inverness, using sources of material in the Regimental library. It has been written in response to the hundreds of questions about the Regiment which are received at Regimental Headquarters each year.

The booklet is not intended to be a comprehensive history of the Regiment, and no literary merit is claimed for it. But it is hoped that it will serve as a book of quick reference, which will provide an outline of the story of the Regiment and give supplementary information in the Annexes, so that the reader or the researcher who wishes to study a particular aspect in greater detail has a start-point for further reading.

The Regimental Trustees would like to put on record their gratitude to the Highlands and Islands Development Board for financial assistance in the publication of the booklet.

ISBN 0 9508986 0 0

Printed by Sunprint, 36 Tay Street, Perth and 40 Craigs, Stirling. In association with Peter Gray (Scotland) Ltd.

Field Marshal His Royal Highness, Prince Philip Duke of Edinburgh, KG, KT, OM, GBE, Colonel in Chief of the Queen's Own Highlanders.

Contents

CHAPTER I — THE REGIMENTS BEFORE 1881

1. CLAN BACKGROUND OF THE REGIMENTS

Kenneth MacKenzie, Earl of Seaforth (1744-1781) who raised the 78th (later 72nd) Highlanders in 1778.

The MacKenzies of Seaforth

The Mackenzies, or Clan Kenneth, first held lands in Kintail in the early 14th Century. For the next 300 years their influence expanded until the clan territory extended across Ross-shire from coast to coast, and also included the island of Lewis. In 1609 Kenneth, Chief of the Clan Kenneth, was created Lord MacKenzie of Kintail, and his son Kenneth became 1st Earl of Seaforth in 1623. He took his title from Loch Seaforth in the island of Lewis.

The Clan MacKenzie were staunch supporters of the Stuart Kings, and so became inextricably involved in the tragic politics and wars of the time. For his support of the Jacobite Rising of 1715, William Dubh, the 5th Earl, was attainted and his peerage and his lands were forfeited. Thanks to the recommendation of General George Wade, the General Officer Commanding Scotland, William Dubh was pardoned in 1726, and the family managed to recover its lands in 1741, on payment of a crippling sum of nearly

£23,000. When the 1745 Jacobite Rising took place only four years later, the 5th Earl's grandson, Lord Fortrose, had no alternative but to remain uncommitted, whatever the traditional loyalties of his house. This enforced change of heart had its reward in 1771 when his son Kenneth was created Earl of Seaforth in the Irish peerage.

But the restoration of the Seaforth lands and title came at a bleak time in Highland history. The Government, in its determination that there should never be another Jacobite Rising, had set about dismantling the clan system with uncompromising severity. While the disarming of the Highlanders removed the military threat, the deliberate repression also brought a time of misery for the whole country.

Faced with economic ruin and the destruction of the traditional way of life in the Highlands, the clan chiefs realised that one way to provide employment and bring money to their tenants was by raising regiments of Highland infantry. When in 1771 Kenneth Earl of Seaforth offered to raise a regiment for the King in gratitude for the restoration of his title, his motives were more than just patriotic: there were compelling social and economic reasons as well, because a regiment would bring employment and income to his clansmen, and possibly even prize money too; and the authority to raise a regiment meant that he had the gift of commissions to offer to his kinsmen.

By 1778, after three years of war in the American colonies, recruiting problems led the government to accept with gratitude the Earl of Seaforth's offer to raise a Highland regiment. Kenneth Earl of Seaforth commanded his 78th Highlanders for three years until he died on the voyage out to India. He had no male heir, and so his cousin Colonel Thomas MacKenzie-Humberston succeeded him as Chief of the Clan MacKenzie and Colonel of the 78th. But he died at Bombay in 1783 from wounds received at sea in a fight against the Mahrattas.

Francis Humberston MacKenzie, younger brother of Thomas MacKenzie-Humberston, succeeded as Mackenzie of Seaforth and as 21st Chief of Clan Mackenzie in 1783. He sat as MP for Ross-shire from 1784-1790. After the death of his brother Thomas, there was no direct connection between the 72nd Highlanders (as the 78th had been renumbered in 1786) and the Seaforth family, for Francis Humberston MacKenzie of Seaforth had no military service and so could not be appointed Colonel.

After the outbreak of war in 1793 his chance came when the Government again required extra infantry regiments. He applied to raise his own regiment of Highlanders from the Clan MacKenzie lands, and was authorised to do so by Letter of Service in March 1793. He was commissioned as Lieutenant Colonel Commandant of the 78th.

Francis Humberston MacKenzie of Seaforth (1754-1815) who raised the 78th Highlanders in 1793.

He held the Colonelcy of the 78th for three years and then passed it on to his brother in law, Colonel Alexander MacKenzie of Belmaduthy. In 1797 Colonel Francis Humberston MacKenzie of Seaforth was created Lord Seaforth and Baron MacKenzie of Kintail. He continued his military interest by raising and commanding the Ross-shire Militia, and was eventually promoted Lieutenant General in 1808.

He became Governor of Barbados in 1801 and did much to improve the working conditions of the slaves on the sugar plantations. But his own West Indian estates contributed to his financial ruin and he was obliged to sell the family estates including Kintail.

The male line of the family ended with him, for his four sons predeceased him. His great grandson Colonel J. A. F. H. Stewart-MacKenzie, was created Baron Seaforth of Brahan in 1921, and was Honorary Colonel of the 4th Bn Seaforth Highlanders TA. He was the last member of the family to hold the title of Lord Seaforth and died without heir in 1923.

In 1978 the Lord Lyon King of Arms recognized Major The Right Hon The Earl of Cromartie as 'Cabar Feidh', Chief of Clan MacKenzie. Lord Cromartie served as a regular officer in the Seaforth Highlanders and won the MC serving with the 4th Seaforth in France in 1940. Thus the connection between Clan MacKenzie and the Regiment is still strong.

The Camerons of Erracht

Although the forebears of Clan Cameron have lived in Lochaber since time immemorial, the first clan chief who can be established historically is Donald Dubh, traditionally the 11th Chief. He came to power in the late 14th Century, and unified the Lochaber tribes into a clan which earned an awesome reputation for its fighting qualities and for loyalty to the Sovereign.

Ewen MacAllan of Lochiel, 13th Chief and grandson of Donald Dubh, married twice. The present Chiefs of Clan Cameron, the Camerons of Lochiel, are descended from him by his first wife; and the Camerons of Erracht were descended from him by the second. For generations the Camerons of Erracht held their lands on a wadset lease from Lochiel, and held the position of chieftains in the hierarchy of the clan.

The defeat of the Jacobites at Culloden in 1746, brought the traditional way of life in the Highlands to an end. The loyalty which Clan Cameron had shown to Bonnie Prince Charlie and the Stuart cause brought severe retribution from the Government. Highlanders were forbidden by Act of Parliament to carry arms or wear the Highland dress; the Episcopal Church was proscribed; Fort William was strongly garrisoned by regular troops; the leaders of Clan Cameron were exiled or imprisoned; the Lochiel estate was forfeited to the Crown; and Achnacarry, and many of the houses in Lochaber were destroyed.

But despite this harsh repression after Culloden, life in Lochaber had to go on. One of the few prominent members of Clan Cameron to escape exile or imprisonment was Ewen Cameron of Erracht, who had been prevented by ill health from joining the Jacobite army. He was still resident at Erracht and so, in the absence of the exiled Lochiel family, he was one of the natural leaders of the local community in Lochaber. His eldest son Alan was born at Erracht in 1750, grew up in Lochaber, and also earned a position of respect and responsibility.

Alan Cameron was educated in Inverness and at Aberdeen University and, having returned to Erracht to run the farm, he became a prominent and popular figure in Lochaber. However in 1772 he had a serious dispute with a neighbour and kinsman, Alexander Cameron of Muirshearlich, and killed him in a duel. Faced with a possible charge of murder, he was forced to go abroad.

His five years in the West Indies and North America turned out to be highly eventful. When the War of Independence broke out he was working in the Indian Department in the North American colonies, and volunteered for service with the Crown. He was commissioned in the Queen's Royal Regiment of Rangers and employed on intelligence work. But his activities led to his capture by the American rebels and to two and a half years as a prisoner of war. Three times he managed to escape, but was recaptured each time, and was badly injured when he fell off a roof in attempting to break out of Philadelphia gaol. In 1778 he was exchanged for an American rebel prisoner and was returned to London, still a cripple.

For the next fifteen years he lived in London, and his fortunes improved. In 1779 he married Ann Phillips, 14 year old daughter of Nathaniel Phillips, a wealthy merchant and owner of estates in the West Indies. Alan Cameron's father died the same year, and so he succeeded to the wadset lease and title of Erracht. In London he became a prominent figure in the Scottish community, playing a leading part in the political lobby to obtain the repeal of the Act of Proscription of the Highland dress. Among his friends were William Pitt the Prime Minister, and Henry Dundas the Secretary for War.

During this time in London, Alan Cameron of Erracht developed the idea of raising a Clan Cameron regiment. He had had military experience in America, he was well respected in Lochaber, and now he had the financial backing of a wealthy father-in-law. The idea had acceptable prospects as a financial venture, and it promised to do something practical to help the devastated economy of Lochaber by providing an ideal form of employment for the young men of Clan Cameron, with their traditional fighting qualities.

He made repeated applications to the Government for permission to raise a regiment, but he was unsuccessful until the commitments of the war with France resulted in an increase in the number of infantry regiments above the normal peacetime establishment of 77. On 17th August 1793, Alan Cameron of Erracht was authorised by Letter of Service to raise the 79th Regiment of Foot, and was commissioned as its Major Commandant.

Alan Cameron of Erracht commanded the 79th himself from 1793 until 1808, when he handed over command to his eldest son Lieutenant Colonel Phillips Cameron. He remained as Colonel of the 79th until he died as Lieutenant General Sir Alan Cameron of Erracht KCB in 1828. Nicknamed 'Cia mar tha' from his normal Gaelic greeting, he was very much the father figure of the Cameron Highlanders.

Although four sons served in the 79th, there are now no male descendants who bear the name Cameron of Erracht. But Erracht's ambition that the 79th should be the regiment of Clan Cameron was fulfilled. The 79th, and

their successors the Queen's Own Highlanders, have had many members of Clan Cameron as officers and soldiers. The Camerons of Lochiel have served with great distinction as Regular, Militia and Territorial officers of the regiment. The Regiment today remains intensely proud of its Cameron and Lochaber origins.

Alan Cameron of Erracht (1750-1828) who raised the 79th Highlanders (or Cameronian Volunteers) in 1793.

2. THE 72nd HIGHLANDERS FROM 1778 TO 1881

The Raising of the 78th (later 72nd) or Earl of Seaforth's Regiment

January-May 1778

On 29th December 1777 Kenneth Earl of Seaforth received his commission as Lieutenant Colonel Commandant, and on 8th January 1778 the Letter of Service was signed which authorized him to raise his Highland regiment. There followed four months of hectic recruiting to find the 47 officers and 1082 men required to fill the establishment.

The earlier Highland regiments had already tapped the manpower of the Highlands, but Lord Seaforth took every advantage of the traditional loyalty of his clan, and managed to recruit the majority of his men from Ross-shire and Lewis. He made up the number with about 300 men from the Lowlands, England and Ireland. In May 1778 he concentrated his men at Elgin for the mandatory inspection by a General Officer, and on 15th May 1778 the regiment was passed by Major General Robert Skene as fit for service. It was designated the 78th Regiment of (Highland) Foot.

Uniform of the 78th (later 72nd) Highlanders

1778

The 78th wore the normal uniform of Highland infantry at the time, which was the kilt and belted plaid of Government (or Black Watch) tartan, with red jacket, red and white hose, and black buckled shoes. In the 18th Century each regiment was distinguished by its facing colour ('facing' was the material used to 'face' or partly line the jackets), by the type of lace on its jackets, and by the pattern of loops in which the lace was arranged. The 78th had yellow facings and the lace loops were 'bastion' shaped.

The regiment wore the 'hummel bonnet' embellished with ostrich feathers, a forerunner, although much smaller of the feather bonnet of today. The Grenadier Company wore mitre caps of bearskin.

The regiment received its first stand of Colours provided by the Earl of Seaforth.

'The Mutiny of the Macraes'

September 1778

A few days after its embodiment and inspection the Earl of Seaforth's regiment marched out of Elgin. Great Britain

Uniforms of the 78th (later 72nd) Highlanders in 1778.

(From a painting by R. Simkin)

was under threat of invasion by the French, and so the 78th was deployed first to Aberdeen, and then to Edinburgh and on the west coast, to counter any French attack. Before leaving Edinburgh there was the famous incident known as 'the affair of the Wild Macraes'.

One of the characteristics of the Highland regiments when they were raised was that the soldiers, while keen to fight for king and country, were accustomed, under the clan system, to proper leadership and to a standard of discipline that was traditionally fair. They soon found that the Government, under pressure to find troops for the war, was not always scrupulous in keeping to the terms of the Letters of Service, the contracts under which the regiments were raised. There were about seventeen instances of 'Mutiny' where Highland soldiers refused to carry out orders which seemed to them to be in breach of their contracts.

One of the most celebrated cases occurred in the Earl of Seaforth's regiment in September 1778. The 78th had been ordered to move to the Channel Islands but, when they paraded for embarkation, half the regiment refused to march to the ships at Leith. Led by a group of Kintail men, 'the Wild Macraes', they marched instead to the summit of Arthur's seat where they entrenched themselves. Their grievances concerned their pay and bounty money, the unfamiliar rigidity of military discipline, and a rumour that the regiment had been sold to the East India Company.

It was to the credit of the Commander in Chief in Scotland, of Lord Seaforth and his officers, and also of the mutineers themselves, that an honourable compromise was reached. A Court of Inquiry found that their complaints had no basis, while the mutineers, having aired their grievances and demonstrated the traditional independence of the Highlander, were granted immunity from disciplinary action.

The 78th (later 72nd) in the Channel Islands   1778-1781

The 78th eventually sailed from Leith in October and, on arrival in the Channel Islands, were split up with half the regiment in Guernsey and half in Jersey. They expected to remain there for the winter and then to sail for the war in America but, in April 1779, the French made an abortive attempt to land in Jersey. They were repulsed without difficulty by Major Thomas MacKenzie Humberston and five companies of the 78th who, with the Jersey Militia and Artillery, deployed on the cliffs at St Ouen's Bay.

The 78th (later 72nd) at the Battle of Jersey   1781

In January 1781 a French force made a more determined effort to capture Jersey when, led by Baron de Rullecourt, a force of 1,200 troops attempted a surprise landing during the night. About 700 French troops got ashore and succeeded in occupying the capital of Jersey, St Helier. But although the Lieutenant Governor of Jersey capitulated to the French, the British garrison and the Jersey Militia counter-attacked the invaders. Major Francis Pierson of the 95th (Yorkshire) Regiment, who was the senior British officer present, led a force which included the five companies of the 78th Highlanders. They advanced into St Helier and, after a brisk street fight, killed Baron de Rullecourt and released the Lieutenant Governor.

The 78th earned much credit for their decisive and effective action in recapturing the capital of Jersey and in thwarting the French attempt to seize the island.

The 78th (later 72nd)'s Voyage to India   1781-1782

The 78th left the Channel Islands in May 1781 and embarked at Portsmouth for India. Their ten month voyage was one of the most miserable episodes in the history of the regiment. The Earl of Seaforth died of a heart attack on 27th August 1781 while the fleet was off West Africa. By the time the 78th arrived in Madras on 31st March 1782, nearly 250 men had died of scurvy and tropical diseases.

The 78th (later 72nd) on service with the East India Company   1782-1798

At the time when the 78th arrived in India for service with the East India Company only a small part of India, including Bengal, Madras and part of the East Coast, was actually under British rule. The object of the East India Company was trade rather than conquest but, as it operated in direct competition with the French, its treaties and trading agreements had had to be backed by military strength. For the next 15½ years the regiment was to take part in campaigns among the independent Indian states by which the East India Company expanded its trade and its influence.

The 78th landed at Madras in 1782 at the start of the hottest part of the summer, greatly weakened by disease, and still dressed in full Highland uniform. For several months it was to suffer greatly from sickness and heat exhaustion, but its comfort was improved by the issue of tropical uniform of white trousers and gaiters, and the red jackets were worn with the linings removed. The round hat, with white linen cover, was worn instead of the feather bonnet. The regiment was to be out of Highland dress until its return to Great Britain in 1798.

The 78th (later 72nd)'s first actions in India   1782-1783

During its first year in India, the 78th had a chance to recover from the voyage and to acclimatise to the heat. There was a minor engagement at Arnee, and a naval battle against the French in which a detachment of Highlanders acted as Marines. Its first major actions were the successful captures of the port of Cuddaldore from the French, and of the fort of Palghautcherry from Tippoo, Sultan of Mysore.

Reduction in the Army, The 78th renumbered as the 72nd   1783-1786

When the war in America ended in 1783 the regiments raised for service in the war were all due to be disbanded. But the military commitment in America was superceded by the deteriorating circumstances in India, and so the regiments serving there were retained on the establishment. The 78th were thus fortuitously reprieved.

The soldiers of the 78th had been enlisted for 'three years or until the end of the Rebellion', and so when the war in America ended they were entitled to be discharged. 300 opted to serve on in India for a bounty of 10 guineas, while the remainder returned home. The regiment was brought up to strength by volunteers from other less senior regiments which were ordered to Britain for disbandment.

The disbandment of regiments at home resulted in the 78th being renumbered in 1786 as the 72nd Regiment of Foot.

An Officer of the 78th (later 72nd) Highlanders in India 1782.

After it had been renumbered, the 72nd received new Colours provided by Major General James Murray, Colonel of the Regiment. These were its second Stand of Colours.

The 72nd in the Carnatic Campaign   1789-1792

Tippoo, Sultan of Mysore, had remained a constant threat to the East India Company's activities in South India. Having failed to persuade France to stir up war with Britain in 1789, he invaded the protected state of Travancore. For the next three years the Madras Army tried to bring Tippoo to battle.

The 72nd formed part of the European Brigade which successfully captured a series of hill forts in preparation for the invasion of Mysore. In 1791 the 72nd earned particular praise from Lord Cornwallis for their part in the attack on Bangalore, and in December 1791 they successfully stormed the strongly held hill fortresses of Savendroog and Outra Durgam. They were present at the capture of Tippoo's capital, Seringapatam, which brought the campaign to an end.

A welcome outcome of the campaign was the payment of prize money by the East India Company to the troops which had taken part in the campaign. A soldier's share was £14, rather more than a year's wages.

The 72nd in campaigns against the French and Dutch
1793-1796

The East India Company's affairs now took on a more international look. In 1793 the 72nd took part in the seige and capture from the French of the fortified settlement of Pondicherry. In 1794, following the French Revolution, Holland had been defeated by the French and had been forced into an alliance. The Madras government was able to send an expedition against the Dutch colony of Ceylon. The force, which included the 72nd, landed at Trincomalee in 1795 and, after a short campaign with no major engagements, the Dutch capitulated. Ceylon, (now Sri Lanka) was added to the East India Company's territory.

72nd BATTLE HONOURS

For their service in India and Ceylon from 1782 to 1798 the 72nd were awarded the Battle Honours:
'CARNATIC'
'HINDOOSTAN'
'MYSORE'

The 72nd at Perth   1798-1800

When the 72nd were eventually ordered to return home, after 17 years abroad, the Government was faced with a desperate shortage of men for its military commitments in the colonies and to protect Great Britain against Revolutionary France. The regiment was ordered to draft men to other regiments, while a cadre of officers, sergeants and drummers returned to Great Britain to recruit. It was based at Perth from 1798 to 1800 while it built up its numbers, was reissued with Highland dress, and received its third stand of Colours.

Recruiting for the 72nd in 1800

The 72nd had not found recruiting easy in Scotland, because the war with France had needed an unprecedented expansion in the Army, and recruiting parties of other regiments had taken almost every available man. By 1800 its strength was still only 214, and so it was ordered to move to Ireland which was traditionally a more productive source of recruits.

All the Scottish regiments were faced with the same recruiting problem, and so the Government took the drastic action of ordering the Fencible regiments to produce volunteers for the regular army; the Colonels of the Fencibles being allowed to recommend one officer for a regular commission as an Ensign (i.e. 2/Lt) for every 50 volunteers. The 72nd thus gained 589 men and 13 Ensigns from the Fencibles.
(Note. Fencible soldiers were enlisted for the defence of Great Britain, and had no obligation to serve overseas. They were not normally allowed to transfer to the regular army).

The 72nd in Ireland   1800-1805

The 72nd spent five years in Ireland, being stationed first at Newry, and subsequently split up, with companies dispersed widely. The regiment combined recruiting with maintenance of law and order, the duties including guarding the mail coaches, seizing illicit whiskey stills, and other police work.

The 72nd at the Capture of the Cape of Good Hope
1805-1806

When France had defeated the Dutch in 1794, and forced Holland into an alliance, the harbours of the Cape of Good Hope had been opened to French warships. This threat to the route to India, and the need for a halfway port on the journey to the East, prompted Britain to seize the Cape in 1795; but it was returned to the Dutch in 1802 after the Peace of Amiens. In 1805 as Napoleon prepared to invade Great Britain, the Government assembled a secret expedition, led by Lt Gen Sir David Baird, to occupy the Cape again. The force included a Highland Brigade consisting of the 71st, 72nd and 93rd Highlanders. The expedition landed at Lospards Bay on 6th January 1806, despite the fire of a party of Dutch skirmishers, and it then pursued the defenders to the Blue Mountains and inflicted a quick and convincing defeat.

72nd BATTLE HONOUR
For their service at the capture of the Cape of Good Hope, the 72nd were awarded the Battle Honour:
'CAPE OF GOOD HOPE 1806'

The 72nd in Cape Colony and Mauritius
1805-1821

The 72nd were to spend 16 years abroad on colonial garrison duty. After the capture of the Cape of Good Hope they were stationed at Simon's Town, Cape Town and Stellenbosch. In December 1810 the regiment took part in an expedition to capture the French island of Mauritius, where the colony surrendered to the British without resistance. The 72nd remained as garrison in Mauritius for three years, returning to Cape Town in 1814. They had a short excursion to India when they were sent for service against the Rajah of Nepal. But, on arrival at Calcutta, they found the war was over and so the regiment returned to Cape Colony, where it remained until 1821.

2nd Battalion 72nd
1804-1816

In 1804 a 2nd Battalion was authorised. It remained in Great Britain as the feeder battalion for the 1st/72nd in South Africa and Mauritius. It served mainly in Ireland. After the Napoleonic Wars the Army was reduced in strength and the 2nd/72nd was disbanded at Londonderry in 1816.

The 72nd change to Infantry of the Line
1809

On 11th April 1809 the War Office decided on a drastic reduction in the number of Highland regiments on the grounds that the population of the Highlands could not provide enough recruits. The 71st, 72nd, 73rd, 74th, 75th and 91st Highlanders were ordered to cease being Highland and to discontinue wearing the Highland Dress. The 72nd had to adopt the tropical uniform for a regiment of the line, with red jacket, white trousers and round hat.

(Note: This most unpopular of orders left only five Highland Regiments on the Establishment, the 42nd, 78th, 79th, 92nd and 93rd. The order left not only resentment, but a determination in each regiment to regain the Highland status. In the event this was achieved, the 72nd becoming Highlanders again in 1823. The final stage was the Army Reforms of 1881 when the 72nd, 73rd, 75th and 91st all regained the kilt).

Despite the loss of the kilt and the Highland name, the 72nd did manage to preserve much of its Highland character. It continued to use Scottish drum beats, it kept its pipers (although on an unofficial basis), it preserved its Scottish traditions, and the officers and soldiers were predominantly Scottish. It also incorporated minor distinctions in its uniform, such as the thistles engraved on officers cross belt plates and embroidered on their coat tails.

The 72nd in the early Kaffir War
1817-1821

The British Government had originally had no intention of extending the limits of Cape Colony. But the Dutch settlers who had been displaced tended to spread up the east coast of South Africa, and this brought them up against the Bantu tribes which had for two centuries been expanding their territory Southwards.

The 72nd spent four years patrolling and manning frontier posts in the east of Cape Colony to prevent the Kaffir tribes raiding the Boer settlements.

The 72nd return to Great Britain
1822

The 72nd left South Africa in December 1821, and returned to Great Britain. It remained in the South of England until 1823 when it moved to the Channel Islands for garrison duty.

The 72nd become a Highland Regiment again
1823-1825

In a letter from the Horse Guards dated 19th December 1823, the 72nd received the most welcome news that it was to become a Highland regiment again with the title 'The 72nd or Duke of Albany's Own Highlanders'. It was to be dressed in trews instead of the kilt.

After 14 years as a line regiment, the 72nd was to fulfil its ambition of becoming a Highland regiment again, and it undertook the conversion with the greatest enthusiasm. In September 1824 it returned to Scotland, after 24 years absence, and was quartered at Edinburgh Castle. It set about recruiting in the Highlands, and achieved a thorough infusion of new blood.

It took at least a year to produce the new uniform. It was unique in the Army: in deference to the Duke of Albany, the 72nd was to wear trews of Royal Stuart tartan in the Prince Charles Edward Stuart sett; it wore red coatees and feather bonnets like other Highland regiments. A radical change of uniform such as this meant that a complete set of buttons, badges, dirks, piper's sporrans and other accoutrements had to be designed, approved and manufactured. The final stage was the presentation of new Colours to the 72nd on Bruntsfield Links, Edinburgh on 1st August 1825. The Colours, which were the fourth Stand to be carried by the regiment, were provided by the Colonel of the Regiment, General Sir John Hope, and presented by Lady Hope. The Colours bore the new regimental badge, the Cipher 'F' and Coronet of Prince Fredrick, Duke of York and Albany, in the corners.

The 72nd Highlanders in about 1840.   *(From a print published by W. Spooner)*

The 72nd in Ireland and London   1825-1828

By 1825 the 72nd was fully restored to being a Highland regiment in name, dress and in the nationality of most of its men, and it was sent to Ireland in the familiar peace keeping role. It moved to London in 1827, being quartered in the Tower of London, and took part in ceremonial duties with the Household troops. Its distinctive uniform of feather bonnets, red coatees and trews gave it such a head start over the Foot Guards that it caught the attention of the Duke of Wellington.

The 72nd in Cape Colony   1828-1840

In 1828 the 72nd left London for Canterbury, and thence for Gravesend, where it embarked for South Africa once more. It was to remain in Cape Colony for 12 years of garrison duty, interrupted by a year of operations against the Kaffirs.

The 72nd in the Kaffir War   1834-1835

In 1834 the Kaffirs, one of the main Bantu tribes who had for years harrassed the European settlers in the East of Cape Colony, made a particularly strong raid and removed a large proportion of the settlers cattle. As part of the military reaction to the Kaffir attack, an expedition which included the 72nd was mounted. The regiment took a prominent part in the campaign in which the Kaffirs were firmly subdued, the cattle recovered, and Kaffir territory up to the Kei river annexed.

The 72nd in England   1840-1841

The 72nd returned to Great Britain in 1840. It received its fifth Stand of Colours at Windsor Castle on 8th July 1841. They were presented by the Duke of Wellington and the parade was watched by Queen Victoria, Prince Albert, and the King of Prussia.

The 72nd in the Industrial Riots   1842

It was a time of industrial unrest in Britain and in 1842 the 72nd, having moved by train to Manchester, was deployed among the manufacturing towns of Lancashire. It had the unpleasant task of riot control and was ordered to open fire on rioters at Preston and Blackburn.

The 72nd in Ireland   1843-1844

In April 1843 the 72nd moved to Ireland where it spent over a year on internal security and garrison duties.

The 72nd in Gibraltar   1844-1848

In November 1844 the 72nd embarked for Gibraltar. Its time there was spent on garrison duties and on improving the fortifications. Among the other regiments there were the 79th Cameron Highlanders and during this, the first occasion when the two regiments served together, a firm friendship was established between them.

riots occurred, before returning to Barbados. During its time in the West Indies, detachments also served in St Lucia, Demerara, Grenada and Tobago.

ie 72nd Highlanders in 1854.
(From a print published by R. Ackermann)

The 72nd in the West Indies   1848-1851

In February 1848 the 72nd left Gibraltar for Barbados. uring its first year it had a bad outbreak of yellow fever in nich four officers and 59 soldiers died. The regiment ent from December 1849 to May 1851 in Trinidad where

The 72nd in Canada   1851-1854

The 72nd left Barbados for Halifax, Canada in July 1851. In September it marched to New Brunswick and returned to Halifax in 1853.

It was a particularly frustrating period for the 72nd. The world's attention at the time was very much on the Russian threat to the Middle East and India, and war seemed imminent. Many of the regular army regiments were being withdrawn from Canada, and the depot Companies of the 72nd in Great Britain were required to send drafts to bring the 42nd and 79th up to strength. In Canada the 72nd awaited sailing orders with the greatest impatience. They eventually left Canada for Ireland in October 1854, by which time the Crimean War had started and Sebastopol was under siege.

The 72nd in Ireland   1854

On their return from Canada in October 1854, the service companies of the 72nd joined up with the depot companies and the regiment was reorganized on a war establishment. But the depot companies in Ireland had been ordered to supply every available man to bring the other Highland regiments up to establishment, and so the 72nd found itself with its service companies more than 300 men under strength. However, such was the pressure to provide reinforcements for the Crimea, that the 72nd was ordered to sail for Malta in December 1854 leaving its depot companies in Ireland to recruit.

hotographs taken in 1856 of soldiers who had served in the Crimea.

pe Major John MacDonald,
nd Highlanders.

Privates William Noble, Alexander Dawson and John Harper, 72nd Highlanders.

Colour Sergeant Andrew Taylor, 72nd Highlanders.

The 72nd in Malta   1855

The regiment arrived in Malta in January 1855 and, despite its impatience to reach the war in the Crimea, it remained there until May.

The 72nd in the Crimea   1855-1856

The regiment eventually sailed for the Crimea and arrived at Balaclava on 29th May 1855. Before it had even disembarked it was ordered to join the British expedition to destroy the Russian port of Kertch, but it did not have to land.

The 72nd joined the Highland Brigade which was commanded by Sir Colin Campbell. The brigade included the 42nd, 79th and 93rd Highlanders. Between June and the fall of Sevastopol in September, the 72nd took their share of duty in the trenches during the siege operations. They also spent a period at Kamara where the Highland Brigade was sent to support the Sardinians against an expected attack. From October 1855 until the withdrawal of the army from the Crimea in July-July 1856, the 72nd lived in the hutted camp established for the Highland Division at Kamara. (The arrival of the 1st and 2nd Bns The Royal Scots, the 71st and the 92nd Highlanders had allowed the formation of the Highland Division).

72nd BATTLE HONOUR

For their service in the Crimea, the 72nd were awarded the Battle Honour:

'SEVASTOPOL'

The 72nd in Great Britain   1856-1857

The 72nd disembarked at Portsmouth on 31st July and paraded next day at Aldershot for inspection by Queen Victoria. It was then sent to the Channel Islands, until in April 1857 it moved to Shorncliffe where it was in the same garrison as the 79th.

On 24th August 1857 the 72nd received its sixth Stand of Colours from HRH The Duke of Cambridge, the Commander in Chief.

The 72nd arrive in India for the Mutiny Campaign
1857-1858

In August-September 1857 the 72nd sailed from Portsmouth to Bombay, where it was complete by early January 1858. Although they fought in a separate theatre from the well known events in the Ganges valley, they did take part in the most successful subsidiary campaign in Central India, with the aim of containing the spread of the mutiny and pursuing bands of rebels.

The 72nd and the attack on Kotah   1858

Their first major engagement was the attack on Kotah, where the British resident and his sons had been murdered by mutineers, and the loyalty of the Rajah was suspect. The fortified town was attacked by three columns, the first of which included 260 men of the 72nd. They managed to storm through a gate blown in by the engineers, and to seize the bastion which was their objective. Then, exploiting this success, the column seized another gate and entered the city. The other columns were equally successful, and Kotah, with over 70 guns and a large magazine, was captured.

Lieutenant A. S. Cameron, VC

Lt A. S. CAMERON WINS THE VICTORIA CROSS, 30t MARCH 1858

The attack on Kotah was particularly memorable for th bravery of Lt Aylmer Cameron of the 72nd. When th second gateway was captured the column came und heavy fire from a strongly built house. Lt Cameron dashe in to the house and reached the upper floor where he kille three of the rebel musketeers before being severe wounded. However he survived, and for his prompt an gallant action was awarded the Victoria Cross. It was th first VC to be won by the 72nd.

The 72nd pursue the rebels

In June 1858 the 72nd, after a month in barracks Neemuch, was split up again among the columns formed pursue the rebels. In October a column, which included t 72nd, marched 110 miles in just over three days to preve the city of Bhopal falling to the rebels. The 72nd remaine in the field until January 1859, with detachments c operations until May. One party was estimated to hav marched over 3000 miles during the campaign.

72nd BATTLE HONOUR

For their service in the Indian Mutiny campaign, t 72nd were awarded the Battle Honour:

'CENTRAL INDIA'

The 72nd in India after the Mutiny   1859-18

The 72nd remained in India after the Mutiny campai until 1865, being stationed at Mhow, with detachments Indore. During this last year in India they moved to Poo for a few months and then embarked for home in late 186

The 72nd in Great Britain   1866-187

The 72nd were posted first to Edinburgh, where t service companies and depot companies joined up March 1866 in Edinburgh Castle. In May 1867 the regime moved by sea and rail, complete with its families, to ca at Aldershot until October. It then moved to Manchest until February 1868 when it went to Ireland again. In 1871 was ordered to India.

The 72nd in India   1871-1878

The 72nd moved to India in early 1871 and arrived at Bombay. It left its depot companies in Ireland. For the next seven years the 72nd was to be stationed in the garrison towns of what is now Pakistan; in Umballa (1871), Peshawar (1873), Nowshera (1875), Cherat (1875), Sialkot (1876). In 1878 it was ordered to march for Afghanistan to join the Kurram Valley Field Force, and this was to lead to one of the most distinguished campaigns in the history of the 72nd.

The 72nd and 91st Depot at Stirling   1873-1881

From 1873 until the Army Reforms of 1881, the Depot of the 72nd was based at Stirling. Under the 'Localisation' scheme the regiment was linked with the 91st Highlanders, and its recruiting area was Kinross, Clackmannan, Stirling, Dunbarton, Argyll, Bute and Renfrew.

The 72nd in India received regular drafts from the joint Depot, and also reinforcements from the 91st, its linked regiment, serving as the home battalion in Great Britain.

The Afghanistan Campaign   1878

The campaign in Afghanistan was the British reaction to the aggressive attitude of the Russians, who for years had been pushing towards India. Although Afghanistan, sandwiched between Russia and India, was traditionally neutral, the Afghans had alarmed the British Government by agreeing to accept a Russian embassy, while at the same time refusing to allow Great Britain to establish a Mission in Kabul. In 1878 the British Government decided to establish the Mission, by force if necessary, and despatched Major General Frederick Roberts VC with a force to do so.

The 72nd at Peiwar Kotal   1878

In November 1878 General Roberts led his force into Afghanistan and found the way blocked by the Afghan army which occupied a strong, stockaded, hilltop position at the Peiwar Kotal pass. However, careful reconnaissance revealed a possible route by which the position could be outflanked, and General Roberts sent part of his force, including the 72nd, to approach from the flank. On 2nd December 1878 the Right Wing of the 72nd Highlanders with the 5th Gurkhas, after a night approach march, scaled a precipitous ridge to storm the flank of the Afghan position, allowing the remainder of General Robert's force to attack from the front. The Afghan army was comprehensively defeated, and the British force captured 21 guns with large amounts of ammunition and food.

The Treaty of Gandamack   1879

The 72nd spent the winter in Afghanistan in intensely cold conditions and with the constant threat of further hostilities. However in May 1879 Yakoob Khan, Amir of Afghanistan, agreed at the Treaty of Gandamack to accept the British Mission.

The settlement was short lived for, only six weeks after the British Mission was established at Kabul, its staff was massacred by an Afghan mob. General Roberts was again sent in, this time with instructions to occupy Kabul.

The 72nd at Charasiah   1879

As the force advanced into Afghanistan in October 1879 it was again faced with an Afghan army, 12,000 strong, holding a hilltop position at Charasiah, which effectively blocked the track to Kabul. General Roberts once more found a possible approach route from a flank, and the 72nd Highlanders with the 5th Gurkhas were given the task of the flank attack. They succeeded in scaling and occupying a hill from which the main Afghan position could be enfiladed, and the Afghan army was again defeated. The battle of Charasiah was the last occasion when the 72nd carried its Colours in battle.

General Roberts entered Kabul on 13th October 1879. His force captured 200 guns and 7,000 rifles and, to demonstrate his superiority, he also marched through the city with bands playing.

Officers of the 72nd in Kabul, 1879.

The 72nd in the occupation of Kabul   1879-1880

General Robert's force occupied the Sherpore cantonment outside Kabul for the winter of 1879-1880. The Afghans were at first subdued, but their morale soon improved and resistance stiffened. By December it had reached the stage of a Jehad, or Holy War. The British force of about 5,000, based on Kabul, operated aggresively in the surrounding countryside, but it was unable to prevent the Afghans massing an army of over 100,000 which threatened to engulf the small British force.

The 72nd took part in a number of fierce actions against the Afghans in the hills round Kabul between 11-23 December 1879.

Lance Corporal George Sellar, VC

L/CPL GEORGE SELLAR WINS THE VICTORIA CROSS, 14TH DECEMBER 1879

On 14th December 1879, during operations against the Afghan positions on the Asmai Heights outside Kabul, Lance Corporal George Sellar reached the enemy position well ahead of the attacking party, and took on the Afghans with his rifle and bayonet. In the hand-to-hand fighting he was severely wounded by an Afghan with his knife. General Roberts had witnessed the incident through his glass, and L/Cpl Sellar was awarded the Victoria Cross for his gallantry.

The 72nd on the march from Kabul to Kandahar   1880

During 1880 the 72nd remained at Kabul until August, and the Afghan resistance waned for a time. Then, in late July, news came of the disaster at Maiwand near Kandahar, where a British column had been attacked, losing over 1,100 casualties. General Roberts was ordered to take his force, which included the 72nd Highlanders, to the relief of Kandahar without delay.

The famous march was never intended to break any speed records, but it was, by any standards, a remarkable feat of organisation. General Roberts set out after only three days preparation to march a force of 10,000 troops, with 11,000 animals and 8,000 camp followers, through over 300 miles of hostile, trackless country. The temperature varied daily as much as 80°F; from 110° at midday to freezing point at night. The march was accomplished in 22 days without any losses from enemy action.

The 72nd at Kandahar

When General Robert's Force reached Kandahar, found the Afghan army, under Ayub Khan, in position among the hills to the North West of the town, ar preparing to attack. General Roberts wasted no time an next day, on 1st September 1880, he attacked them. Th 72nd were part of the left flanking attack which cleared th enemy position and finally defeated the Afghans. The co to the 72nd was two officers and 11 men killed, and th included the Commanding Officer Lt Col F. Brownlow.

72nd BATTLE HONOURS

For their service in the Afghanistan campaign, the 72n were awarded the Battle Honours:

> 'PEIWAR KOTAL'
> 'CHARASIAH'
> 'KABUL 1879'
> 'KANDAHAR 1880'
> 'AFGHANISTAN 1878-80'

The 72nd in India   1880-188

Two weeks after the battle of Kandahar the 72n marched out of Afghanistan and then travelled by train t rejoin the families and rear details at Mean Meer. They ha been on campaign for nearly two years. In November 188 they moved to Lucknow.

The 72nd become 1st Bn Seaforth Highlanders   188

Under the Army Reforms of 1881 the 72nd Duke c Albany's Own Highlanders were amalgamated with th 78th Highlanders (Ross-shire Buffs). The 72nd became th 1st Battalion Seaforth Highlanders and the 78th becam the 2nd Battalion. Of particular significance to the 72nd 73rd, 75th and 91st, four of the regiments which had lost th kilt in 1809, was the restoration of their old uniform.

To the 72nd, the change meant a radical difference i both the uniform and character of the regiment. Instead o being linked with the 91st Argyllshire Highlanders, with strong Campbell background, they were now amalgamate with a partner which shared the distinction of having bee raised by the MacKenzie of Seaforth family.

Instead of a Depot at Stirling and a territorial area i Argyll and the Central Lowlands, it had a Depot at For George and a territorial area which included the ol MacKenzie lands of Ross-shire and Lewis. Instead of th trews of Prince Charles Edward Stuart tartan, it was t wear the kilt of MacKenzie tartan. To the genera satisfaction of the regiment, the clock had been put back 7 years.

The name of the new regiment was at first described a 'Seaforth Highlanders (Ross-shire Buffs)', but this wa amended in November 1881 to include the old title of th 72nd, so that the full name was:
'SEAFORTH HIGHLANDERS (ROSS-SHIRE BUFFS THE DUKE OF ALBANY'S)'.

3. *THE 78th HIGHLANDERS FROM 1793-1881*

The Raising of the 78th Highlanders   March-July 1793
On 7th March 1793 Lt Col Francis Humberston MacKenzie of Seaforth was granted his Letter of Service authorising him to raise a Highland regiment, and also his commission as the Lieutenant Colonel Commandant of it. The regiment was assembled at Fort George and was inspected by Lt Gen Sir Hector Munro on 10th July 1793. It was designated the 78th (Highland) Regiment of Foot, and was the first regiment to be added to the army when the government authorised an expansion of the infantry to meet the threat of war with France after the French Revolution.

Uniform of the 78th Highlanders   1793
The 78th wore the normal uniform of the Highland regiments at the time, with red jacket, kilt and belted plaid, sporran, red and white hose, and feather bonnet. The tartan worn was the 42nd Black Watch (or Government) tartan, with the addition of the red and white stripes. It is likely that the 78th were the first regiment to wear this tartan which later became known as the MacKenzie tartan. The 71st, which was also a MacKenzie regiment, seem to have adopted the 78th tartan in 1797. The facings of the regiment were buff.

There were some variations in the dress of the 78th. The pipers wore buff jackets with green wings, and a green hackle in the feather bonnet. The fashion at the time was to form a band of music with uniform distinctively different from the rest of the regiment; the bandsmen of the 78th were dressed in the kilt of Royal Stuart tartan, with white jackets.

Two features of the uniform of the 78th were to prove notably long lasting; the kilt of MacKenzie tartan has been worn by the regiment ever since the 78th was raised, and it is worn by the Queen's Own Highlanders today, (except for pipers, drummers and bandsmen who wear 79th tartan kilt); and the buff facings have also survived to the present day uniform.

The 78th received its first stand of Colours which were provided by Lt Col F. H. MacKenzie of Seaforth.

The 78th in Guernsey and Newport   1793-1794
In August and October 1793 the 78th left Scotland in two halves for service in the Channel Islands. Their role was to support the French Royalists in Brittany in their resistance to the French Revolution in France.

It was a time of constant reinforcement of the coastal garrisons against invasion by the French. The 78th left Guernsey in January 1794 for Newport, then returned to Guernsey in March.

2nd Battalion 78th raised   1794
On 8th February 1794, Lt Col F. H. MacKenzie of Seaforth, as Lieutenant Colonel Commandant of the 78th, was authorised to raise a further battalion. The 2nd Battalion 78th was inspected and passed as fit for service in June 1794, also at Fort George, and it too received its Colours, provided by Seaforth. In July the 2nd/78th was officially designated the 'Ross-shire Buffs', the name being derived from the buff facings of the regiment.

Uniforms of the 78th Highlanders in 1793
(From a painting by R. Simkin)

The 1st Bn/78th in the Netherlands   1794-1795
In September 1794 the 78th went on active service for the first time. By ill luck it happened to be one of the most ill-organised ventures in which the British Army has ever been used. A British and Hanoverian expeditionary force, commanded by Prince Frederick, Duke of York and Albany, fought a campaign in the Netherlands in conjunction with Austrian and Dutch allies. The object of the war was to check the advance of the armies of Revolutionary France. After a modestly successful start, the campaign took a bad turn when Britain's Austrian allies were heavily defeated by the French, leaving the British force isolated in the Netherlands and in danger of being overrun.

Among the reinforcements sent out to join the Duke of York's army were the 1st Bn 78th Highlanders and also the newly raised 79th Cameron Highlanders. The 78th took part in three engagements with the enemy. The regiment had its first taste of action at the defence of Nimjegen on 4th November 1794, when it made a gallant sortie against a besieging battery of French artillery. In late December the 78th made a successful counter-attack against an enemy force which had crossed the frozen River Waal. And on 5th January 1795 it repelled, by good discipline and fire control, a charge by the French Cavalry.

The 78th took part in the British withdrawal to Germany in the intense cold of early 1795, and were eventually embarked at Bremerhaven in April. They had lost over 350 men through enemy action and due to the severe weather.

2nd Bn 78th at the capture of the Cape of Good Hope   1795

In May 1795 Holland, having been defeated by France and forced to become the revolutionary 'Batavian Republic', with a permanent garrison of French troops, declared war on Great Britain. The Dutch Colony at the Cape of Good Hope had thus become an enemy port, and so it posed a serious threat to the security of the sea route to India.

The 2nd Bn 78th were ordered to join a secret expedition despatched to seize the Cape of Good Hope from the Dutch. They landed at the Cape in July 1795, and after two months of resistance by the Dutch settlers, the colony capitulated after the towns of Wynberg and Cape Town had been taken.

The 1st Bn 78th on the Expedition to L'Isle Dieu   1795-1796

Meanwhile, on their return from the disastrous campaign in the Netherlands, the 1st Bn 78th Highlanders were stationed for short periods in Chelmsford, Harwich, and Southampton. In August 1795 they too were sent off on an expedition. The force was intended to give military support to the French Royalists in Brittany who were still opposing the Revolution in France. The 1st/78th landed on the island of L'Isle Dieu, off the coast of Brittany. But the resistance of the French Royalists had collapsed, and so the force was withdrawn. On its return to England in January 1796, the 1st/78th was quartered at Poole.

The 1st and 2nd Battalions 78th amalgamated   1796

In November 1795 the 1st and 2nd Battalions of the 78th were ordered to amalgamate. The 1st Bn sailed from England in March 1796, and the amalgamation took place at Cape Town in June 1796.

The 78th arrive in India   1797

The 78th left South Africa in November 1796 for their first period of service in India, and arrived at Calcutta in February 1797. By coincidence they arrived just a month before the 72nd were to leave India for home.

By 1797 the East India Company had expanded the territory under its control into three Presidencies; Bengal, Madras and Bombay. Within these territories trade prospered, and Britain benefitted by an enormous inflow of merchandise. But outside the presidencies, anarchy prevailed. In the south Tippoo, Sultan of Mysore, with his French trained army, and further north the Mahrattas, kept India in a state of permanent turmoil.

Despite the threats of this unstable situation, the 78th spent the next six years on uneventful garrison duty in Bengal, Oudh, and on the east coast of India. They did not take part in the conquest of Mysore and the defeat of the southern Mahrattas which were happening at the time.

The 78th in the 2nd Mahratta War   1803

Their turn came in 1803 when the Governor General of India, the Marquess of Wellesley, launched a military campaign led by his younger brother, Major General The Hon Arthur Wellesley (later to become the Duke of Wellington), against the northern Mahrattas whose French trained army was continually raiding British territory.

The 78th were sent by sea to Bombay and then marched to Poona. Wellesley's first step was to secure a firm base for his operations, and so he besieged the Mahratta fortress of Ahmednuggar. The attack was headed by the European Infantry of the army, the 74th and 78th Highlanders, and to the astonishment of the Mahrattas the fortress was taken in four days. Wellesley now had the base and communications centre which he needed for his campaign.

The 78th at Assaye   23rd September 1803

On 23rd September 1803 Wellesley and his army of 7,000 encountered the main Mahratta army of over 40,000 men, apparently starting to retreat, and so he immediately decided to attack in order to catch them strung out on the march. But he had been wildly misinformed, and the Mahratta army, with over 100 cannon to Wellesley's 22, and with a 20 to one superiority in cavalry, was drawn up in a strong position in the angle formed by the junction of two rivers, beside the village of Assaye.

Wellesley decided on the only possible course; to attack the Mahrattas from the flank, so that their overwhelming fire power could not be brought to bear. By personal reconnaissance he found a ford over the Kaitna river, which allowed his army to cross and deploy across the narrow neck of land, thus using the two rivers both to deny the enemy room to manoeuvre and also to protect his own flanks. As Wellesley's army attacked, the Mahratta line wheeled to face him.

The attack was launched in three echelons, with the 78th in the all-important position on the left flank of the leading echelon. They were the first of the infantry to reach the Mahrattas realigned front line, and their determined attack played a critical part in the capture of the Mahratta guns and the consequent rout of their infantry.

In later years the Great Duke of Wellington rated the tactics of the battle of Assaye as the best thing he had ever done on the battlefield.

78th BATTLE HONOUR

For their part in the battle of Assaye the 78th Highlanders were awarded the battle honour:

'ASSAYE'

They were also granted the badge of the Elephant superscribed 'Assaye', which is the collar badge of the Queen's Own Highlanders, and is one of the devices on the Regimental Colour today.

The Assaye Colour

The three British regiments at Assaye, the 74th and 78th Highlanders and the 19th Light Dragoons, were presented with Honorary third Colours by the East India Company. (It is not known what happened to the original 'Assaye' Colour of the 78th, but a replica was made in 1889 and is now in the regimental chapel at Fort George).

The 78th at Argaum   1803

After Assaye, Wellesley wasted no time in following up the defeated Mahrattas. He was joined by a further column to give him a total of 11,000 men. On 29th September 1803 he caught up with the Mahratta army, still 30,000 strong. By advancing through shoulder high corn he was able to approach unobserved, and to attack at last light. The 78th were on the right of the assaulting line, and the attack took its direction from them. By 11 p.m. Wellesley's army had won a further devastating victory and had captured the remaining Mahratta guns, and their ammunition, Colours, elephants, camels and baggage train.

The 78th at Gawilghur   1803

The final battle of the Mahratta war was the attack on the supposedly impregnable hill fortress of Gawilghur. It took a siege of a week before it was successfully breached and stormed. Wellesley's superiority, established during the campaign, resulted in a collapse of Mahratta morale and resistance before a general assault was necessary.

The fall of Gawilghur was followed by a peace treaty with the Rajah of Berar, which left the British Government and the East India Company in control of the major part of central India.

The 78th in Bombay and Goa   1804-1811

After the Mahratta war the 78th remained in and around Bombay for three years. The campaign had produced prize money for all the troops who had taken part, although a private soldier's share was only 13 rupees.

Since 1799, when Portugal's colonies, being allied to Great Britain, had come under threat of French attack, the British had maintained a garrison in the colony of Goa which belonged to Portugal. The 1st Bn 78th spent a period of uneventful garrison duty in Goa from 1807 to 1811.

2nd Battalion 78th raised   1804

In 1804, when the invasion of Great Britain by the French seemed imminent and Britain's army was dangerously over-stretched to meet the country's world wide military commitments, the Government authorised the raising of a number of 2nd Battalions. Most of these were intended to be 'feeder' battalions with the task of recruiting and training reinforcements for the 1st Battalions overseas. But the 2nd Bn 78th Highlanders had an unusually interesting record of service in its 13 years existence, and it experienced extremes of triumph and disaster.

It was raised by Maj Gen Alexander MacKenzie Fraser, who had succeeded his brother-in-law, Lord Seaforth, as Colonel of the Regiment. The 2nd Bn 78th Highlanders was inspected at Fort George on 6th December 1804.

2nd Bn 78th under training with Sir John Moore   1805

To counter the threat of invasion, large bodies of troops were being concentrated for training in the South of England, and so the 2nd Bn 78th embarked at Fort George in early 1805 for training in the South. They spent six months at Hythe, under the command of Maj Gen Sir John Moore, who at the time was developing his ideas on discipline and tactics, and on the training of light infantry troops, which were to prove so effective in the Peninsula war. When the 2nd Bn 78th was ordered abroad in September 1805, it had achieved a high standard of discipline, morale and training.

2nd Bn 78th In Gibraltar   1805-1806

The 2nd Bn 78th sailed for Gibraltar in late 1805, but their journey was adventurous. A large fleet of French and Spanish ships forced the British transports to seek refuge in the mouth of the River Tagus. Their plight was suddenly and dramatically relieved by the historic British naval victory at the Battle of Trafalgar, and they sailed on to reach Gibraltar safely.

Uniforms of the 2nd Bn 78th Highlanders (Ross-shire Buffs) in 1806.   (From a painting by R. Simkin)

2nd Bn 78th in Sicily   1806

The Kingdom of the Two Sicilies, which comprised the South of Italy and the island of Sicily itself, had joined the alliance against Napoleon. But in 1806 the French, under Napoleon's elder brother Joseph Bonaparte, invaded the Kingdom and deposed King Ferdinand. A British force was sent to Sicily to support the King, and in May 1806 the 2nd Bn 78th sailed from Gibraltar to join it.

2nd Bn 78th at Maida   1806

When the 2nd 78th reached Sicily, the French seemed poised to invade the island itself, and so the British troops in Sicily were ordered to attack the mainland of Italy to preempt the invasion. The British force of 4,800 under General Sir John Stuart landed in Calabria, the 'toe' of Italy, and on 4th July 1806 attacked the French force of General Regnier who had roughly 6,400 troops.

The British in two ranks met the French who were deployed in three and, after a brisk musketry duel, the British charged with the bayonet. The French, met by musketry of an accuracy and intensity which they had not before experienced, broke and fled. The battle was a remarkable demonstration that British linear tactics, combined with the enormous improvements that had been achieved in discipline, musketry and training, could defeat the hitherto irresistible French columns.

2nd Bn 78th BATTLE HONOUR

For its part in the campaign the 2nd Bn 78th was awarded the Battle Honour:

'MAIDA'

The 2nd Bn 78th in the Expedition to Egypt   1807

In 1806 Turkey entered the was as allies of the French, and closed the Dardanelles to Russian shipping. A British fleet was sent to bombard Constantinople on behalf of the Russian allies, but was forced to withdraw rather ignominiously in the face of the Turkish defences. Great Britain therefore opted for an attack on Turkey and, selecting what seemed the most vulnerable point of the Ottoman Empire, ordered British troops to land again in Egypt.

As a result of this chain of international events, the 2nd Bn 78th in Sicily joined an expedition of 5,000 men which landed at Alexandria in March 1807 and occupied the city successfully. It was hoped that the Egyptian Mamelukes would rebel against their Turkish rulers and join forces with the British expedition.

The Disaster at El Hamet   1807

The Mameluke rising never materialised and the British force, attempting half heartedly to capture the town of Rosetta, was itself attacked by the Turks. It was caught most vulnerably deployed in scattered positions. On 21st April 1807 three companies of the unfortunate 2nd Bn 78th were surrounded at El Hamet by an overwhelming force of Turkish cavalry and, after a gallant resistance, were either killed or captured. The regiment lost 163 killed, including the Commanding Officer, Lt Col Patrick MacLeod of Geanies.

The 2nd Bn 78th return to England   1807-1808

The British force, with the remainder of the 2nd Bn 78th, withdrew to Alexandria and held the city until September. Then, because there seemed to be no intention of reinforcing or evacuating the force, the commander negotiated a truce with the Turks. The prisoners were released and the 2nd Bn 78th returned to Sicily and thence to England, arriving in early January 1808.

The Legend of Drummer MacLeod and Pte Thomas Keith

One of the most intriguing stories of the 78th concerns the fate of two Highlanders taken prisoner at El Hamet. They had become the property of a Turkish officer who removed them from Cairo, and so they were not repatriated with the remainder. Both turned Mohamedan and had successful careers in the Ottoman Empire. Drummer MacLeod, from Lewis, took the name Osman, and 'Osman Effendi' became a well known doctor in Cairo. Private Thomas Keith, an apprentice gun maker from Leith, had been the regimental armourer of the 2nd Bn 78th. He took the name of Ibrahim, and his skill with weapons earned him military promotion. He became a cavalry leader and by 1815 was Ibrahim Aga, Governor of Medina. He was killed the same year in a cavalry charge at Medina.

The 2nd Bn 78th in Great Britain   1809-1814

On its return to Britain the 2nd Bn 78th was quartered in the south of England where it was required to despatch drafts to the 1st Bn 78th in Goa. The regiment moved to Fort George in early 1809, leaving a draft of 370 men under orders for India. The headquarters remained at Fort George until 1811 and then moved to Aberdeen until 1814.

The draft of the 78th at Walcheren   1809

The draft for India got no further than Cowes when it was diverted to join the Earl of Chatham's expedition to Walcheren in Holland. It was intended to be a strong raid on the French occupied port of Antwerp, with its dockyards and arsenals. However the British force suffered from the joint disasters of malaria, which struck 11,000 men out of a total of 40,000, and from a wholly incompetent commander. The expedition was withdrawn in disarray.

The 1st Bn 78th in the Capture of Java   1811

Ever since the French had defeated the Dutch and forced them into an alliance, the Dutch Colony of Java had been in French hands. The Dutch had previously held it since 1596, and considered it their most valuable Colony. In 1811 the British Government of India decided to eject the French occupation force. The 1st Bn 78th joined the expedition and sailed from Bombay in March 1811.

As the force landed in Java, the French garrison abandoned the capital Batavia to the invaders, and withdrew to a defensive position at Weltervreeden. On 10th August 1811 the British force attacked the French, forcing them to retreat to an even stronger position at Fort Cornelis. On 25th August the British attacked again and, in a fiercely fought three hour assault against a well-prepared position, routed the French. Among the total of 154 British and Indian troops killed, was Brevet Lt Col William Campbell, the Acting Commanding Officer of the 78th. The French lost the remarkable figures of over 1000 killed, 3000 wounded, and 6000 taken prisoner, while 430 French guns were captured.

However the French commander, General Jansens, managed to avoid capture, and it was not until 18th September that a pursuing force, which included the 1st Bn 78th, compelled him to sign an unconditional surrender of the Colony. Mr Stamford Raffles (later the founder of the Colony of Singapore) was appointed Governor of Java.

The 1st Bn 78th in the occupation of Java   1811-1816

The 1st Bn 78th remained in Java for five years. They spent the first few months in the port of Sourabaya where the regiment's families arrived from Goa to join them. Then in 1812 the Sultan of Djakarta, who strongly resented the European settlement of his island, rebelled against the rule of the East India Company. A force of about 1000 troops, including the 1st Bn 78th, was sent to check the revolt, and it successfully stormed the Sultan's fortified krattan (the Palace), deposed the Sultan, and appropriated his treasure.

The 1st Bn 78th remained in Java for five years, and were regularly involved in minor expeditions and incidents with rebellious local tribes. Its most persistent enemies, however, were the climate and tropical disease, which caused over 600 casualties.

1st Bn 78th BATTLE HONOUR

The service of the 1st Bn 78th Highlanders in Java was rewarded in 1818 by the Battle Honour:
'JAVA'

The Shipwreck of the 1st Bn 78th   **1816**

In September 1816 the 1st Bn 78th left Java for Bengal. The Headquarters of the regiment had an uneventful journey, but the ship 'Frances Charlotte', with six of the companies on board, struck a rock off Preparis, a small uninhabited island north of the Andamans, and sank. The companies with their families, managed to reach Preparis, about 12 miles away, where they existed precariously for five weeks until they were rescued. A number died of starvation, drowning and exposure and, apart from the human misery of the event, the regiment lost its baggage, records and £2000 of regimental funds in the shipwreck.

The survivors were eventually picked up and taken to Calcutta, where they arrived in December 1816.

The 1st Bn 78th return to Great Britain   **1817**

The 1st Bn 78th sailed for Great Britain in March 1817 on the 'Prince Blucher', by happy chance the ship which had rescued the shipwrecked companies from Preparis island. The regiment arrived at Portsmouth and then sailed for Aberdeen arriving in July. It had been abroad for 21 years.

The 2nd Bn 78th at Merxem   **1814**

The demands for men to keep the 1st Bn 78th up to strength in Java had prevented the 2nd Bn achieving the numbers needed to make it fit for further active service. However in January 1814, despite being less than 300 strong, it left Aberdeen for Holland, and took part in the advance on Antwerp. It particularly distinguished itself on the outskirts of the town when it routed a force of four French battalions at the village of Merxem.

The 2nd Bn 78th in Holland and Belgium   **1814-1816**

After the abdication of Napoleon in March 1814, the 2nd Bn 78th remained in Holland and Belgium on garrison duty. When Napoleon returned to France in 1815 and launched his final campaign towards Brussels, the 2nd Bn 78th had been so further reduced in numbers by sickness that they remained in reserve at Nieuport and were not present at Waterloo. The battalion eventually returned to Great Britain in February 1816, and remained at home until it was amalgamated with the 1st Battalion.

The 1st and 2nd Battalions 78th amalgamated   **1817**

In Aberdeen the 1st and 2nd Battalions amalgamated to form one regiment again.

The 78th in Scotland   **1817**

The amalgamated 78th had only a short stay in Scotland, but its deployment was an interesting comparison with the Army today. The headquarters were based in Aberdeen, and detachments were garrisoned in Perth and in the Highlands at Fort George, Fort William and Fort Augustus. In August 1817 companies of the 78th were sent to Glasgow to aid the civil power in riot control in Calton. While escorting prisoners to gaol they were so fiercely attacked by a mob that they had to open fire.

The 78th in Ireland   **1817-1826**

In November 1817 the 78th moved to Belfast. It remained in Ireland for nine relatively uneventful years. In 1818 it received new Colours, the third stand to be carried by the regiment.

Uniforms of the 78th Highlanders (Ross-shire Buffs) in 1822.   (From a painting by R. Simkin)

In 1821 the 78th were brigaded with the 42nd, 79th and 93rd for the visit to Dublin of King George IV. The only kilted regiment in the Army not present, the 92nd, were abroad in Jamaica at the time.

The 78th in Ceylon   **1826-1837**

In 1826 the 78th sailed for Ceylon, and it remained on the Island for 11 years. The only real enemy was disease, and the regiment lost 299 officers and men, mainly from cholera.

The 78th in Great Britain   **1838-1841**

The 78th left Ceylon in 1837 and arrived in Ireland in February 1838. Among its more unusual acquisitions was a young elephant, presented to the regiment in Ceylon, which was trained to march in front of the Regimental Band. (It was subsequently presented to the Edinburgh Zoo when the 78th left for India in 1842).

In 1838 there had been serious disturbances in Canada, and extra regiments had to be sent out to reinforce the garrison and to support the Canadian Militia regiments. The 78th was ordered to send volunteers, and the regiment was thus reduced to well below strength. In 1839 it moved back to Scotland in order to recruit, and was stationed first in Glasgow and then in Edinburgh. By 1840 it was up to strength again.

In 1839 the 78th received new Colours, the fourth stand to be carried by the regiment.

In 1840 there were serious industrial riots in Lancashire, and the 78th was sent to Manchester for over a year on peace-keeping duties. It returned to Ireland in November 1841.

Uniforms of the 78th Highlanders (Ross-shire Buffs) in 1834. *(From a painting by R. Simkin)*

The 78th return to India   1842

In early 1842 news arrived in Britain of the greatest disaster which was to happen to British troops in the East in the 19th Century. A force of 4,500 British and Indian troops, with 12,000 camp followers, had been attacked and massacred by the Afghans while withdrawing from Kabul to India. Only one man, Dr. William Brydon, had escaped to tell the tale.

With face-saving retaliation a priority for the Government, the 78th were hurriedly embarked for India to take the place of troops required in Afghanistan. They arrived in Bombay in July 1842, over 1,000 strong, and spent the next three years in Poona and Karachi.

The 78th Highlanders (Ross-shire Buffs). *(From a print published by W. Spooner C.1840)*

Cholera strikes the 78th   1844-1845

In 1844 to 1845 the 78th suffered tragedy on a scale which it never met in battle in the 19th Century, when it was decimated by cholera. During the time in Bombay and Poona there had been occasional minor outbreaks of the disease, but casualties from tropical illness had to be accepted as a recurrent hazard of service in India. In 1844 the 78th was moved to Karachi and marched to Sukkur, in Sind. On its arrival cholera broke out on an appalling scale. In eight months the regiment lost 535 officers and men, and 202 of its wives and children. In early 1845 the survivors of the regiment returned to Bombay, just over 300 strong. A monument in St Giles Cathedral, Edinburgh is a sad memorial to this miserable epidemic.

The 78th restored to strength   1845

But the 78th made a remarkable recovery from this disaster. By allowing the 78th depot companies to recruit generally throughout Great Britain and Ireland, and with the addition of 100 volunteers from the 2nd Queens Regiment, then leaving India for home, the regiment was restored to strength by the end of the year.

This influx of 732 men, few of whom were Scottish inevitably changed the composition of the regiment. Having been 91% Scottish, the 78th was now composed of 47% Scotsmen, 30% English and 23% Irish. But, as is so often the case, the character of the regiment survived, and many of these were the men who were to earn the 78th its high reputation in the campaigns in Persia and the Indian Mutiny.

The 78th remained based in the Bombay Presidency, in Poona, Kirkee and Belgaum for four years.

The 78th Highlanders (Ross-shire Buffs). *(From a print published by R. Ackermann 1846)*

78th Highlanders (Ross-shire Buffs) 1852
(From a painting by R. Simkin)

The 78th in Aden   1849-1853

The Colony of Aden had been captured by an expedition from Bombay in 1839. The British garrison there was drawn from the regiments in Bombay, and the 78th took their turn at this hot and unrewarding duty for over three years. The 78th was divided between Bombay and Aden from late 1849 to early 1853.

Life in this inhospitable station was occasionally interrupted by minor friction with the Sultan of Lahej, from whom Aden had been captured. The monotony of military garrison life is well commemorated by the famous pipe tune 'The Barren Rocks of Aden', composed by Piper James Mauchline of the 78th during the 78th's time there. The tune is said to have been 'improved' by Pipe Major Alexander MacKellar of the 78th, who is sometimes credited with its composition).

The 78th in Poona   1853-1857

In 1853 the 78th moved to Poona, half the regiment returning from Aden and half from Bombay. In 1854 the regiment received new Colours, the fifth Stand to be carried. These Colours were to see much action in the campaigns in Persia and India which ensued.

The 78th in the expedition to Persia   1857

As the British had expanded their trade and extended their control of India, they had come up against the Russians, also expanding from the other direction. The country of Afghanistan, on the north west frontier of India, became the buffer state whose neutrality had to be preserved at all costs as a barrier to further Russian

expansion. Persia was also in the 'No-Mans Land' between the rival powers. When the Shah of Persia, prompted by the Russians, besieged the Afghan town of Herat, Britain had to intervene with force. An expedition was sent from India to the Persian Gulf.

It successfully captured the port of Bushire to use as a base, and then waited until further reinforcements arrived from India. The 78th were sent from Poona as part of these reinforcements.

The 78th at Koosh-Ab   1857

The British Commander of the expedition to Persia, Lt Gen Sir James Outram, soon realized that the Persians were assembling a large army to recover Bushire, and so he took the initiative and marched to attack them. With surprising lack of opposition, Outram's force located and captured the enemy camp, and the Persians fled as they approached. However the Persian cavalry summoned up the courage to make a half hearted attack on the British force as it withdrew during the night near the village of Koosh-Ab. Outram took up a defensive position and waited until daylight on 8th February 1857 when he deployed into line and attacked the Persians. In a rather one-sided engagement the Persians were routed losing 700 dead, while the British and Indian force lost only 10. The 78th did not have any casualties at all, despite being on the right of the first line of the attack.

The 78th at Mohomrah   1857

In the next few weeks, the Persians managed to concentrate their army again and fortified a camp at Mohomrah beside the Shat-el-Arab river. General Outram employed a system of combined operations, using the guns of his fleet to bombard the Persians, while his transport steamers landed the army. The 78th again led the advance on the Persian position, but the prospect of another attack was too much for the enemy and they abandoned their position and fled.

78th BATTLE HONOURS

For their service in the Persian campaign the 78th were awarded the Battle Honours:
> **'KOOSH-AB'**
> **'PERSIA'**

The 78th and the start of the Indian Mutiny   1857

The 78th arrived back in India in May 1857 to find the country in a state of emergency. In April 1857 Sepoy troops (Indian troops trained by Europeans) had started to mutiny against British rule. Within a few weeks the discontent had spread through the Sepoy regiments in Bengal, which represented four fifths of the East India Company's army.

On their arrival in Bombay, the 78th were ordered to continue by sea to Calcutta, and arrived in June 1857. Their first task was to disarm the Sepoy troops of Barrackpore, and four companies then moved to Allahadad where they joined Maj Gen Sir Henry Havelock's column which was to march to relieve the besieged garrison of Cawnpore.

The 78th at the recapture of Cawnpore 1857

On 12th July 1857 the 78th had its first encounter with the enemy when Havelock's column routed a small force of mutineers at Futtehpore. It was the enemy's first defeat of the campaign. Three days later Havelock won another small action at Aong. On 16th July the column arrived at Cawnpore.

Havelock's men were to find one of the most horrifying scenes of the Indian Mutiny. Cawnpore had been besieged by a force of about 3000 mutineers under Dandhu Panth, known as Nana Sahib, a rebel Mahratta Rajah. The garrison of 900, about half of whom were women and children, had held out for three weeks. Then with the assurance of safe conduct, they had been allowed to leave the city by boats down the River Ganges, but had been brutally attacked by the mutineers. The surviving women and children had subsequently been butchered and thrown down a well.

On 16th July, the day after this killing, Havelock's Column reached Cawnpore. In a series of quick attacks in which the 78th played the key role, the Nana Sahib's army was briskly defeated. Next day Havelock's column entered Cawnpore and made their grisly discovery. The brutal excesses of the Nana Sahib were an incident which the British army did not forget or forgive during the campaign.

The 78th in the Advance to Lucknow 1857

General Havelock's next task was to reach Lucknow where the garrison of about 1,700 British and loyal Indian troops was besieged by about 60,000 mutineers. Havelock's column was itself only 1,500 strong, but even that would almost double the garrison, and so he crossed the river Ganges and marched for Lucknow.

Andrew Bogle, awarded the VC as a Lieutenant 1857.

Lt ANDREW BOGLE WINS THE VICTORIA CROSS AT OONAO — 29th JULY 1857

On 29th July 1857 Havelock's column met an enemy force in the strongly defended town of Oonao. During the assault on the town, Lieutenant Andrew Bogle of the 78th showed particular gallantry in leading the attack on a house which was strongly held by enemy musketeers. For his bravery he was later awarded the Victoria Cross, the first member of the 78th to win it.

Havelock's Column is delayed

Six miles further on Havelock was again forced to clear a rebel position by a frontal attack on the village of Bashiratganj. Although these two attacks had been successful, they had cost nearly 100 casualties. To add to the difficulties, cholera had broken out reducing the strength of the column to about 850 fit men, and so Havelock was forced to wait for reinforcements. The mutineers took advantage of his halt and reoccupied a position at Boorbia-ki-Chauki just beyond Bashiratganj.

Lt Joseph Crowe, VC 1857

Lt JOSEPH CROWE WINS THE VICTORIA CROSS AT BOORBIA-KI-CHAUKI — 12th AUGUST 1857

However on 11th August, despite his shortage of men General Havelock attacked again. Next day the four companies of 78th Highlanders, now reduced to about 100 men, led the attack with a spirited bayonet charge. Havelock undertook to recommend for the Victoria Cross the first man into the enemy position, and Lieutenant Joseph Crowe thus became the second member of the 78th to win the VC.

The 78th arrive at Lucknow September 1857

The action against the mutineers had again reduced the numbers to below a worthwhile fighting strength, and so Havelock once more withdrew his column to Cawnpore. Here the remainder of the 78th joined the force, followed by another column of about 1500 men under General Sir James Outram. At last the relief column could muster a division of over 3,000 men, and in late September it marched on Lucknow. It reached the Alam Bagh, a Royal palace in a walled garden outside Lucknow, on 23rd September 1857.

In the town of Lucknow the British garrison was surrounded in the Residency, two miles away on the far side of the rebel held town, and so the hardest part of the expedition was still to come.

On 25th September Havelock's column, leaving its sick and wounded, its 5000 native camp followers, its ordnance stores and its commissariat at the Alam Bagh, fought its way across the canal bridge at Char Bagh. It then skirted round the town of Lucknow to try to avoid getting involved in street fighting. After a long hot day of continuous fighting it reached the Residency in the evening to an emotional welcome from the defenders.

It had been a costly fight, the 78th losing 41 killed and 81 wounded.

THE 78th WIN SIX VICTORIA CROSSES AT LUCKNOW

The relief of the garrison was rewarded by six Victoria Crosses for the 78th.

Lt H. T. MacPHERSON — 25th SEPTEMBER 1857

During the advance through Lucknow Lt Herbert MacPherson, the Adjutant of the 78th Highlanders, led a most gallant bayonet charge against an enemy gun position and captured two nine pounder cannon. He was awarded the VC for his bravery.

Brig Gen Sir Herbert MacPherson, awarded the VC as Lieutenant and Adjutant in 1857.

ASSISTANT SURGEON VALENTINE McMASTER — 25th SEPTEMBER 1857

The Victoria Cross was awarded to the regiment as a whole for its gallant advance to the Residency on 25th September 1857. The 78th voted on who should wear it, and it was awarded to Assistant Surgeon Valentine McMaster for his bravery in treating and rescuing the wounded under fire. He had also carried the Queen's Colour during the final stages of the advance to the Residency.

Assistant Surgeon Valentine McMaster VC 1857.

SURGEON JOSEPH JEE — 25th and 26th SEPTEMBER 1857

During the advance through Lucknow, and during the recovery of the casualties next day, Surgeon Joseph Jee of the 78th tended the wounded under heavy fire and remained with them until they were taken to safety. He was awarded the VC for his gallantry over the two days.

Surgeon Joseph Jee VC 1857

C/Sgt STEWART MacPHERSON — 26th SEPTEMBER 1857

The day after the 78th reached the Residency, the fighting continued as the wounded were brought in and the position secured. Colour Sergeant Stewart MacPherson managed to bring in a wounded man from his company under very heavy fire, and was awarded the VC for his courage.

Colour Sergeant Stewart MacPherson VC 1857.

Pte HENRY WARD — 25th and 26th SEPTEMBER 1857

During the advance on the Residency many of the wounded had to be left behind until they could be recovered later by dhoolie (a covered stretcher). Capt H. Havelock, the son of the General, had been wounded and left behind with a wounded soldier of the 78th, with Private Henry Ward as a guard. Pte Henry Ward managed to bring in the dhoolie with the two casualties safely, under heavy fire. He was awarded the VC for his bravery and resourcefulness.

Private Henry Ward VC 1857

Private James Hollowell VC 1857

Pte JAMES HOLLOWELL — 26th SEPTEMBER 1857

On the day after the advance on the Residency, when the wounded were being collected, one of the bearer parties lost its way and was besieged in a house by a large number of rebels. Pte James Hollowell took the lead in repelling a series of fierce attacks, and eventually the party was rescued. He was awarded the VC for this gallant defence.

The 78th at The Defence of Lucknow September-November 1857

The arrival of Havelock's column at the Residency brought a slight breathing space for the garrison because it doubled the strength of the defenders, but it did not raise the siege. For the next seven weeks the 78th found themselves part of the besieged garrison.

The 2nd Relief of Lucknow — 17th November   1857

In November a column commanded by the Commander in Chief in India, Sir Colin Campbell, reached the Alam Bagh. It then fought its way round Lucknow to reach the beleaguered Residency on 17th November 1857.

The 78th in the Defence of the Alam Bagh   1857-1858

A week after Sir Colin Campbell's second relief of Lucknow, Sir Henry Havelock died of dysentery. It was clear that the Residency was untenable without a much stronger garrison, and so it was abandoned and a new defensive position was established outside Lucknow beside the Alam Bagh. Here General Outram's force, including the 78th, held their ground from November 1857 to March 1858 until Sir Colin Campbell could muster a strong enough force to recapture Lucknow from the rebels. The 78th in their position at the Alam Bagh took part in minor defensive actions. During the final attack on Lucknow by Sir Colin Campbell's force, which now had over 25,000 troops including four infantry divisions, the 78th held the firm base at the Alam Bagh. The recapture of Lucknow took 19 days fighting and was complete by 21st March 1858.

78th BATTLE HONOUR

For their part in the relief and defence of Lucknow the 78th were awarded the Battle Honour:
'LUCKNOW'

NCOS and men of the Light Company 78th Highlanders in 1859, including Pte Henry Ward, VC on the right.

The 78th at the capture of Bareilly   1858

In March 1858 the 78th joined the Rohilkand Field Force in what, for them, was to be the last phase of the campaign. Marching north west out of Oudh the force, which also included the Highland Brigade (the 42nd, 79th and 93rd Highlanders), attacked the rebels at Bareilly and captured the town. The 78th remained in garrison at Bareilly until January 1859 when it received welcome orders to return to Great Britain.

The 78th leave India   1859

The 78th returned to Bombay where its families rejoined it after an absence of over two years. After a rapturous welcome and an official banquet, the regiment embarked for home 532 strong. Of the regiment which had arrived in India 17 years earlier, only 59 were still serving with it.

In September 1859 the 78th arrived at Fort George where the service companies and depot companies joined up.

Piper and Corporal of the 78th Highlanders (Ross-shire Buffs) 1861.   (From a print published by Day & Son)

The 78th 'The Saviours of India' in Great Britain   1859-65

The 78th was the first of the regiments which had taken part in the Indian Mutiny campaign to arrive back in Scotland, and the reports of their military successes, and in particular the first relief of Lucknow, caught the public's imagination. The regiment, hailed as the 'Saviours of India', was feted in Nairn and Inverness, and there were social events at Rosehaugh, Brahan and elsewhere in the north.

When the 78th moved to Edinburgh in February 1860, the welcome continued. There were banquets in Edinburgh and Hamilton, Lady Havelock (widow of General Sir Henry Havelock) presented the campaign medals, and in 1861 the regiment erected on Edinburgh Castle esplanade the well known monument in the form of a Runic Cross.

78th Highlanders (Ross-shire Buffs) 1859
(From a painting by R. Simkin)

In 1861 the 78th moved on to Aldershot where they were inspected by the Duke of Cambridge and received the welcome news that all those who had served in Havelock's first relief of Lucknow were to receive an additional year's service.

Moving on to Shorncliffe in 1862, the 78th were presented with a magnificent silver centre piece and cup by the counties of Ross and Cromarty, and the pipe major was given a banner by Keith Stewart-MacKenzie of Seaforth.

The regiment's final year at home was spent in Dublin. After six festive years it left for Gibraltar in August 1865.

The 78th in Gibraltar   1865-1867

The regiment spent an uneventful period of garrison duty at Gibraltar, marred only by occasional outbreaks of cholera.

The 78th Highlanders (Ross-shire Buffs) in Canada 1869.

The 78th in Canada   1867-1871

The 78th sailed for Canada in July 1867 and landed at Montreal. Next year, on 30th May 1868, new Colours were presented on the Champs de Mars at Montreal by Lady Windham, wife of General Sir Charles Windham the Commander of the British Forces in North America. They were the sixth Stand of Colours of the 78th.

The regiment moved to Halifax in 1869 where it spent two years, with a detachment at St John's, New Brunswick.

The 78th in Ireland   1871-1873

The 78th left Canada in late 1871 for a turbulent tour in Northern Ireland, The regiment was stationed in Belfast, with four companies in Londonderry. In August 1872 there were particularly vicious riots between Roman Catholics and Protestants in Belfast, followed by disturbances in Lisburn. In early 1873 there were more riots in Monaghan, Downpatrick and Ballymena. The 78th earned praise for their steadiness and patience. Contemporary comment, in its praise for the regiment's impartiality in these sectarian squabbles, bears a marked similarity with modern commendation of the Army's role in Ulster.

The 78th Highlanders (Ross-shire Buffs) 1877
(From a painting by R. Simkin)

The 71st and 78th Depot at Fort George   1873-1881

Under the Localisation Scheme of 1873, until the Army Reforms of 1881, the 78th Highlanders were linked with the 71st Highland Light Infantry. The two regiments had much in common, for both were Ross-shire regiments originally, (the 71st had been raised by John MacKenzie, Lord MacLeod); both wore MacKenzie tartan, although the 71st wore it as trews; and both had buff facings.

The joint Depot was set up at Fort George, and the two regiments were allocated a recruiting area of Orkney, Shetland, Caithness, Sutherland, Ross and Cromarty, Inverness, Nairn and Moray.

The 78th at Fort George   1873-1874

In May 1873 the 78th left Belfast and returned to Fort George where it joined the newly established joint Depot

of the 71st and 78th. But Fort George was so overcrowded that two companies had to be accommodated at Aberdeen. These provided the Queen's Guard at Ballater in 1873.

The 78th in Great Britain   1874-1879

In 1874 the 78th moved to Aldershot where it was brigaded with the 42nd, 79th and 93rd Highlanders in a Highland Brigade commanded by Maj Gen W. Parke, late of the 72nd. The four regiments had served together at the final capture of Lucknow in 1858, and it was a friendly reunion for the few veterans of the Indian Mutiny who were still serving. The brigade was inspected by The Czar of Russia.

In 1875 the 78th moved to Dover, in 1876 to Edinburgh, and in 1878 back to Ireland. The main task during this series of peacetime garrison postings was to supply regular drafts to the linked regiment, the 71st, then stationed in Malta.

In 1879 the 78th left Ireland for India.

The 78th return to India   1879

The 78th arrived in Bombay in March 1879 and went by train to Poona. It was the fifth time it had been stationed there.

The 78th in Afghanistan   1879-1881

The war in Afghanistan had broken out in 1878 and, when news was received of the attack on a British column at Maiwand, the 78th were sent to Afghanistan. After a time employed on protection of the lines of communications, they arrived at Kandahar in November 1880, and spent an extremely cold winter in Afghanistan. The 78th returned to India in May 1881 and were stationed at Sitapur.

78th CAMPAIGN HONOUR

Although the 78th did not take part in the fighting of the Afghanistan campaign, their long marches and hard work guarding the lines of communication were recognised by the award of the campaign honour:
'AFGHANISTAN 1879-80'

The 78th become 2nd Bn Seaforth Highlanders   1881

Under the Army Reforms of 1881 the 78th Highlanders (Ross-shire Buffs) were amalgamated with the 72nd Duke of Albany's Own Highlanders. The 78th became the 2nd Battalion Seaforth Highlanders and the 72nd became the 1st Battalion.

It was a logical amalgamation with the only other regiment which had been raised by the Seaforth family. For the 78th there was little change to the arrangements under the localisation scheme of 1873. The depot remained at Fort George, and the territorial area was unchanged, except for the loss of Inverness-shire and Nairn which became the territorial area of The Queen's Own Cameron Highlanders.

Neither was the uniform of the 78th to change much, for the 72nd were only too pleased to return to the kilt which they had lost in 1809. The Seaforth Highlanders adopted the MacKenzie kilt of the 78th. The only major concession by the 78th was in changing to the yellow facings of the 72nd; but even this was altered in 1899 when the Seaforth Highlanders were allowed to change to the buff facings of the old 78th.

4. THE 79th CAMERON HIGHLANDERS FROM 1793-1881

The Raising of the 79th Cameronian Volunteers   1793

On 17th August 1793, Alan Cameron of Erracht was granted the Letter of Service which authorised him to raise the 79th Regiment of Foot, or Cameronian Volunteers. On the same date he was commissioned as Major Commandant of the new regiment.

He had always intended that it should be the Clan Cameron regiment, and the main source of recruits was therefore Lochaber, Appin, Mull and North Argyll. His brother Captain Ewen Cameron raised a complete company from Lochaber which assembled at Fort William in November 1793. But competition for recruits was fierce at the time, as there were many Fencible regiments being raised; and the Duke of Gordon, who was in the influential position of being feudal superior of much of Lochaber, was also hoping to be allowed to raise a regiment (the 100th Regiment, later known as the 92nd Highlanders, was authorised in February 1794). Erracht had to send his recruiting parties to draw men from all over the Highlands, from the main cities such as Edinburgh, Glasgow, Aberdeen and Perth, and also from the industrial towns where many Highlanders had sought work.

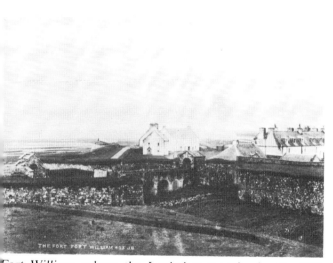

Fort William, where the Lochaber recruits for the 79th mustered in 1793.

(Photograph by courtesy of West Highland Museum)

In selecting a base for his Headquarters, and accommodation for nearly 700 men, he was left with little choice. The coastal towns were full of Fencible regiments protecting the country against invasion by the French, and the only large barracks, at Fort George, were occupied by the 78th Highlanders who were being raised. The only available town, with a small military barracks and enough inns to accommodate the recruits, was Stirling; and so it became the first headquarters of the 79th.

On 4th January 1794 the 79th were paraded in the King's Park at Stirling for inspection by a General Officer, and passed as fit for service. Erracht had achieved the full establishment of 654. The 79th were the second regiment to be added to the Army's establishment in the French Revolutionary wars, the first being Lord Seaforth's 78th Highlanders.

Uniform of the 79th   1794

The 79th wore the normal uniform of the Highland regiments at the time, with red jackets, kilt and belted plaid, sporran, red and white hose, and feather bonnets. Their most distinctive feature was their tartan, for it was the only military tartan which was not based on the 42nd Black Watch (or Government) tartan. By tradition the 79th tartan was designed by Alan Cameron's mother and, although the story of its origin has been lost, it is probably a variation of a sett which was popular in Lochaber at the time. The 79th, or Cameron of Erracht tartan, has always been a matter of particular pride to the regiment. With the MacKenzie tartan of the 78th, it is still used by the Queen's Own Highlanders today, being worn by the pipers, drummers and bandsmen of the regiment. The facings of the 79th were green.

The first stand of Colours, provided by Major Alan Cameron of Erracht, were taken into use at Stirling in January 1794.

The 79th in Ireland   1794

As soon as the 79th was passed as fit for service, the regiment received marching orders for service in Ireland. They left Stirling on 11th January 1794 and marched to Portpatrick where they embarked for Belfast. During five months in Ireland, the issue of uniform and equipment was completed.

The service in Ireland had its advantages, for it allowed the regiment to be put on the Irish establishment. This meant an increase in strength to 1000 rank and file, and also allowed Major Cameron of Erracht to be promoted to Lieutenant Colonel Commandant.

The 79th in the Netherlands   1794

In June 1794 the 79th received orders for active service. They left Ireland for Southampton where they joined the reinforcements for the Duke of York's expedition to the Netherlands. It was a stroke of ill fortune, which they shared with the 78th, that their first taste of active service had to be in one of the British Army's worst conducted campaigns.

The Duke of York's expedition, with Britain's Austrian and Dutch Allies, had been intended to halt the advance of the French Revolutionary Army. But the Austrians had been defeated and the British force, in danger of being overrun, was left to withdraw through Germany to the port of Bremen. The campaign coincided with one of the hardest winters on record, when the cold was so intense that it was said that even the brandy froze in the bottles. The 79th lost 200 men, nearly all from the effects of the cold.

The threat to draft the 79th   1795

The 79th returned from their ordeal in April 1795 and were stationed in Newport, Isle of Wight. Their stay there was short, thanks to a degree to Colonel Alan Cameron of Erracht and his famous interview with the Duke of York.

On his return from Holland Erracht had heard of plans to draft the 79th to four other regiments. As his Letter of Service gave the specific undertaking that his regiment should never be drafted, he sought an interview with the Commander in Chief of the Army, HRH The Duke of

York. Erracht told him in no uncertain terms that 'to draft the 79th is more than you or your Royal father dare do'; to which the Duke of York countered; 'The King, my father, will certainly send the regiment to the West Indies'. Losing his temper Erracht told the Duke of York that 'You may tell the King, your father, from me, that he may send us to hell if he likes, and I'll go at the head of them, but he daurna' draft us'.

The 79th in the West Indies   1795-1797
Erracht had saved his regiment but, perhaps not surprisingly, the 79th sailed for the West Indies on 10th July 1795. For the unfortunate 79th the West Indies fulfilled their dreadful reputation for tropical disease. In two years the yellow fever and malaria which decimated nearly every regiment which served there, had killed 267 of the 79th. With his regiment reduced to below effective strength, Erracht had no option but to allow 229 of the survivors to be drafted to other regiments, mainly to the 42nd Highlanders, and to return to Great Britain with his officers, NCOs and drummers to find new recruits for the 79th.

The 79th in Great Britain   1797-1798
On his arrival back in London Colonel Cameron of Erracht wasted no time in complaining to the Commander in Chief about the drafting of his regiment, and he had the satisfaction of a more sympathetic hearing this time. It was a difficult time for recruiting, because the army was expanding to meet the commitments of the French war, and there was intense competition among the regiments for recruits. Erracht was allowed to establish his headquarters in Inverness, and the 79th was authorised to recruit throughout Britain. Erracht had lost none of his skill and persuasion as a recruiter and, against all the odds, by June 1798 he was able to parade a regiment 780 strong.

In September 1798 the 79th sailed for garrison duty in Guernsey.

The 79th in the Netherlands   1799
In August 1799 the 79th embarked again for active service against the French in the Netherlands. This time they joined Sir John Moore's Brigade in the Duke of York's Anglo-Russian army. Again, however, it was a difficult and unhappy campaign, much hampered by the canals and ditches which favoured the Franco-Dutch defenders. In one of the few successes of the campaign the 79th had their first major engagement with the enemy when they took part in a successful flanking attack on a French position near the coast at Egmont-op-Zee.

79th BATTLE HONOUR
For their part in the successful attack on the French position, the 79th were awarded the battle honour:
'EGMONT OP ZEE'

Raids against the Spanish ports   1800
The 79th returned to England in late October and were quartered at Chelmsford until April 1800. The regiment's next active service was in August 1800, when it joined an expedition intended to attack the Spanish arsenals at Ferrol and Cadiz. But, through lack of resolute generalship, the attack on Ferrol was abandoned and the force never landed at Cadiz. The 79th were eventually landed in Malta.

Private, 79th Highlanders or Cameronian Volunteers 1799.   (From a painting by Major J. W. Van Oorschot

The Campaign in Egypt   180
In 1798 Napoleon had landed in Egypt with the object o forming a base for the conquest of India. But the French fleet had been located and destroyed at Aboukir Bay by Admiral Nelson, and Napoleon had returned to France abandoning his army in Egypt.

The 79th took part in Sir Ralph Abercromby's expedition which was sent to attack the marooned French army. The expedition was prepared with unusua imagination, and the fleet and the troops were put through a thorough programme of training in beach landing a Marmorice Bay in Turkey. The practice paid off, and fo once the brigades and regiments were landed in the correc order, despite heavy French fire.

As the British force advanced on Alexandria, the 79th fought a successful engagement with the French nea Aboukir, and then took part in the battle of Alexandria which led to the fall of Cairo and the surrender of the French.

79th BATTLE HONOUR
For their part in the campaign in Egypt the 79th wer awarded the Battle Honour:
'EGYPT

They were also granted the badge of the Sphinx superscribed 'Egypt' which is one of the devices on the Regimental Colour today.

The 79th in Minorca and the United Kingdom   1801-1807

After the 79th left Egypt, they spent six months in Minorca which was at the time a British possession. Then in 1802 they returned to Dundee and spent six months recruiting. In early 1803 they moved to Ireland, where they were employed on keeping the peace and in the often unpopular duty of confiscating illicit whisky stills. It was during one of these operations that they had their first encounter with Irish rioters.

In December 1805 the 79th moved to Kent and, while there, they paraded with the 92nd Highlanders for the funeral at St Paul's Cathedral, London, of Admiral Lord Nelson, who had been killed at the battle of Trafalgar. During 1806-1807 the regiment was stationed in Essex at Colchester, Weeley and Harwich.

2nd Battalion 79th   1804-18

In 1804, when a French invasion of Great Britain seemed imminent, and the infantry was stretched to its limits to meet its commitments of defending India and the colonies, the Government authorised a number of Colonels to raise 2nd battalions for their regiments. The main role of the 2nd battalions was to act as 'feeder' battalions for the regiments overseas.

The 2nd Battalion 79th was raised at Stirling in 1804-05, and was commanded at first by Lt Col Phillips Cameron, 22-year-old son of Col Alan Cameron of Erracht. The 2/79th served in Great Britain, supplying drafts to the 1st Battalion which was abroad in the Peninsula Campaign and in Belgium. After the battle of Waterloo brought the Napoleonic wars to an end, the 2/79th was disbanded in August 1815. Its last Commanding Officer was Lt Col Nathaniel Cameron, Sir Alan Cameron of Erracht's second son.

The 79th are redesignated   1804 and 1806

The original name of the 79th had been the 'Cameronian Volunteers'. This was certainly not Erracht's choice of name, and was probably a clerical mistake by the War Office. In 1804 the name was changed to the 'Cameronian Highlanders'. Two years later, apparently at the request of both the 79th and the 26th Cameronians, the 79th were redesignated as 'Cameron Highlanders'.

The 1/79th at the Siege of Copenhagen   1807

In 1807 Napoleon and Czar Alexander of Russia met at Tilsit and agreed that France and Russia, with the involuntary alliance of Austria, Denmark and Portugal, would impose a trade embargo against Britain. The Danish fleet was to be siezed by a French army and used to enforce this blockade. But the British government reacted quickly, and an expedition was sent to occupy Zealand and secure the Danish fleet before the French could reach it.

The 1/79th embarked at Harwich in July to join Lord Cathcart's expedition. After a three day siege Copenhagen surrendered and the Danish fleet was taken over. In the captured city the 79th were billeted in the citadel, until November 1807 when they sailed back to Great Britain in the commandeered Danish ships.

The 1/79th in the expedition to Sweden   1808

The 1/79th took part in a brief expedition to Sweden in May 1808, but the army was not ordered to land and the regiment returned to Portsmouth.

The 1/79th in Portugal   1808

The first long campaign of the 79th was the Peninsula War, where they established a lasting reputation as a reliable and courageous fighting regiment.

In 1807 Napoleon invaded Portugal and the French occupied Lisbon. Next year he deposed the King of Spain and gave the throne to his own brother Joseph Bonaparte. Lt Gen Sir Arthur Wellesley (later the Duke of Wellington) was sent to Portugal with a British force in 1808. Landing north of Lisbon, he fought the skilful defensive battle of Vimiero which forced the French to withdraw from Lisbon.

The 1/79th were embarked for Portugal at the time of the battle of Vimiero, and they arrived the following week. As his regiment joined the British troops occupying Lisbon, Colonel Alan Cameron of Erracht was appointed to command a brigade and, after 15 years in command of the 79th, he handed over to his eldest son Lt Col Phillips Cameron.

The 1/79th at Corunna   1809

After the Convention of Cintra, the peace agreement which followed Vimiero, General Sir John Moore was appointed Commander in Chief of the British forces in the Peninsula. In 1809 he marched into Spain with 20,000 troops, including the 1/79th. His plan was to cooperate with the Spanish armies in attacking the long lines of communication of the French Armies in the Peninsula. But the Spanish troops were no match for the French, and Moore found himself surrounded and outnumbered. He was forced to retreat through the Galicia mountains in bitter December weather. Although his army was successfully evacuated by the fleet from Corunna, Moore himself was killed during the successful rearguard action.

79th BATTLE HONOUR

For their part in the successful withdrawal to Corunna, the 1/79th were awarded the Battle Honour:
'CORUNNA'

79th Cameron Highlander in 1813.
(From a print by W. Heath from a sketch by Capt Unetts, published by T. McLean)

The 1/79th in the Walcheren Expedition   1809

The 1/79th returned from Corunna to Weeley in Essex in February 1809, and in July they were sent to Holland with the Earl of Chatham's army which was intended to attack Antwerp. But during two months in Walcheren, the British Force was so badly attacked by Walcheren fever (a form of malaria), that its strength was reduced by over a quarter, and it had to be withdrawn without achieving its aim.

The 1/79th in the defence of Cadiz   1810

In January 1810 the 1/79th returned to Portugal. They were quickly reembarked with Sir Thomas Graham's force and sent to the relief of Cadiz, which was besieged by the French army of Marshal Victor. The 1/79th took part in the defensive operations which saved Cadiz from capture.

The 1/79th at Busaco   1810

The 1/79th returned to Lisbon in August 1810 and rejoined the British Army of Portugal. When they arrived in September, Wellington was engaged in withdrawing to his carefully and secretly prepared defences, the lines of Torres Vedras, where he planned to block the French advance on Lisbon during the winter months of 1810-11. He had selected several possible defensive positions from which he could fight the French, and he made his stand on the mountain ridge at Busaco.

The 1/79th were in Lt Gen Sir Brent Spencer's 1st Division, in the centre of the British line, and were drawn up on the reverse slope of the ridge, with picquets on the forward slope. The 1/79th was fortunate in that the two French columns attacked the left and right of Wellington's line. One picquet of the 1/79th was overrun, but the regiment avoided the main impact of the French columns.

Through a most carefully sited defensive position and skilful use of reserves, Wellington defeated the French offensive at Busaco. He was then able to retire to the security of the lines of Torres Vedras for the winter, leaving Massena's French Army to waste away through starvation and desertion.

79th BATTLE HONOUR

For their part in the victory of Busaco in 1810 the 79th were granted the Battle Honour:
'BUSACO'

The 79th at Fuentes D'Onor   1811

After a miserable and frustrating winter outside the British lines at Torres Vedras, the French withdrew from Portugal in March 1811. Wellington's army followed up their retreat, and the 1/79th had a sharp engagement with Ney's rearguard at Foz d'Aronce. In April 1811 the British re-entered Spain, but further progress was impossible while the French still held the Spanish fortresses of Almeida, Cuidad Rodrigo and Badajoz.

Wellington's first siege was Almeida, but his operations were disrupted by Marshal Massena who marched a French army to try to relieve the garrison. Wellington had to abandon the siege and take up a defensive position on a line of low hills behind the gorge of the River Dos Casas.

The 1/79th, in the 1st Division, were on the right of the British line on the hill above the village of Fuentes D'Onor. The full weight of the French attack, in three closely packed columns, came through the village, driving the allied sharpshooters back up the narrow streets. But before the French could consolidate their hold on the village,

An officer of the 79th Cameron Highlanders.
(From a print published in 1828 by W. Heath)

Wellington launched his counter-attack. The 79th and 71st Highlanders charged down hill into the streets, and drove the French back with bayonets until the village was recaptured.

Next day the 79th and 71st held on to the village against the most determined French attacks. In what was some of the heaviest fighting that the 79th experienced in the Peninsula war, the regiment lost 287 casualties, including their Commanding Officer Lt Col Phillips Cameron, Erracht's eldest son. The 79th had lost almost a third of its strength, but it had made its mark in the campaign.

79th BATTLE HONOUR

For its gallant service in the battle which prevented the French from raising the siege of Almeida, the 79th were awarded the Battle Honour:
'FUENTES D'ONOR'

The 1/79th at Salamanca   1812

The casualties at Fuentes d'Onor, followed by several bad outbreaks of dysentery and fever, reduced the 1/79th to such a low fighting strength that they did not take part in further operations for a year. However by early 1812 they had been brought up to strength by drafts from the 2nd Battalion, and in June 1812 they joined Wellington's advance into Northern Spain.

On 22 July 1812 Wellington succeeded in catching Marshal Marmont's French army deployed on the march near Salamanca and, in a quick concentrated attack, inflicted a most decisive defeat. The 1/79th, as part of the 1st Division, took part in the action but, being deployed on a flank, were only lightly engaged.

79th BATTLE HONOUR
For their part in the victory over the French, the 79th were awarded the Battle Honour:
'SALAMANCA'

The 1/79th at the siege of Burgos   1812
In August 1812 Wellington's army, including the 1/79th, entered Madrid to a heroes welcome from the Spanish. But an attempt to take the fortress of Burgos in September failed through lack of seige artillery and trained sappers and miners. One of the few successes of the siege was the capture of the Hornwork by a light battalion made up of Light Companies of five regiments including the 79th, and commanded by Major The Hon E. C. Cocks of the 79th. The siege at Burgos cost the 79th 125 casualties, including the gallant Maj Cocks who was killed on 8th October.

The 1/79th at the Battle of the Pyrenees   1813
After withdrawing to the security of Portugal for the winter of 1812, Wellington's army advanced again into Spain in 1813. He defeated the French at Vitoria, where the 79th were not engaged because the 6th Division had been detached to bring up ammunition and stores. The army had now reached the North East of Spain and were entering the Pyrenees mountains.

On 28th July 1813 Marshal Soult's French army attacked across the Pyrenees in a desperate attempt to relieve their garrison at San Sebastian. The 1/79th, in Packenham's 6th Division, were hastily deployed into a blocking position at Sorauren where, despite being outnumbered, they successfully checked the French advance. The 6th Division then attacked and annihilated the French Rearguard.

79th BATTLE HONOUR
For their part in the successful operations against the French at Sorauren, the 79th were awarded the Battle Honour:
'PYRENEES'.

The 1/79th at the Battle of the Nivelle   1813
In September 1813, with the three main continental powers, Russia, Prussia and Austria, allied together against Napoleon, Wellington took the opportunity to enter France from the South West while Napoleon was preoccupied with his eastern frontiers.

On 9th November 1813 the 79th entered France, and next day they took part in the assault across the River Nivelle which cleared the French out of a well-entrenched defensive position.

79th BATTLE HONOUR
For their service in the Battle of the River Nivelle the 79th were awarded the Battle Honour:
'NIVELLE'

The 1/79th at the Battle of the River Nive   1813
As the advance continued up the coast of France, the 1/79th, in the 6th Division, moved North to Bayonne where Soult's army again faced them. In order to attack from the flank, Wellington put half his force across the flooded River Nive and attacked astride the river. The 79th took part in this five day operation which forced the French army to withdraw from Bayonne.

79th BATTLE HONOUR
For their part in the attack on the French on the River Nive, the 79th were awarded the Battle Honour:
'NIVE'

The 1/79th at the Battle of Toulouse   1814
The 1/79th spent two months outside Bayonne and then, in February 1814, Wellington moved North towards Bordeaux. Here the third largest city of France opened its gates and declared itself for King Louis. On 30th March 1814, as his empire collapsed, Napoleon abdicated and Paris surrendered to an Allied army.

Unfortunately this news did not reach Wellington who had now arrived at Toulouse in pursuit of Marshal Soult's army. In the final battle of the Peninsula War, Wellington's army crossed the River Garonne and attacked the French positions on Mont Rave, a 600 ft. hill which dominated the impregnable city of Toulouse. Sir Denis Pack's Highland Brigade, consisting of the 42nd, 79th and 91st, charged and captured the French redoubts of 'La Colombette' and 'Le Tour des Augustins', and then held them against determined counter attacks.

The 79th lost 233 casualties in what was one of the most distinguished actions of the Peninsula War. Next day Wellington entered Toulouse, and news arrived from Paris of Napoleon's downfall.

79th BATTLE HONOUR
For their part in this battle, and for their service in the campaign, the 79th were awarded the Battle Honours:
'TOULOUSE'
'PENINSULA'

1/79th in Ireland   1814-1815
After five years of active service in the Peninsula, the 1/79th sailed in July 1814 for Ireland where they were reinforced by the 2nd Battalion. In January 1815 they embarked for North America, but the ships were driven back by gales and, by the time they were ready to sail again, the move had been overtaken by international events. The deposed Emperor of France, Napoleon Bonaparte, had escaped from exile in Elba and arrived in Paris on 20th March 1815. Instead of moving to America, the 79th left Ireland for Belgium in May 1815.

Napoleon's last campaign   1815
The first two Allied armies in the field against Napoleon were the Duke of Wellington's British, Dutch, Belgian and German force which he assembled in Belgium, and Marshal Blücher's Prussians. Further afield, Russian, Austrian and Spanish armies were also on the march.

Napoleon decided to take the offensive without delay by striking at Wellington's and Blücher's armies, aiming to defeat them in turn. Leaving Paris, the French army followed the axis of the Brussels road, crossing the frontier South of Charleroi. As news of Napoleon's advance reached Wellington in Brussels, his army was still widely dispersed in the garrison towns of Belgium.

The 1/79th at Quatre Bras   1815

At 10 p.m. on 15th June, the 1/79th in quarters in Brussels were put at immediate notice to march. They fell in on the Place Royale at midnight, and by sunrise on 16th June were on the march. 22 miles South of Brussels, the Allied army took up a hasty blocking position at the crossroads of Quatre Bras, level with the Prussians who were about three miles to the east at Ligny.

Sir James Kempt's brigade, which included the 1/79th, arrived at Quatre Bras at about 3 p.m., and took up a position on the Namur road on the left of the Allied line. For the next six hours the 1/79th resisted continual attacks by skirmishers and charges by the French cavalry. In this critical preliminary to Waterloo the regiment, with 27 killed and 277 wounded, was reduced to almost half its effective fighting strength.

The 1/79th at Waterloo   1815

Next day Wellington broke contact with the French at Quatre Bras and withdrew to a previously reconnoitred position on the ridge of Mont St Jean, two miles South of the village of Waterloo. Here the survivors of Quatre Bras concentrated with the rest of the Allied army. The 1/79th, in Kempt's Brigade of Sir Thomas Picton's Division, were sited on the East side of the main Brussels-Charleroi road, in the centre of the Allied line.

On 18th June 1815 the French attack began at 11.20 a.m. with an attack on the strongpoint of Hougoumont on Wellington's right. Then at 1 p.m. the French started a heavy artillery bombardment. The 1/79th lay down on the reverse slope and allowed the cannon balls to pass overhead. At about 2 p.m., four divisions of French infantry attacked the centre and left of the Allied position, and Picton moved his division up into line to meet them. The 1/79 stood along the hedge-lined sunken road which followed the line of the Mont St Jean Ridge. As the massed French columns approached, Picton ordered his division forward of the road. The 79th pushed through the hedge and, drawn up in line, they engaged the French columns with a devastating volley at close range. Then they followed it up with a bayonet charge which sent the French infantry down the hill in disorder. The routed French infantry were then charged by the British heavy cavalry, the Union Brigade pushing through the gaps in Picton's Division and thundering downhill into the bewildered French infantry.

But Picton had been killed during this action, and his Division was now heavily attacked by the French cuirassiers. The 1/79th formed square and regained their position on the ridge under fierce cavalry attack. This moment of intense enemy pressure was the scene of one of the best known incidents of individual bravery, when Piper Kenneth MacKay, of the Grenadier Company of the 79th,

Piper Kenneth McKay of the 79th Cameron Highlanders at the Battle of Waterloo 1815.
(From a painting by Lockhart Bogle)

stepped outside the security of the square playing the ancient rallying tune 'Cogadh no Sith' ('War or Peace' — the Gathering of the Clans), to encourage the hard-pressed 79th.

At last, about 8.15 p.m., the French retreated. They had narrowly failed to break through Wellington's line, and were now attacked in the flank by the Prussians.

The 79th had held their ground throughout the day, but at heavy cost. Reduced to just over 200 strong, and commanded by the senior unwounded officer, Lieutenant Alexander Cameron, a nephew of Sir Alan Cameron of Erracht, the regiment moved forward as Wellington gave his famous order for the whole line to advance. They bivouacked that night at the farm of La Belle Alliance where Wellington and Blucher met.

Of the 675 who had left Brussels two days earlier, the 1/79th had lost 456 casualties, of whom 103 were killed. The 79th shared with the 42nd and 92nd Highlanders and the 28th Regiment the distinction of being the four British regiments specifically mentioned by the Duke of Wellington in his Waterloo Dispatch.

79th BATTLE HONOUR

For their service in the Waterloo campaign the 79th were awarded the Battle Honour:
'WATERLOO'

The 79th in France   1815-1818

After Waterloo the 1/79th took part in the Allied occupation of Paris and remained in France for three years. They were brought up to strength with drafts from the 2nd Battalion before the 2/79th were disbanded in December 1815. The 79th were present at the Reviews in Paris by the Emperors of Austria and Russia, the King of Prussia, and the Dukes of Kent, Cambridge and Wellington.

The first Stand of Colours of the 79th had been in such bad condition after the rigours of the Peninsula War that a new set was ordered on their return in 1814. But the Colours were not ready when the 1/79th were ordered to move to Brussels, and so the 1st Battalion had to borrow the Colours of the 2nd Battalion to carry at Waterloo. The 79th received their second Stand of Colours in Paris in 1815.

The 79th in England and the Channel Islands   1818-1820

In October 1818 the 79th left France for England and were stationed in Chichester. They moved to the Channel Islands in March 1819 and were split up between Jersey, Guernsey and Alderney.

The 79th in Ireland   1820-1825

The 79th moved to Ireland in May 1820 and spent five years there. They had a full share of duties in aid of the civil power, including two turbulent years in Limerick.

Piper 79th Cameron Highlanders 1853
(From a painting by E. Lami. By courtesy of the Victoria and Albert Museum).

In 1821 the 79th were brigaded with the 42nd, 78th and 93rd for the visit of King George IV to Dublin. The only other kilted regiment in the Army, the 92nd, were abroad in Jamaica.

The 79th in Canada   1825-1836

The 79th moved to Canada in 1825, arriving at Quebec in October. In 1828 the regiment moved to Montreal, and on 18th June received its third Stand of Colours on the Champs de Mars. In 1829 they moved to Kingston, and the detachments included the garrison of Fort Henry. In 1831 the regiment moved to Toronto, and then in 1833 returned to Quebec where it remained until returning to Scotland in 1836.

An officer of the 79th Cameron Highlanders with his family, C. 1835.
(From a painting by William Kidd RSA)

The 79th in Great Britain   1836-1840

In October 1836 the 79th landed in Glasgow, moving in 1837 to Edinburgh and in 1838 to Dublin. During 1839-1840 the regiment was sent to the North of England for duty against the Chartist rioters in the industrial towns.

Ensign 79th Cameron Highlanders 1853.
(From a painting by E. Lami. By courtesy of the Victoria
and Albert Museum)

Corporal 79th Cameron Highlanders 1853.
(From a painting by E. Lami. By courtesy of the Victoria
and Albert Museum)

The 79th in Gibraltar   1841-1848

The 79th left Great Britain for Gibraltar in December 1840 under the acting command of Major The Hon Lauderdale Maule. He succeeded to command of the 79th in 1842. The regiment was to spend six-and-a-half years in garrison at Gibraltar, an uneventful time in terms of active service, but a period of unprecedented regimental stability and prestige.

Colonel Maule was a powerful and respected commanding officer whose absorbing interest was the quality and appearance of his regiment. He had a deserved reputation as a man of influence in the Army, and his brother, Captain The Hon Fox Maule (later 11th Earl of Dalhousie), was a prominent politician and became Secretary of War in 1846. During his 10 years in command, Colonel The Hon Lauderdale Maule made many improvements to the uniform of the 79th. New badges, accoutrements, sporrans, sgian dubhs, dirks were introduced. Among his innovations which were followed by other regiments were the Glengarry bonnet, the green tunics for the pipers, and the red and green hose which replaced the universal red and white.

The 79th in Canada   1848-1851

In 1848 the 79th sailed for Canada, their departure being commemorated in Pipe Major John MacDonald's famous pipe tune, 'The 79th's Farewell to Gibraltar'. The arrival in Canada was less auspicious, for the ship carrying most of the mess plate was wrecked in the St Lawrence river.

The 79th spent three years in Quebec until returning to Scotland in 1851.

The 79th in Great Britain   1851-1854

On their return to Great Britain the 79th were based in Stirling and then in Edinburgh Castle. On 18th November 1852 a representative party attended the funeral of the Duke of Wellington in London. In 1853 the regiment took part in the Camp of Exercise at Chobham, the first peacetime manoeuvres held by the Army in Great Britain.

The 79th move to the Crimea   1854

When war with Russia broke out in 1854, the 79th were at Portsmouth. They received their fourth Stand of Colours shortly before embarking for Turkey. In June 1854 they joined Sir Colin Campbell's Highland Brigade at Varna, in Bulgaria, together with the 42nd and 93rd Highlanders.

After a couple of months at Varna the British and French allied army embarked for the Crimea and landed at Kalamita Bay on 14th September 1854.

The 79th at the Battle of the Alma   1854

After landing the army marched on the city and port of Sevastopol. The first Russian troops encountered in any strength were holding a line of hill top positions beyond the River Alma. On 20th September 1854 the Allied Army carried out a frontal assault in which the lack of tactical manoeuvre was fortunately compensated by the determination of the British regiments. On the left of the line the Highland Brigade waded the River Alma under heavy artillery fire, fought their way up to the crest, re-formed, and charged the Russian redoubts with the bayonet. The Russians retreated in confusion.

9th BATTLE HONOUR

For their part in the victory over the Russians at this first battle of the Crimean war the 79th were awarded the Battle Honour:

'ALMA'

The 79th in the Crimea   1854-1856

Bypassing Sevastopol, the army captured the port of Balaclava as a base for operations. Its main aim was to besiege and capture the strongly fortified port of Sevastopol, and for a year the British, French and Sardinian allies conducted a costly and disheartening siege. The 79th took their turn in the trenches and held positions around Balaclava, until Sevastopol eventually fell on 8th September 1855. In May 1855 the regiment took part in the expedition to capture the towns of Kertch and Yenikale.

The 79th suffered the well known hardships of the winter of 1854-55, and from the outbreaks of cholera that hit the army so hard in Bulgaria and in the Crimea. The extent of the epidemic is highlighted by the fact that, of 367 Cameron Highlanders who died in the war, only nine died as a result of enemy action.

9th BATTLE HONOUR

For their part in the siege and capture of Sevastopol, the 9th were awarded the Battle Honour:

'SEVASTOPOL'

The 79th return to Great Britain   1856

On their return from the Crimea in June 1856, the 79th were reviewed by Queen Victoria at Aldershot. They were then stationed at Dover with their former comrades of the Highland Brigade, the 42nd and the 93rd, and in June 1857 moved to Dublin.

The 79th move to India   1857

When news arrived of the mutiny by the Sepoy regiments in India, the 79th were quickly brought up to a strength of 1000 rank and file with volunteers from other regiments. They embarked for India and arrived in Calcutta in November 1857.

In December the 79th moved up to Allahabad, and in January 1858 had their first brush with the mutineers when they attacked a party of rebels at Secundragunge and captured 600, without loss. The regiment then joined Sir James Outram's force near the Alam Bagh position outside Lucknow in February 1858.

The 79th in the final capture of Lucknow   1858

After Sir Colin Campbell had arrived to take command, the operations to recapture Lucknow began on 4th March 1858. The 79th, in Sir John Outram's Division, carried out a flanking attack, crossing the river Coomtee and advancing up the far bank, while the main force advanced through the outskirts of Lucknow itself. The 79th took part in the attacks on a series of rebel-held positions, and finally crossed over the river on a bridge of casks and recaptured the abandoned Residency. On 19th March 1858, in the attack on the last rebel stronghold in the outlying Musa Bagh, the 79th captured the Colours of the 7th Oude Irregular Infantry.

79th BATTLE HONOUR

For their part in the recapture of Lucknow in March 1858 the 79th were awarded the Battle Honour:

'LUCKNOW'

The 79th at the capture of Bareilly   1858

After the fall of Lucknow, the 79th joined Sir Colin Campbell's Rohilkand Field Force which advanced up to the River Ganges in pursuit of the Sepoy mutineers. In the capture of Bareilly in May 1858 the Highland Brigade of the 42nd, 79th and 93rd Highlanders formed the first line of the attack.

The 79th Cameron Highlanders in India C. 1860.

The 79th in the last stages of the Indian Mutiny Campaign   1858-1859

The 79th fought several further engagements, including the relief of Shahjahanpore, before spending the hottest part of the summer at Cawnpore. In the final stages of the campaign the 79th's actions included the storming of Rampore Kussia, the crossing of the River Gogra, the capture of Baubasia and Bundwa Kote. The campaign ended in January 1859.

The officers of the 79th Cameron Highlanders at Rawalpindi in India 1864.

The 79th in India after the Indian Mutiny   1859-1871

After the Indian Mutiny, the 79th were to remain in India for garrison duty until 1871. They were stationed at Mean Meer (1859), Ferozepore (1861), Nowshera (1862), Peshawar (1862), Rawalpindi (1864), Roorkee (1866), Delhi (1869), Kamptee (1869-1871).

The garrison life of India was peaceful, although the 79th sent four companies to operate on the North West Frontier in 1863-64. The main enemy was fever, and the 79th lost 336 officers and men from disease in their 13 years in India.

The 79th become 'The 79th Queen's Own Cameron Highlanders'   1873

On their return to Great Britain in 1871, the 79th were stationed for two years at Parkhurst, Isle of Wight, and provided the Guards of Honour and ceremonial duties whenever Queen Victoria was in residence at Osborne nearby. It was this period which led to the Queen's special affection for the 79th. She presented the fifth Stand of Colours to the 79th at Parkhurst on 17th April 1873, and in July ordered that the regiment should be designated 'The 79th Queen's Own Cameron Highlanders'.

On becoming a Royal regiment the facings of the 79th were changed from Green to Blue, and the regiment was given as its badge the 'Thistle ensigned with the Imperial Crown.' The badge remains part of the badge of the Queen's Own Highlanders today.

The 42nd and 79th Depot at Perth   1873-1881

Under the Localisation Scheme of 1873, and until the Army Reforms of 1881, the 79th were linked with the 42nd Royal Highlanders. The joint depot of No. 57 Sub District was established at Perth, and the two regiments were allocated a recruiting area of Kincardine and Forfarshire. Under this arrangement it was the home battalion's duty to keep the overseas battalion up to strength with drafts. The system was put to the test when the linked 42nd were sent at short notice to join General Wolseley on the Gold Coast in 1873, and the 79th was required to supply a draft of 132 volunteers to bring them up to strength for the Ashanti Campaign.

The 79th in Great Britain   1871-1879

After two years at Parkhurst, the 79th moved to Aldershot in 1873. During the summer manoeuvres of 1874 they were brigaded with the 42nd, 78th and 93rd, and it was a friendly reunion for the few remaining veterans of the Indian Mutiny who were still serving. In 1875 the 79th moved to Edinburgh Castle, in 1876 to Fort George, and in 1878 to Glasgow. The regiment provided the Royal Guard at Ballater for 1876, 1877 and 1878. In 1879 the 79th sailed for Gibraltar where they relieved the linked regiment, the 42nd Royal Highlanders.

The Army Reforms   1881

Under the Army Reforms of 1881, the 79th were the only single battalion infantry regiment to escape amalgamation. The old regimental numbers were officially discontinued and so the 79th became 'The Queen's Own Cameron Highlanders.'

The Camerons were given a territorial area of Inverness-shire and Nairn, and were allocated the Depot which was still being built at Inverness. When it had been started in 1876 it had been intended for the combined Depot of the 71st and 78th Highlanders. Now it was to become the Depot of The Queen's Own Cameron Highlanders. However Cameron Barracks, as it was now called, was not completed until 1886 and so, until then, the Camerons Regimental Depot was accommodated at Fort George with the Seaforth Depot.

5.   THE DEPOTS BEFORE 1881

Officers of the 42nd and 79th Highlanders at the shared No. 57 Brigade Depot at Perth in 1873.

The Depot Companies

Until the Crimean War of 1854-1856, an infantry regiment did not have a permanent base or depot in Great Britain. When it was sent on foreign service the regiment divided into two parts, The Service Companies going abroad, and the Depot Companies remaining in Great Britain or Ireland to recruit and to train reinforcements for the Service Companies. There were no permanent territorial links, and the Depot Companies at home were given normal military roles, such as garrison duty or aid to the civil power.

The Depot Battalions

In order to improve recruiting for the regiments serving in the Crimean War, the Depot Companies of several regiments were grouped together in the industrial towns. After the war, in 1856, this centralization was taken a stage further by the formation of Depot Battalions.

Depots Attached to Home Service Battalions   1870

In 1870 the Depot Battalions were replaced by a system of pairing, under which the Depot Companies of regiments overseas were attached to Regiments at home. The 72nd stationed at Cork, had the Depot Companies of the 71st attached; the 78th, stationed in Nova Scotia, left their Depot Companies with the 93rd in Aberdeen; and the 79th, stationed in India, left their Depot Companies with the 2nd in Aldershot.

Localisation of Depots   1873

Under the 'Localisation Scheme' of 1873, 70 infantry regimental Sub-Districts were established, based on population figures and county boundaries. Each Sub-District supported two line regiments, and had a permanent Brigade Depot consisting of two skeleton companies from each of its two line regiments. Each Brigade Depot also included the HQ and permanent staff of the local Militia regiments.

Under the 1873 scheme the 72nd and the 91st Argyllshire Regiment were linked and shared a Depot at Stirling, the 71st and 78th were linked and shared a temporary Depot at Fort George, and the 42nd and 79th were linked and shared a Depot at Perth. Because Fort George was considered unsuitable accommodation for the Depot of the 71st and 78th, the building of a new Brigade Depot was begun at Inverness.

Permanent Depots   1881

Under the Army Reforms of 1881 the 72nd and 78th were amalgamated to form the Seaforth Highlanders, and were given a permanent Depot at Fort George. The 79th remained as the only single battalion regiment in the Infantry, and were allocated as their Depot the half built barracks at Inverness, which had been started for the 71st and 78th. The Depot of the Camerons was accommodated temporarily with the Depot of the Seaforth at Fort George, until 1886 when the Cameron Barracks were completed.

Officers and NCOs of the 71st and 78th Highlanders and the Highland Rifle Militia at the shared No. 55 Brigade Dep
at Fort George, in 1877.

6.   *THE MILITIA BATTALIONS OF THE REGIMENT*
BEFORE 1881

The Militia battalions of the regiment originated in the Napoleonic Wars when the regular army was so stretched by its commitments in India and the colonies, and also by sending expeditionary forces to the continent of Europe, that it could not provide an adequate force for the defence of Great Britain and Ireland against invasion by the French. The Militia regiments were intended mainly for home defence, and they supplemented the regular army garrisons. In a secondary role they were also used to control riots and disturbances in the industrial towns during the turbulent times of the Industrial Revolution.

Under the 'Scotch Militia Act' of 1802 the responsibility for providing officers and raising men for the Militia was delegated to counties. Each county was allocated a share c commissions and was required to run a ballot in ever parish to select men for 3 year periods of service. After th Napoleonic Wars, the Militia was seldom called out fc service and the ballots lapsed until in 1852 voluntar service superceded the ballot system.

The shortage of recruits for the regular army during th Crimean War was largely overcome by allowing Militi soldiers to volunteer for the regular army. The success o this prompted a re-organisation of the Militia. Eac regiment was given a permanent training staff of regula officers and NCOs, and a small barracks and stores.

THE ROSS-SHIRE MILITIA 1798-1881

The 96th Ross-shire, Caithness, Sutherland and Cromarty Rifles C.1855, at Fort George.

The 96th Highland Rifle Militia C.1860.

The officers of the 96th Highland Rifle Militia, Fort George 1869.

Pipe Major Ronald MacKenzie and the pipers of the 96th Highland Rifle Militia at Fort George in 1880.

THE ROSS, SUTHERLAND, CAITHNESS AND CROMARTY, OR 2nd NORTH BRITISH MILITIA
1798-1802

The regiment was raised in 1798 by Colonel Francis Humberston MacKenzie, Lord Seaforth (who had also raised the 78th Highlanders, Ross-shire Buffs). It was embodied at Fortrose and Dingwall and served on garrison duty in Scotland until 1802 when all but the permanent staff were disbanded. The regiment wore the normal uniform of a line regiment.

THE 5th ROSS, CAITHNESS, SHETLAND AND CROMARTY MILITIA   1803-1831

The regiment was embodied again in 1803, under a slightly changed designation, and served for 11 years on garrison duty throughout Great Britain until being disbanded in 1814. It was re-embodied again in 1815 and served in Northern Ireland for a year before being disbanded again. Thereafter it was called out for training periodically, but was not required to leave the north of Scotland.

THE 96th ROSS, CAITHNESS, SUTHERLAND AND CROMARTY MILITIA   1831-1854

In 1831 the regiment was renumbered the 96th Militia. The long period of peace meant that little, if any, formal training was required to be carried out. The ballots were not held and the permanent staff was not kept up to strength.

THE 96th ROSS-SHIRE, CAITHNESS, SUTHERLAND AND CROMARTY RIFLES   1854-1860

During the Crimean War the Ross-shire Militia was embodied once again at Dingwall in 1855. Designated as Rifles, and given the role of a Rifle Corps, it was dressed in green uniform similar to the Rifle Brigade. After the Crimean war a Militia barracks was built in Dingwall to house the permanent staff and stores of the regiment.

THE 96th HIGHLAND RIFLE MILITIA   1860-1881

In 1860 the regiment changed its name to the Highland Rifle Militia, and its uniform was changed to Highland dress. The new uniform had been designed in 1855 by the artist R. R. McIan, well known for his sketches of the 'Clans of the Scottish Highlands'. It included a rifle green doublet, MacKenzie tartan kilt and flat blue bonnets. In 1866 the uniform was further embellished with belted plaid, diced hose and brown spats, and a 'set up' bonnet with a grouse wing.

In 1867 the stores and arms were moved from Dingwall to Fort George, and the Militia barracks in Dingwall converted to quarters for the permanent staff. The move was mainly intended to allow the Militia men to be assembled and dismissed well away from the 'pot houses' (i.e. pubs) of Dingwall.

In 1870 the regiment changed from its rather elaborate kilted uniform to MacKenzie tartan trews, green tunic, and green shacko.

THE INVERNESS-SHIRE MILITIA 1802-1881

THE INVERNESS, BANFF, ELGIN AND NAIRN
MILITIA   1802-1804

The Inverness Militia, as they were known, were enrolled in 1802 and first embodied in February 1803. The regiment was raised by Sir James Grant of Grant, Bart, Lord Lieutenant of Inverness-shire. It wore the normal uniform of a line regiment. The Commissions and the liability to raise recruits were shared out among the counties of Inverness, Banff, Elgin and Nairn on a basis of the population figures.

The regiment received its Colours in 1803.

THE 10th INVERNESS, BANFF, ELGIN AND NAIRN
MILITIA   1804-1833

The Inverness Militia were numbered the 10th Militia in March 1804. During the Napoleonic Wars the regiment served throughout Great Britain on garrison duty, returning from Portsmouth to Inverness in 1814 to be disembodied. Thereafter it was called out periodically for training.

THE 76th INVERNESS, BANFF, ELGIN AND NAIRN
MILITIA   1833-1855

In 1833 the Inverness Militia were renumbered the 76th. During the Crimean War they were embodied at Inverness.

THE 76th HIGHLAND LIGHT INFANTRY
MILITIA   1855-1881

The Crimean War gave the Inverness Militia new impetus. The Master of Lovat became the Commanding Officer, the uniform was changed to Highland dress with the kilt of Hunting Fraser tartan, and the regiment was redesignated as the 76th Highland Light Infantry Militia. (There was no connection with the regular regiment, the 71st Highland Light Infantry). In 1856 the Militia barracks were built in Telford Street, Inverness, to house the permanent staff and stores. From 1858 to 1871 the regiment carried out its annual training period at Fort George, and after 1872 at Muir of Ord.

Pipe Major MacLennan and the pipers of the 76th Highland Light Infantry Militia C.1870.

The Band of the 76th Highland Light Infantry Militia C.1868.

The Colour Sergeants of the Highland Light Infantry Militia 1877.

The Permanent Staff of the Highland Light Infantry Militia 1877.

7.   THE VOLUNTEER BATTALIONS OF THE REGIMENT UP TO 1881

Although a large number of Volunteer regiments were raised during the Napoleonic Wars, they were discontinued after 1815. In 1859-1860, when renewed hostility by the French triggered off a wave of patriotism in Great Britain, many new Volunteer corps were formed. The Territorial Army of today is directly descended from these Volunteers of 1859-1860.

They were first formed as independent companies, whose uniform was largely at the discretion of the volunteers themselves. A set of 'Regulations for the Volunteer Force' was published in 1861, which gave instructions for the administration, discipline, and training of the volunteers. For convenience, the companies were grouped into 'Administrative battalions', but retained a high degree of autonomy. Constitutionally they remained under the jurisdiction of the Lords Lieutenant of the counties.

In 1871, under the 'Regulation of the Forces Act', the Volunteers were transferred to the Secretary of State for War, so that they became subject to the Articles of War and the Mutiny Act.

Under the 'Localisation' plans of 1873, the Volunteers were put under the command of the Brigade Depots which were formed. This was their first formal alignment with the Regular Army.

Under the Army Reforms of 1881, the Volunteers became an integral part of the territorial regiments.

1st ROSS-SHIRE (ROSS-HIGHLAND) RIFLE VOLUNTEERS

The Ross-shire Rifle Volunteers were first raised as six companies during 1860-61.

1st Invergordon 1860	Grey tunic and trousers.
2nd Dingwall 1860	Grey tunic and trousers.
3rd Avoch 1860	Grey tweed jacket and knickerbockers.
4th Knockbain 1860	Light grey tunic and trousers.
5th Alness 1861	Grey tunic and trousers.
6th Alness 1861	Grey tunic and trousers.

In 1861 these six companies were incorporated in the 1st Administrative Battalion, Ross-shire Rifle Volunteers. In 1864 the battalion was given a common uniform of red tunics and blue trousers, except that No. 3 Company chose to wear the MacKenzie kilt.

Three more companies were added in 1866-67.

7th Evanton 1866	Red tunic and MacKenzie kilt.
8th Moy 1866	Red tunic and MacKenzie kilt.
9th Gairloch 1867	Red tunic and MacKenzie kilt.

In 1873 the battalion came under the command of 55 Brigade Depot at Fort George. In 1875 it adopted a common uniform of red doublet and MacKenzie trews, except for 3, 7, 8, 9 Companies who continued to wear the kilt. In 1880 it was consolidated as the 1st Ross-shire (Ross-Highland) Rifle Volunteers with headquarters at Dingwall.

After the Army Reforms of 1881, the battalion became an integral part of the Seaforth Highlanders (Ross-shire Buffs, The Duke of Albany's).

The Ross-shire Rifle Volunteers and 1st Volunteer Battalion Seaforth Highlanders 1860-1908.
(From 'Records of the Scottish Volunteer Force' by Maj Gen J. M. Grierson)

1st SUTHERLAND (SUTHERLAND HIGHLAND) RIFLE VOLUNTEERS

The Sutherland Rifle Volunteers were first raised as eight companies in Sutherland, Caithness, Orkney and Shetland during 1859-1861.

Sutherland
1st Golspie 1859	Grey tunic and trousers.
2nd Dornoch 1859	Grey tunic and trousers.
3rd Brora 1860	Grey tunic and trousers.
4th Rogart 1861	Red doublet and Sutherland kilt.

Caithness
1st Thurso 1860	Grey tunic and trousers.
2nd Wick 1861	Grey tunic and trousers.
3rd Halkirk 1861	Grey tunic and trousers.

Orkney and Shetland
1st Lerwick 1860	Grey tunic and trousers.

In 1864 the companies were incorporated in the 1st Administrative Battalion Sutherland Rifle Volunteers. Two more companies were added in 1867.

Sutherland
5th Bonar Bridge 1868.

Caithness
4th Watten 1867.

In 1864 the Orkney and Shetland Company changed to red tunic with dark grey trousers, and in 1867 the Sutherland companies adopted Sutherland tartan kilt and

The Sutherland Rifle Volunteers 1860-1908.
(From 'Records of the Scottish Volunteer Force' by Maj Gen J. M. Grierson)

belted plaid. HRH The Prince of Wales (later King Edward VII) became Honorary Colonel of the battalion in 1866.

In 1873 the battalion came under command of 55 Brigade Depot at Fort George. In 1880 it was consolidated as the 1st Sutherland Highland Rifle Volunteers, with headquarters at Golspie.

Under the Army Reforms of 1881, the battalion became an integral part of the Seaforth Highlanders (Ross-shire Buffs, The Duke of Albany's).

1st ELGIN RIFLE VOLUNTEERS

The Elgin Rifle Volunteers were first raised as six companies during 1860-61.

1st Forres 1860	Dark grey tunic and trousers.
2nd Elgin Citizens 1860	Elcho grey tunic and trousers.
3rd Elgin Artisans 1860	Elcho grey tunic and trousers.
4th Rothes 1860	Elcho grey tunic and trousers.
5th Fochabers 1861	Dark grey tunic and trousers.
6th Carr Bridge 1861	Elcho grey tunic and trousers.

In 1860 the companies were incorporated as the 1st Administrative Battalion, Elgin Rifle Volunteers. In 1862 the whole battalion changed its uniform to red tunics, and blue trousers, except that the 6th Company adopted red doublets and Grant tartan kilt.

Three companies were added between 1863-1871.

7th Lhanbryde 1863.
8th Garmouth 1867.
9th Grantown 1871.

In 1873 the battalion came under Command of 55 Brigade Depot at Fort George. In 1880 it was consolidated as 1st Elgin Rifle Volunteers, with headquarters at Elgin.

Under the Army Reforms of 1881 the battalion became an integral part of the Seaforth Highlanders, (Ross-shire Buffs, The Duke of Albany's).

The Elgin Rifle Volunteers and 3rd Volunteer Battalion Seaforth Highlanders 1861-1908.
(From 'Records of the Scottish Volunteer Force' by Maj Gen J. M. Grierson)

1st INVERNESS-SHIRE (INVERNESS HIGHLAND) RIFLE VOLUNTEERS

The Inverness-shire Rifle Volunteers and 1st Volunteer Battalion Cameron Highlanders 1860-1908. (From 'Records of the Scottish Volunteer Force' by Maj Gen J. M. Grierson)

The Band of the Inverness-shire Rifle Volunteers C.1870.

The Inverness-shire Rifle Volunteers were first raised as seven companies in 1859-1861.

1st Inverness 1859	Dark grey tunic and trousers.
2nd Lochaber 1860	Dark grey tunic and trousers.
3rd Inverness Merchants 1860	Slate grey tunic and trousers.
4th Inverness Clachnacuddin 1860	Elcho grey tunic and trousers
5th Inverness Celtic 1860	Grey doublet, Celtic tartan kilt.
6th Badenoch 1861	Elcho grey tunic and trousers.
7th Beauly 1861	Elcho grey tunic and Fraser tartan trews.

In 1860 the companies were incorporated as the 1st Administrative Battalion Inverness-shire Rifle Volunteers. In 1863 the uniforms were changed, and all companies adopted the Elcho grey doublet, and the 1st Company wore 42nd tartan trews. All the other companies wore the kilt and belted plaid, the 2nd Company wearing

79th or Cameron of Erracht tartan, the 3rd, 4th and 5th Companies 42nd tartan, the 6th Company Hunting MacPherson tartan, and the 7th Company Fraser tartan.

Three more companies were raised during 1867-1869.

8th Portree 1867	MacDonald of the Isles tartan kilt.
9th Campbelltown of Ardersier 1867	42nd tartan kilt.
10th Roy Bridge 1869	MacKintosh tartan kilt.

In 1873 the battalion came under the command of 55 Brigade Depot at Fort George. In 1880 it was consolidated as the 1st Inverness-shire (Inverness Highland) Rifle Volunteers, with headquarters at Inverness, and its uniform was changed to red doublets, buff facings and 42nd tartan kilt for all companies.

Under the Army Reforms of 1881 the battalion was at first attached to No.72 Regimental District but in 1883, when No. 79 Regimental District was set up, the battalion became an integral part of The Queen's Own Cameron Highlanders.

The 1st Inverness-shire Rifle Volunteers at Inverness C.1880.

CHAPTER II THE REGIMENTS FROM 1881-1914

1. REGULAR ARMY BATTALIONS

1st BATTALION SEAFORTH HIGHLANDERS 1881-1914

The 1st Seaforth in Aden   **1882**

In February 1882 the 1st Seaforth left India for Aden to finish off the foreign tour. The garrison of Aden was found from the British troops serving in India. After only four months there, the 1st Seaforth were warned for active service in Egypt, and in early August they were reinforced by two companies of the 2nd Seaforth (the former 78th) sent from Lucknow.

The 1st Seaforth move to Egypt   **1882**

In 1882 insurrection had broken out in Egypt when the Egyptian Army, led by the Egyptian Minister of War, Arabi Pasha, had revolted against the Khedive (or Turkish Viceroy) in protest against government corruption and foreign interference in the country's affairs. At the Khedive's invitation, Great Britain sent an expeditionary force led by Sir Garnet Wolseley to restore order. The force came mainly from Britain and the Mediterranean garrisons, but was augmented by an Indian Contingent which included the 1st Seaforth from Aden.

The 1st Seaforth at Tel-el-Kebir   **1882**

The British force landed at Ismailia. General Wolseley's intention was to march on Cairo, following the line of the Sweetwater Canal, a cutting which took fresh water from the Nile to Ismailia. The Egyptian Army took up a strong defensive position in the desert to block the British advance. Faced with the prospect of attacking a well-entrenched position, held by about double his own strength, Wolseley decided to gain surprise by approaching with a silent night march and then attacking at dawn.

During the attack on the Tel-el-Kebir position on 13th September 1882 the Indian Contingent, led by the 1st Seaforth, had the task of advancing along the side of the Sweetwater Canal to protect the flank of the main attack, and then of preventing the Egyptians escaping. The night advance was a notable success and, as Wolseley's attack went in, the 1st Seaforth charged and captured a battery of four guns and then cleared a series of infantry and gun positions. The British force took the Egyptian position in under 30 minutes, but it had a hard fight and needed time to consolidate and collect its casualties. The Indian Contingent was given the task of following up the Egyptian retreat, and it reached Zag-a-Zig by evening. It had achieved the remarkable feat of covering 33 miles in the day, despite the intense heat of the Egyptian summer.

1st SEAFORTH BATTLE HONOURS

For their part in the campaign in Egypt, the 1st Seaforth were awarded the Battle Honours:
'TEL-EL-KEBIR'
'EGYPT 1882'

1st Bn Seaforth Highlanders, Edinburgh Castle 1887.

The 1st Seaforth return to Great Britain   **1882**

The 1st Seaforth took part in the grand review before the Khedive in Cairo, and then embarked for England. The reinforcements from the 2nd Battalion returned to Lucknow.

There was a heroes welcome for the 1st Seaforth on their arrival in England and during their time at their new station at Parkhurst, Isle of Wight. They took part in the great review by Queen Victoria on Horse Guards parade, and were inspected by the Queen at Parkhurst in January 1883. In 1884 the battalion had the sad duty of parading at the funeral of HRH Prince Leopold Duke of Albany, Queen Victoria's fourth son, who had in 1882 been appointed Honorary Colonel of the 3rd Militia Bn Seaforth Highlanders.

In 16th August 1884 the 1st Seaforth received new Colours from Queen Victoria at Osborne House. They were the seventh Stand of Colours to be carried by the battalion and its predecessors.

The 1st Seaforth at Windsor and Aldershot   **1885**

The revolt of the Mahdi in the Sudan, and the murder by the Dervishes of General Charles Gordon in Khartoum, resulted in another expeditionary force being required. The 1st Seaforth therefore took over public duties from the Foot Guards at Windsor from February to September 1885. During this period the old Colours, the sixth Stand which had been retired in 1884, were presented to Queen Victoria and hung in Windsor Castle.

On the return of the Guards from the Sudan, the 1st Seaforth marched to Aldershot and remained there for the rest of the year.

The 1st Seaforth in Edinburgh   1886-1888

In January 1886 the 1st Seaforth moved by sea from Portsmouth to Edinburgh where they were to spend two years in Edinburgh Castle. The battalion made the most of its return to Scotland after 19 years abroad by sending parties of soldiers into the territorial area which it had been allocated in 1881. Parties visited the Orkneys, Caithness, Sutherland, Ross-shire, Skye and Lewis; the old fourth Stand of Colours was laid up in Dingwall; and the regiment found in the Highland counties a deep interest in their territorial regiment. These tours did much to pioneer a better recruiting system. Between 1882-1888 the 1st Seaforth, as the home battalion, sent out over 1000 men to the 2nd Battalion in India. The recruiting tours of the Highlands succeeded in attracting a high proportion of Highlanders to the regiment, and in maintaining an enviable calibre of recruit.

On the ceremonial and public duties side, the 1st Seaforth provided the Royal Guard at Ballater for 1886 and 1887, and the ceremonial troops for the General Assembly of the Church of Scotland.

1st Bn Seaforth Highlanders, Officers and men of the Royal Guard at Ballater 1886.

The 1st Seaforth in Glasgow   1888-1889

The 1st Seaforth moved from Edinburgh to Glasgow in March 1888 and were quartered in Maryhill Barracks for a year. They provided all the guards and duties for the great International Exhibition which was visited by the Queen.

The 1st Seaforth in Ireland   1889-1895

The 1st Seaforth spent six generally uneventful years in Dublin, Fermoy and Tipperary. The requirement of keeping the 2nd Battalion in India up to strength with drafts meant that at times the Seaforth Highlanders had to be open to General enlistment, as the territorial area itself could not keep pace with the number of men needed. This accounted for the significant proportion of Englishmen and Irishmen in the regiment before World War I.

The 1st Seaforth in Aldershot   1895-1897

The 1st Seaforth moved to Aldershot in early 1895 and spent two years there. The main event of each year was the Autumn Manoeuvres, conducted in full dress uniform.

The 1st Seaforth in Malta   1897-1898

The 1st and 2nd Battalions exchanged duties as the home and foreign service battalions in early 1879. The 1st Seaforth were posted to Malta where they arrived in February 1897 less than 500 strong, and were brought up to strength by over 500 men of the 2nd Battalion from India who had not finished their overseas service.

The 1st Seaforth in the Occupation of Crete   1897

During 1897 the 1st Seaforth took part in an unusual operation, the International Occupation of Crete. The island was under Turkish military rule, but had a mixed population of Greeks and Turks. Strong pressure from the Greeks for union of Crete with Greece, and constant guerilla warfare between Greeks and the Turkish soldiers, led to war being declared between Greece and Turkey. An International Occupation Force was formed with contingents supplied by Great Britain, France, Russia, Italy and Austria.

The 1st Seaforth spent from March to September in Crete in what was a forerunner of a United Nations peace-keeping contingent. The only force used was naval bombardment of the insurgent's position by the Allied Fleets.

The reconquest of the Sudan   1898

After the revolt by the Mahdi against Turkish rule in the Sudan, the British Government had, at the Khedive's invitation (The Turkish Viceroy of Egypt), sent General Charles Gordon to occupy the Sudanese capital Khartoum. But the Mahdi and his Dervish troops had murdered Gordon and established a Mahdist state independent of Egypt. The Mahdi died in 1885, and his successor the Khalifa allowed Sudan to slide into anarchy. In 1897 the British and Egyptian Governments agreed to send an Egyptian Army expedition under Major General Sir Herbert Kitchener to recover the Sudan. In November 1897 Kitchener, opposed by a large Dervish army, requested a brigade of British troops as reinforcements. The British Brigade, which was sent to Sudan in early 1898, was made up of the 1st Warwicks, 1st Lincolns, 1st Seaforth and 1st Camerons.

The 1st Seaforth move to Egypt   1898

The 1st Seaforth moved from Malta to Cairo in March 1898 and were sent south to join Kitchener's army in the north of Sudan. They travelled by train, by Nile river boat, on Kitchener's desert railway, by sailing boat, and the last stage was by camel.

The 1st Seaforth at the Battle of the Atbara River 5th April 1898

The first major action of the campaign was an attack by three brigades of Kitchener's force on a strongly held Dervish 'dem' (defensive position) beside the dried up Atbara River. In the British brigade the 1st Camerons led, with the task of breaching the zariba (thorn fence), followed by the other three British regiments, with the 1st Seaforth in the centre, with orders to enter the breaches and fight through the 'dem'. In a short but fierce fight, the 1st Seaforth cleared the position, but lost two officers and six soldiers killed.

After the Battle of the Atbara 1898, the 1st Seaforth and 1st Camerons bury the dead.

The 1st Seaforth at Omdurman   2nd September 1898

After the victory at the Atbara River, Kitchener's force was reinforced by a further British Brigade, and continued south up the Nile towards Omdurman and Khartoum. By 2nd September it was within five miles of Omdurman when it was confronted by a Dervish army of about 60,000 troops. The British force took up a defensive position behind a zeriba, with its back to the Nile where a fleet of gunboats supported it. The Dervishes attacked with great determination but could not defeat an army which was armed with modern rifles which it used most effectively, and which had the fire support of Maxim machine guns, artillery and gunboats.

The 1st Seaforth, in the centre of the British Brigade, first engaged the Dervish attack at 1,800 yards range, and no Dervish got closer than 800 yards to them. As the Dervish attack petered out the British brigades advanced on Omdurman, and the 1st Seaforth reached the town in the evening.

The battalion returned to Cairo after the battle.

1st SEAFORTH BATTLE HONOURS

For their service in the Sudan Campaign the 1st Seaforth were awarded the Battle Honours:
'ATBARA'
'KHARTOUM'

The 1st Seaforth in Egypt   1898-1903

The 1st Seaforth were to remain in Cairo until 1903. This was over the period of the South African War and, to the chagrin of the 1st Battalion, it was the 2nd Seaforth at Fort George who were sent to the war. The 1st Battalion remained in Cairo sending strong drafts of men, and two companies of Mounted Infantry, to the 2nd Battalion in South Africa. The 1st Seaforth were reinforced by the 3rd (Militia) Bn who volunteered for overseas service and were in Cairo for nearly 18 months.

The 1st Seaforth return to India   1903

The 1st Seaforth sailed from Egypt to Bombay in February 1903 and were stationed at Nasirabad. Much of their training was carried out in the same area as that in which the 72nd had fought in 1858. In late 1905 the battalion moved to Nowshera. It spent the summer of 1907 at Ghora Dhaka in the Murree Hills.

The 1st Seaforth on the Zakka Khel Expedition   1908

In February 1908 the 1st Seaforth formed part of a punitive expedition on the North West frontier against the Zakka Khel tribe. The Bazar Valley Field Force, of two brigades, in destroying the villages of the rebel tribesmen, had some particularly hard fighting. The 1st Seaforth lost their acting Commanding Officer, Major Hon. D. Forbes-Sempill, killed.

The 1st Seaforth on the Mohmand Expedition   1908

Two months later the 1st Seaforth took part in a further expedition against the turbulent Mohmand tribe on the North West Frontier. Between 30,000-40,000 Mohmands and Afghans were threatening to cross the frontier, and so a force of three brigades was sent to oppose them. The expedition had a tough six week campaign of mountain warfare. The incursion was suppressed with some severity, and 170 fortified towers were destroyed.

The 1st Seaforth in India   until 1914

The 1st Seaforth remained in India until 1914. They were garrisoned in Nowshera (1905-1909), Peshawar (1909), Shahjahanpur (1909), Chaubattia and Bareilly (1910-1912), Agra (1912-1914).

In 1911 King George V visited Delhi for his Coronation Durbar, and on 11th December presented the 1st Seaforth with new Colours. They were the eighth Stand to be carried.

On the outbreak of World War I in 1914 the 1st Seaforth left India for France with the Indian Expeditionary Force.

2nd BATTALION SEAFORTH HIGHLANDERS 1881-1914

The 2nd Seaforth at Lucknow and Bareilly   1882-1889

The 2nd Seaforth moved to Lucknow in early 1882. The 1st Seaforth had moved to Aden to complete their Indian tour, but were then ordered to join an Indian contingent which was to join the British Expedition to Egypt. The 1st Seaforth, having left behind with the 2nd Battalion a large contingent of men who had volunteered to remain in India, were now below strength for active service, and so the 2nd Seaforth therefore sent two companies of reinforcements. They joined the 1st Battalion in Aden and then took part in the 1882 campaign in Egypt, and in the battle of Tel-el-Kebir.

The 2nd Seaforth left Lucknow in 1885 and moved to Bareilly, where they remained until 1889.

The 2nd Seaforth in the Hazara (or Black Mountain) Expedition   1888

During 1888 the 2nd Seaforth joined a punitive expedition against the Asakis and Hassanzais, two tribes of the North West Frontier of India which had murdered a Gurkha officer and caused much local trouble. The 2nd Seaforth were split between two columns which operated for two months in extremely rough, mountainous country, under very arduous conditions. The expedition was frequently attacked, but it succeeded in forcing the tribesmen to submit to the authority of the British Government.

The 2nd Seaforth at Rawalpindi 1889-1893 including the second Hazara Expedition   1891

In 1889 the 2nd Seaforth moved to Rawalpindi. In March 1891 the battalion was again sent to join a punitive expedition in Hazara, and spent three months operating in the mountains of the North West Frontier until the tribesmen again submitted to the Government's terms.

The 2nd Seaforth at Ferozepore   1893-1897

In 1893 the 2nd Seaforth left Rawalpindi for Ferozepore. In March 1895 the British Agent in Chitral, with a small British garrison, was besieged by tribesmen, and a field Force of 15,000 men was assembled at Nowshera to go to their relief. The 2nd Seaforth, in the 3rd Brigade, took part in the advance against the enemy-held Malakand Pass, and then into Swat, Bejaur and Dir. The garrison at Chitral was successfully relieved.

2nd SEAFORTH CAMPAIGN HONOUR

For their service in the expedition to relieve the garrison at Chitral, the 2nd Seaforth were awarded the Battle Honour:

'CHITRAL'

The 2nd Bn Seaforth Highlanders on active service in Chitral 1895.

The 2nd Seaforth at Dover and Fort George   1897-1899

In February 1897 the 2nd Seaforth left India after a foreign tour of 18 years, and returned home to be stationed at Dover. In June it was on parade in London lining the streets for Queen Victoria's Diamond Jubilee. In January 1899 the battalion moved up to Fort George and seemed set for a peaceful tour of duty in the regimental area. It furnished the Ballater Guard for the Queen, the battalion marched through Easter Ross on a recruiting tour; and it received new Colours, its seventh Stand, from Queen Victoria at Balmoral on 29th September. But in October 1899 the South African war broke out and the battalion was soon under orders to leave for Cape Town.

The 2nd Seaforth move to South Africa   1899

In South Africa, the long standing hostility between the Boers (the settlers of Dutch descent) and the British led to the declaration of war on 11th October 1899 between the British Government and the South African Republic.

The 2nd Seaforth were ordered to mobilize on 7th October and had a fortnight to call up reservists and issue kit before sailing from Glasgow on 20th October 1899. On arrival in South Africa the battalion joined the Highland Brigade, together with the 2nd Black Watch, 1st HLI and 1st Argyll and Sutherland Highlanders, under Major General Andrew Wauchope.

Faced with a resourceful enemy, skilled at fieldcraft and marksmanship, the battalion adapted its uniform to suit the conditions in the field. It still wore the kilt and diced hose tops, but for camouflage it used khaki drill jackets, kilt aprons, spats and covers on the sunhelmets. Buttons were left unpolished, sporran badges and medal ribbons discarded, and officers gave up carrying swords.

The 2nd Seaforth at Magersfontein 11th December   1899

The 2nd Seaforth joined Lord Methuen's force which had just fought its way across the Modder River in its advance to relieve the besieged town of Kimberley. About six miles beyond the Modder River the Boers held a well prepared defensive position based on the hill of Magersfontein Kop, which the Highland Brigade and Guards Brigade were ordered to attack.

Methuen's plan was based on his experience at Tel-el-Kebir, when a silent night approach followed by an attack at dawn had caught the Egyptians by surprise. But he underestimated the standard of the Boers tactics. He failed to realize that the Boers, instead of siting their trenches in the traditional way on the top of the range of hills, had dug them at the foot of the hills, sited to cover the ground where they foresaw that the Highland Brigade would form up for an attack on the hill.

The Highland Brigade duly advanced, and at 3.20 a.m. it halted in brigade mass of quarter companies, the closest possible formation. It then began to deploy for the attack, still unaware that the Boer position was only 300-400 yards away. As dawn broke the Boers opened a devastating fire at close range. General Wauchope was killed and the 2nd Seaforth were pinned down by the Boer fire for the rest of the day. Despite many small actions of great gallantry, it was a disastrous day for the Highland Brigade, the unfortunate victims of a defective plan and lack of proper reconnaissance.

The Highland Brigade suffered over 900 casualties of which the 2nd Seaforth had 72 killed and 140 wounded.

This sad day is commemorated in the expressive retreat march 'The Highland Brigade at Magersfontein'.

Morale restored

Magersfontein was only one of the three separate disasters for the British in what was known as 'Black Week'. The Boers were also successful against other British forces at Colenso and Stormberg. In Scotland where the Highland regiments had known nothing but victory for nearly a century, there was intense gloom. A wave of popular sympathy, together with a mass of letters, messages and gifts, helped to restore the morale of the Highland Brigade. The 2nd Seaforth were soon reinforced by drafts from the 1st Battalion and from the Militia and Volunteer battalions. The Highland Brigade received new commander, Maj Gen Hector MacDonald, 'Fighting Mac' the hero of the battle of Omdurman.

The 2nd Seaforth at Paardeberg   190

In early 1900 the arrival of Field Marshal Lord Roberts in South Africa as Commander in Chief of the British forces with General Lord Kitchener as his GOC in C, brought to the campaign the decisiveness which it had lacked. Roberts wasted no time in launching an offensive to relieve Kimberley, and the Highland Brigade advanced again.

The 2nd Seaforth took part in an action at Koedoesberg on 7th February 1900 which drew the Boer defenders away from Kimberley and allowed the cavalry to break through to relieve the garrison. Then in late February over 4,000 Boers under General Cronje were cornered at Paardeberg. On 18th February the 2nd Seaforth took part in an expensive opening attack on the Boers, losing 53 killed and 100 wounded. But the British then changed to siege tactics and, after a further nine days of continual pressure and artillery bombardment the Boers surrendered. It was the first major British military success of the war and did much to restore the self esteem of the British Army.

The 2nd Seaforth in the march to Heilbron   190

The Highland Brigade continued its advance, occupying Bloemfontein on 14th March 1900, and halting there for six weeks to refit and reorganize. In late April they resumed the advance to Pretoria, but were then sent to occupy Heilbron. After marching 120 miles in eight days, against constant minor opposition, and including a fierce action against a Boer attack at Roodeport, the 2nd Seaforth occupied Heilbron.

The 2nd Seaforth in the attack on Retief's Nek   190

On 24th July, in the depth of the South African winter, the 2nd Seaforth took part in the attack on a Boer force of 4,000 under General Prinsloo occupying hill top positions on either side of the Retief's Nek pass. The British advance was made in a blizzard, and the 2nd Seaforth made successful flanking attack. The operation resulted in the second major surrender of Boer troops during the war.

The 2nd Seaforth in the later stages of the Boer War.   1900-190

For the rest of 1900, the 2nd Seaforth took part in various smaller operations, including actions further south at Fauresmith, Jagersfontein and Phillippolis. The gueril warfare involved continual marching in pursuit of small Boer forces and destroying Boer farms.

During 1901 and 1902 the 2nd Seaforth were engaged in the work of building and manning the lines of strategic blockhouses, by which Kitchener aimed to divide up the country into districts and then to clear each area methodically.

After peace was signed at Pretoria on 31st May 1902, the battalion remained in the Transvaal until its return to Great Britain in 1903.

Reinforcements for the 2nd Seaforth in South Africa
1899-1902

During the South African war the demand for reinforcements to keep the regular army battalions up to strength was so great that the Militia and Volunteer battalions of the regiment were allowed to volunteer for service overseas. The 2nd Seaforth received over 2,000 reinforcements, and these included drafts from the 1st Battalion in Cairo, drafts from the Depot, three companies of Volunteers from the 1st Ross-shire, the Sutherland and Caithness, and 3rd Morayshire Volunteer battalions, and a draft from the 3rd Militia battalion. The Territorial system introduced in 1881 was given its first real test, and worked extremely well.

Sgt John MacKenzie Seaforth Highlanders, who won the Victoria Cross in 1900 while on attachment to the West African Frontier Force in Ashantee.

The Colours and Assaye Colour of 2nd Bn Seaforth Highlanders C.1903.

2nd SEAFORTH BATTLE HONOURS

For their service in the South African War, the 2nd Seaforth were awarded the Battle Honours:

'PAARDEBERG'
'SOUTH AFRICA 1899-1902'

The 2nd Seaforth in Ireland   1903-1904

On their return from South Africa in February 1903 the 2nd Seaforth were sent to Dublin. They took part in the Royal Review in the Phoenix Park in July and furnished Guards of Honour for the Kings Levee.

The 2nd Seaforth in Aldershot and Edinburgh   1904-1909

In 1904 the battalion moved to Aldershot, and in 1906 on to Edinburgh where it was quartered in the castle. HRH Prince Leopold, Duke of Albany, had been appointed Colonel in Chief of the Seaforth Highlanders, and in 1907 he paid his first visit to the regiment when he inspected the 2nd Seaforth at Edinburgh.

There was a full share of ceremonial duties, including Guards of Honour for the General Assembly of the Church of Scotland, the Royal Guard at Ballater, and the opening of the Queen Victoria School, Dunblane.

The 2nd Seaforth at Fort George   1909-1912

In 1909 the 2nd Seaforth moved to Fort George. The battalion took full advantage of being in its Regimental area again by training with the Seaforth and Cameron Brigade of the Territorial Force, parading with the 3rd (Special Reserve) Battalion, and sending companies to train and camp at Strathpeffer, Loch Broom, Lossiemouth and Grantown-on-Spey. It went by rail to Thurso and then marched back to Fortrose, crossing the Firth from Chanonry to Fort George in small boats. Next year a similar march was carried out through Morayshire, and in 1911 through Easter Ross.

The 2nd Seaforth in Shorncliffe   1912-1914

In 1912 the 2nd Seaforth moved to Shorncliffe, and they were stationed there when war broke out on 4th August 1914.

1st BATTALION THE QUEEN'S OWN CAMERON HIGHLANDERS 1881-1914

The 1st Camerons move to Egypt   1882

In 1882 the Egyptian Army, led by the Egyptian Minister of War, Arabi Pasha, revolted against the Khedive (or Turkish Viceroy) in protest against the corruption of the Turkish government of Egypt and against foreign interference in Egypt's affairs. At the Khedive's invitation, Great Britain sent to Egypt an expeditionary force to restore order. It was led by Sir Garnet Wolseley.

The 1st Camerons embarked at Gibraltar and, on their arrival in Egypt, joined the Highland Brigade under Maj Gen Sir Archibald Alison, together with the 1st Black Watch, 2nd HLI and 1st Gordons.

The 1st Camerons at Tel-el-Kebir   1882

The 79th were landed with the main force at Ismailia. The plan was to advance on Cairo up the axis of the Sweetwater Canal, a cutting which carried fresh water from the Nile to Ismailia. The Egyptian Army took up a strongly entrenched position in the open desert at Tel-el-Kebir.

Faced with an attack on an enemy of about double his own strength, Wolseley decided to gain surprise by a silent night approach followed by an attack at dawn. The Highland Brigade were to be the left forward brigade of the attack. The force assembled at last light, and waited until 1.30 a.m. when it set out on a silent six mile advance.

The Highland Brigade were within 200 yards of the enemy position before the enemy realized that they were there. As the Egyptians opened fire the Highlanders charged. The 1st Camerons rushed forward with their pipers playing, scrambled over the ditch and parapet, and fought their way through the Egyptian position. After 30 minutes the enemy were routed and the Egyptian army destroyed.

1st CAMERONS BATTLE HONOURS

For their part in the defeat of the Egyptian Army the 1st Camerons were granted the Battle Honours:
'TEL-EL-KEBIR'
'EGYPT 1882'

The 1st Camerons in the Expedition to relieve Khartoum
1884

The 1st Camerons took part in the grand review before the Khedive in Cairo, and the Highland Brigade then remained in Egypt with the Army of Occupation.

The Sudan had been ruled by the Turkish Government in Egypt until 1881 when a religious leader Mohammed Ahmed, the 'Mahdi', had declared a Holy war against the Turks. His Dervish army had thrown out the Egyptian occupation troops. The British Government had sent General Charles Gordon to evacuate the Khedive's troops and government officials from Sudan, but Gordon had been besieged in the Sudanese capital Khartoum.

In November 1884 the 1st Camerons joined Wolseley's expeditionary force which was sent up the Nile to rescue Gordon. But the battalion had got no further than Koroske when news came that the Dervishes had captured Khartoum and murdered General Gordon.

The 1st Camerons with the Sudan Frontier Field Force
1884-1886

The 1st Camerons spent one-and-a-half years operating with the Frontier Field Force on the Sudanese border. Helped by 250 men of the 9th Sudanese Bn of the Egyptian Army, they held the fort of Kosheh against a Dervish force of 7,000, and routed the Dervishes at Giniss. In April 1886 the battalion returned to Cairo.

(To mark the association between the 1st Camerons and the 9th Sudanese during the defence of Kosheh and the attack at Giniss, the 1st Camerons presented them with a Colour. It was carried by the 9th Sudanese until they were disbanded in 1930, and is now in the regimental museum of the Queen's Own Highlanders).

1st CAMERONS BATTLE HONOUR

For their part in the expedition up the Nile and their operations on the Sudan border, the 1st Camerons were awarded the Battle Honour:
'NILE 1884-85'

The 1st Bn The Queen's Own Cameron Highlanders in the desert in Egypt 1885.

The 1st Camerons in Great Britain   1887-1892

The 1st Camerons returned to Great Britain in 1887 to find their future in doubt. It was proposed to convert the regiment in the 3rd Bn Scots Guards but, thanks to vociferous protest from a large list of influential people and societies, the idea was shelved for the time being.

The 1st Camerons were at first stationed at Devonport, and then in 1888 relieved the 1st Seaforth at Edinburgh Castle. The battalion spent four years in Scotland, providing the Royal Guard at Balmoral from 1888-1891.

The 1st Camerons in Malta and Gibraltar   1892-1897

The 1st Camerons spent six uneventful years in the Mediterranean garrisons, stationed in Malta (1892-95), Gibraltar (1895-97) and then moving to Cairo in late 1897.

The reconquest of the Sudan 1898

Since the Madhi's revolt and the murder of General Charles Gordon at Khartoum in 1884, the Sudan had remained independent of Egypt. But under the rule of the Madhi's successor, the Khalifa Abdullahi, it had disintegrated into anarchy, and had become a dangerous and unstable neighbour on Egypt's southern border. In 1897 the British and Egyptian Governments decided to send an Egyptian Army expedition under Major General Sir Herbert Kitchener to recover the Sudan.

The force moved south into Sudan in late 1897, but the Khalifa reacted by sending a large Dervish army against them. In response to Kitchener's request for British troops as reinforcements, a brigade was assembled in Egypt in 1898, made up of the 1st Warwicks, 1st Lincolns, 1st Seaforth from Malta, and 1st Camerons.

In January 1898 the 1st Camerons moved from Cairo by train, then by river boat up the Nile, and finally by Kitchener's desert railway, to join the army at Abu Hamed.

The 1st Camerons at the Battle of the Atbara River   1898

The Dervish army under the Emir Mahmoud had advanced north from Omdurman, and the Dervishes had taken up a strong defensive position beside the dried-up Atbara river. Kitchener's army approached the position by night and, after an artillery bombardment, the British and Egyptian brigades attacked at dawn on 8th April 1898.

The 1st Camerons had the task of advancing in line ahead of the British Brigade, firing as they went, and then of making three breaches in the zeriba (thorn fence) surrounding the Dervish position. The 1st Seaforth, 1st Warwicks and 1st Lincoln followed in column of companies, passed through the breaches and, with the 1st Camerons, cleared the Dervish position.

The Dervish position was over-run, the Emir Mahmoud captured and his army routed. In this short but gallant action the 1st Camerons lost 18 killed.

1st CAMERONS BATTLE HONOUR

For their part in the battle the 1st Camerons were awarded the Battle Honour:
'ATBARA'

The 1st Camerons at Omdurman   1898

After the victory at the Atbara River, Kitchener's force prepared to advance on the Dervish capital of Omdurman. The army was reinforced by a further British brigade and

1st Bn The Queen's Own Cameron Highlanders storm the zeriba at the Battle of the Atbara 1898.

moved south in August. It reached to within five miles of Omdurman, when the Dervish army of about 60,000 troops advanced to meet it. Kitchener's army took up a defensive position behind a zeriba, with its rear protected by the River Nile where it was supported by a fleet of gunboats. On 2nd September 1898 the Dervishes attacked the British and Egyptian position with great determination.

The 1st Camerons, standing beside the 1st Seaforth in the centre of the British Brigade, first engaged the Dervish attack with rifle fire, in section volleys, at 1800 yards. The accuracy and volume of the British rifle fire, supported by the Maxim machine guns and artillery, effectively prevented the Dervishes getting near the British position. As the Dervish attack failed, Kitchener resumed the advance and occupied Omdurman that evening.

(Note. The Dervish capital consisted of two towns each side of the river at the junction of the Blue and the White Niles. Khartoum on the east side was the old centre of government, and included the palace where Gordon had been murdered. Omdurman on the west side was the Dervish capital and included the Mahdi's tomb, an important religious shrine. The battle took place outside Omdurman, but is normally referred to as the battle of Khartoum, from the official capital of Sudan).

1st CAMERONS BATTLE HONOUR

For their part in the victory over the Dervishes, the 1st Camerons were awarded the Battle Honour:
'KHARTOUM'

The 1st Camerons in the Fashoda incident   1898

After the Dervish defeat, the 1st Camerons returned to Cairo, but one company took part in a curious little international incident after the campaign. A French expedition had crossed Africa from the Congo to the Nile to claim the Sudan for France, and had raised the French flag at Fashoda. Kitchener continued up the White Nile by steamer, taking E Company of the 1st Camerons and two Egyptian Army battalions with him. The Egyptian flag was raised a short distance upstream of the French fort at Fashoda, and the French withdrew.

The 1st Camerons move to South Africa   1900

The 1st Camerons were still in Cairo when the war in South Africa broke out in 1899. After the early disasters of

H

the war in December 1899, reinforcements were urgently needed, and the 1st Camerons were sent from Cairo, arriving in South Africa in March 1900.

The 1st Camerons in the advance to Johannesburg and Pretoria   1900
The 1st Camerons joined the 21st Infantry Brigade in General Ian Hamilton's column, and took part in the advance from Bloemfontein to Johannesburg and Pretoria.

The 1st Camerons at the Battle of Diamond Hill   1900
After the fall of Pretoria, the 1st Camerons joined the pursuit of the Boer forces who had escaped from the town. On 11-12th June 1900 the battalion was engaged in the successful attack on the Boer position at Diamond Hill, outside Pretoria.

The 1st Camerons in the Wittebergen   1900
In July 1900 the 1st Camerons joined General Sir Archibald Hunter's force, which included the Highland Brigade, for the operations in the Orange River Colony. They took part in the arduous pursuit of General Prinsloo's army until it was eventually surrounded and captured in the Brandwater Basin in the Wittebergen mountains. The 1st Camerons had a particularly fierce engagement in the capture of Spitzkopf. The operations led to the second major surrender by Boer troops during the war.

The 1st Camerons in the later stages of the Boer War
1900-1902
The 1st Camerons spent the rest of the year in the Orange River Colony on operations round Kroonstad. Their operations included treks to Ladybrand and to the north west of the colony. In 1901 the battalion moved north to the Transvaal, and took part in the work of building and manning the lines of strategic blockhouses by which General Kitchener divided up the country and cleared each area.

During their two-and-a-half years in South Africa, the 1st Camerons completed just under 3000 miles of marching on operational duty.

The battalion lost 24 officers and soldiers killed during the campaign.

SGT DONALD FARMER WINS THE VICTORIA CROSS AT NOOITGEDACHT 1900
On 13th December 1900 the Mounted Infantry Company of the 1st Camerons, operating independently with General Clemens's force, was attacked by a Boer commando at Nooitgedacht, west of Pretoria. Under very accurate and close range Boer rifle fire, Sgt Donald Farmer managed to rescue Lt Sandilands, who had been badly wounded, and brought him to safety. He was awarded the VC for his bravery.

Reinforcements for the 1st Camerons in South Africa
1900-1902
During the South African war the 1st Camerons were reinforced by a Volunteer Service Company from the 1st Volunteer Battalion The Queen's Own Cameron Highlanders, by eight drafts from the 2nd Battalion in Gibraltar, and by volunteers of the 3rd (Militia) Battalion which was embodied during 1900.

1st CAMERONS BATTLE HONOUR
For their service in the South African war, the 1st Camerons were awarded the Battle Honour:
'SOUTH AFRICA 1900-1902'

The 1st Camerons at Inverness   1902-1904
On their return from South Africa, the 1st Camerons were stationed at Fort George. They received a most enthusiastic reception in the Highlands, with a formal welcome and banquet in Inverness. In 1904 the battalion provided the Royal Guard at Balmoral.

The 1st Camerons in Ireland   1904
In 1904, after a farewell banquet at Nairn, the 1st Camerons left Fort George for Dublin. For three years the battalion took part in the largely ceremonial life of the Irish capital, parading for the visits of King Edward VII, and the

Colour Sergeant Donald Farmer VC.

1st Bn The Queen's Own Cameron Highlanders in Dublin 1907.

Duke of Connaught, and for the Prince of Wales, who had been appointed Colonel in Chief of the Camerons in 1902.

In July 1907 there was serious rioting in Ulster, and the 1st Camerons were sent to reinforce the Belfast garrison. The battalion spent a month operating in the docks, and was called out for a major riot in the Falls Road.

The 1st Camerons in Tidworth and Aldershot　1907-1913
In 1907 the 1st Camerons moved to Tidworth and in 1909 to Aldershot. The battalion paraded in London for the funeral of King Edward VII in 1910 and for the Coronation of King George V.

Soon after the 79th Cameron Highlanders of Canada were raised, the 1st Camerons were hosts to a detachment of their Canadian allied regiment when it spent a month in Great Britain for the Coronation ceremonies.

The 1st Camerons in Edinburgh　1913-1914
In 1913 the 1st Camerons returned to Edinburgh Castle. When war broke out in August 1914 they marched out of the Castle for France, the last battalion to occupy the Castle as a peacetime garrison.

2nd BATTALION THE QUEEN'S OWN CAMERON HIGHLANDERS 1897-1914

Under the Army Reforms of 1881 The Queen's Own Cameron Highlanders had been left as the only regiment in the Army to have a single regular battalion, and this was often a difficult and vulnerable position. The lack of a second battalion at home had left the 1st Camerons short of men in the operations on the Nile in 1884-85. There were recurring rumours that the 1st Camerons were to be converted into a 3rd Battalion of the Scots Guards, and in 1887 and 1893 proposals for this were only defeated by intense pressure from influential Highlanders, and eventually by the intervention of Queen Victoria herself.

From the Cameron Highlanders point of view, the obvious solution was to raise a second battalion, and at last in March 1897 the regiment was given authority to do so.

The formation of the 2nd Camerons　1897
The nucleus of the 2nd Camerons came from the 1st Battalion. They left Gibraltar in April 1897 and arrived at Fort George a week later. The battalion was allowed to recruit throughout Scotland, and the plan was to raise three companies in 1897, three more in 1898, and two in 1899. On 29th October 1898 the 2nd Camerons received Colours from Queen Victoria at Balmoral Castle. The battalion also furnished the Royal Guard at Balmoral in 1898.

HM Queen Victoria presents Colours to the newly raised 2nd Bn The Queen's Own Cameron Highlanders at Balmoral 1898.

In December 1898 the 2nd Camerons moved to Aldershot 618 strong, and the final two companies were raised by May 1899.

The 2nd Camerons in the Mediterranean　1899-1903
In October 1899 the 2nd Camerons were sent to Gibraltar to relieve a Guards battalion for the South African war. They supplied the main drafts of reinforcements for the 1st Battalion in South Africa.

In 1902 the 2nd Camerons left Gibraltar for service in the other Mediterranean garrisons. Battalion Headquarters and four companies were stationed in Crete, three companies in Malta and one company in Cyprus. In 1903 the battalion was reunited in Malta.

The 2nd Camerons in South Africa　1904-1907
In April 1904 the 2nd Camerons left Malta for South Africa and were stationed in Pretoria. In 1906 there were disturbances among the African population of Natal and among the Zulus, and so the battalion spent from February to August in Pietermaritzburg, but it was not required to go on active service. In 1907 a contingent was sent to Johannesburg for duty in aid of the civil power during the strikes in the gold fields.

The 2nd Camerons in China　1908-1909
In December 1907 the 2nd Camerons left Pretoria for China. Because of the change of climate from the South African summer to the North China winter, the battalion spent two months acclimatising in Hong Kong before moving to Tientsin.

It was a period of much instability in China, and the European powers all maintained strong guards in their legations in Peking. The 2nd Camerons found themselves serving with an international force made up of contingents from France, Germany, Japan, Russia and the USA.

The 2nd Camerons in India　1909-1914
The 2nd Camerons arrived in Bangalore in December 1909 and remained there for four years. They sent a representative detachment to King George V's Coronation Durbar at Delhi in 1911, and in 1913 won the Championship Cup at the Highland Brigade games at Agra. In 1913 the battalion moved to Poona, where it was stationed when the Great War broke out.

2. THE DEPOTS AND MILITIA BATTALIONS 1881-1914

The Army reforms of 1881 gave each Regular Army regiment a permanent Depot and a territorial area, within which the Militia and Volunteers were integrated with the parent regiment. The Militia became the reserve for the Regular Army, and the Militia regiments were redesignated as Militia battalions of the local regiment, and adopted their uniform. The Depot was the permanent base shared by the Regular and Militia battalions.

In the Army Reforms of 1908 the Militia battalions became Special Reserve battalions, and their establishments were fully integrated with the regimental Depots. In the event of war, their officers and men were liable to be drafted to the Regular Army to fill vacancies when casualties occurred.

DEPOT SEAFORTH HIGHLANDERS, FORT GEORGE

The Depot of the Seaforth Highlanders was established at Fort George in 1881, and was to remain there until the amalgamation of the Seaforth and Camerons in 1961.

DEPOT THE QUEEN'S OWN CAMERON HIGHLANDERS, CAMERON BARRACKS, INVERNESS

The Depot of The Queen's Own Cameron Highlanders was established in 1881 at Fort George, because the Inverness Barracks were still under construction. On 11th June 1886 the Depot of the Cameron Highlanders moved to the completed Cameron Barracks, and it remained there until the Depots of the Seaforth and Camerons were joined together at Fort George in September 1960, shortly before the amalgamation of the two regiments in 1961.

SEAFORTH HIGHLANDERS MILITIA

3rd (MILITIA) BN SEAFORTH HIGHLANDERS 1881-1908

In the Army Reforms of 1881 the Highland Rifle Militia became the 3rd (Militia) Bn Seaforth Highlanders, with a uniform the same as the line battalions of the regiment except that it continued to wear trews instead of the kilt.

In 1882 HRH Prince Leopold, Duke of Albany, was appointed Honorary Colonel of the battalion, but sadly his Colonelcy was short-lived, for he died in 1884.

During the South African War the 3rd (Militia) Bn Seaforth Highlanders was embodied, and volunteered to a man for active service abroad. It was never required to serve in South Africa, but in May 1900 it was sent to Egypt. In Cairo it replaced the 1st Bn Queen's Own Cameron Highlanders, allowing the Camerons to be sent to South Africa, and for 18 months the 3rd Seaforth were quartered in the same garrison as the 1st Seaforth.

CAMPAIGN HONOUR
The battalion was granted the Honour:
'MEDITERRANEAN 1900-01'

3rd (SPECIAL RESERVE) Bn SEAFORTH HIGHLANDERS 1908-1919

In 1908, under the Haldane reforms of the Army, the 3rd (Militia) Battalion became the 3rd (Special Reserve) Battalion of the Seaforth Highlanders. At the same time the permanent staff of the 3rd Seaforth and the Depot were amalgamated into one establishment.

3rd (Militia) Bn Seaforth Highlanders in camp at Fort George C.1907.

THE QUEEN'S OWN CAMERON HIGHLANDERS MILITIA

3rd (Militia) Bn The Queen's Own Cameron Highlanders in camp at Cameron Barracks 1906.

2nd (MILITIA) Bn THE QUEEN'S OWN CAMERON HIGHLANDERS 1881-1897

In the Army Reforms of 1881, the Highland Light Infantry Militia became the 2nd (Militia) Bn The Queen's Own Cameron Highlanders, with a uniform the same as the Regular Army regiment. The 2nd Camerons continued to camp each year at Muir of Ord until 1893, when the issue of the more powerful Lee-Metford rifles made it necessary for the battalion to use the safer Fort George ranges.

3rd (MILITIA) Bn THE QUEEN'S OWN CAMERON HIGHLANDERS 1897-1908

On the formation in 1897 of a second regular battalion for The Queen's Own Cameron Highlanders, the Militia battalion was renumbered as the 3rd Battalion. During the South African war, when the 1st Camerons were serving in South Africa and the 2nd Camerons had been sent to Gibraltar, the 3rd (Militia) Battalion was embodied. It served in Aldershot and in Ireland, at Mullingar.

3rd (SPECIAL RESERVE) Bn THE QUEEN'S OWN CAMERON HIGHLANDERS 1908-1919

In 1908, under the Haldane reforms of the Army, the 3rd (Militia) Bn became the 3rd (Special Reserve) Bn of The Queen's Own Cameron Highlanders. At the same time the permanent staff of the 3rd Camerons and the Depot were amalgamated into one establishment.

On 28th June 1909 the 3rd Camerons were presented with new Colours by Colonel MacKintosh of MacKintosh at Fort George.

2nd (Militia) Bn The Queen's Own Cameron Highlanders in camp at Muir of Ord 1885.

3. THE VOLUNTEER AND TERRITORIAL BATTALIONS 1881-1914

Under the Army Reforms of 1881, the Volunteer battalions became integral parts of the local regiments. Over the years most of them gradually adopted the same uniform and in 1887-1888 were redesignated as Volunteer Battalions of the parent regiments. Their role was limited to home defence and they had no liability to overseas service.

Under the Haldane reforms of 1908, the Volunteer became the Territorial Force (TF). They had the mor ambitious role of a reserve field force for operating, necessary, on the Continent of Europe. The plan wa implemented in 1914 when the Territorial Force wa mobilized and sent to serve in France.

ROSS-SHIRE VOLUNTEERS

1st (ROSS-HIGHLAND) VOLUNTEER BATTALION SEAFORTH HIGHLANDERS   1881-1908

In 1888 the battalion changed its title to conform with its parent regiment, and adopted the full dress of the Seaforth Highlanders, except that the Glengarry was worn instead of the feather bonnet.

During the South African war the battalion sent 110 volunteers for service with the 2nd Seaforth and other regiments in South Africa.

BATTLE HONOUR
The battalion was granted the Honour
'SOUTH AFRICA' 1900-02'

4th (ROSS-HIGHLAND) BATTALION SEAFORTH HIGHLANDERS TF 1908-1914

Under the Haldane reforms of 1908, the battalior became the 4th Seaforth. It was brigaded in the Seaforth and Cameron Brigade of the Highland Territorial Force.

SUTHERLAND VOLUNTEERS

1st SUTHERLAND HIGHLAND RIFLE VOLUNTEERS
1881-1908

Under the Army Reforms of 1881 the battalion was included in the Regimental District of the Seaforth Highlanders but, unlike the Ross-shire and the Moray Volunteers, it did not adopt the name or uniform of the Regular Army regiment. It remained as the 1st Sutherland (The Sutherland Highland) Volunteer Rifle Corps.

In 1884 the Lerwick Company was disbanded and was replaced by a new company at Lairg. In 1890 the addition of another company at Wick and a company at Reay brought the battalion up to a total of twelve companies. The battalion replaced its brass band in 1883 with a band of thirty pipers who wore the Sutherland kilt with Royal Stuart plaid, evidently in honour of the Honorary Colonel, the Prince of Wales.

During the South African war the battalion sent 87 volunteers to serve with the 2nd Seaforth and other regiments.

BATTLE HONOUR
The battalion was granted the Honour:
'SOUTH AFRICA 1900-02'

5th (SUTHERLAND AND CAITHNESS HIGHLAND) BATTALION SEAFORTH HIGHLANDERS TF
1908-191

Under the Haldane reforms of 1908 the battalion became the 5th Seaforth. Although it conformed to its paren regiment in name, it was allowed to retain its own uniforn of Sutherland tartan kilt.

It was brigaded in the Seaforth and Cameron Brigade o the Highland Territorial Division.

Permanent Staff Instructors and Senior NCOs 5th Bi Seaforth Highlanders 1914.

MORAYSHIRE VOLUNTEERS

**rd (MORAYSHIRE) VOLUNTEER BATTALION
EAFORTH HIGHLANDERS   1881-1908**

In 1886 the battalion was authorised to wear the red oublet and MacKenzie tartan trews of the Seaforth Highlanders.

In 1887 the battalion was redesignated to conform with s parent regiment. It adopted the kilt of the Seaforth Highlanders in 1898.

During the South African war the battalion sent 193 olunteers for service with the 2nd Seaforth and other egiments.

BATTLE HONOUR
The battalion was granted the Honour:
'SOUTH AFRICA 1900-02'

**6th (MORAYSHIRE) BATTALION SEAFORTH
HIGHLANDERS TF   1908-1914**

Under the Haldane reforms of 1908 the battalion became the 6th Seaforth. It was brigaded in the Seaforth and Cameron Brigade of the Highland Territorial Division.

INVERNESS-SHIRE VOLUNTEERS

**st (INVERNESS-HIGHLAND) VOLUNTEER
BATTALION, THE QUEEN'S OWN CAMERON
HIGHLANDERS   1881-1908**

In 1887 the battalion was redesignated to conform with he parent regiment. In 1893 it adopted the uniform of The Queen's Own Cameron Highlanders except with the Glengarry instead of the feather bonnet.

During the Boer War, 245 members of the battalion erved in South Africa. The battalion sent the highest roportion of its strength to the war of any battalion in cotland. The main contingents served with the 1st Camerons and the Lovat Scouts.

BATTLE HONOUR
The battalion was granted the Honour
'SOUTH AFRICA 1900-02'

**4th BATTALION THE QUEEN'S OWN CAMERON
HIGHLANDERS TF   1908-1914**

Under the Haldane reforms of 1908, the battalion became the 4th Camerons. It was brigaded in the Seaforth and Cameron Brigade of the Highland Territorial Division.

THE LIVERPOOL SCOTTISH

**8th (SCOTTISH) VOLUNTEER BATTALION, THE
KING'S LIVERPOOL REGIMENT   1900-1908**

The Liverpool Scottish date from the time of the South African War when, on 30th April 1900 the War Office uthorised the formation of the 8th (Scottish) Volunteer Battalion, The King's Liverpool Regiment. In 1901 the Liverpool Scottish were authorised to wear Highland dress, and they chose to wear the kilt of Forbes tartan as a ompliment to their first Commanding Officer, Colonel Christopher Forbes Bell. The headquarters of the Liverpool Scottish were built in Fraser Street, Liverpool in 904.

During the Boer War the Liverpool Scottish sent a volunteer detachment for service in South Africa.

BATTLE HONOUR
The battalion was granted the Honour:
'SOUTH AFRICA 1902'

**0th (SCOTTISH) BATTALION, THE KING'S
LIVERPOOL) REGIMENT TF   1908-1914**

In the Haldane Army reforms of 1908, the Liverpool cottish became the 10th (Scottish) Bn, The King's Liverpool) Regiment TF. The battalion received its 1st tand of Colours from King Edward VII in 1909.

Although the Liverpool Scottish were until 1937 an ntegral part of the King's (Liverpool) Regiment, the ffiliation to The Queen's Own Cameron Highlanders riginated before World War I.

*The King's Liverpool Regiment, 10th Scottish Battalion
1911   (From the painting by R. Caton Woodville)*

CHAPTER III THE REGIMENT IN WORLD WAR I

1. INTRODUCTION

During the First World War the regiments were greatly expanded, and between Seaforth, Camerons, and Liverpool Scottish, there were over 30 battalions. Each battalion has its separate own story, and these vary from the bloodiest battles of the front line to the unspectacular, but nevertheless important roles of home defence and training reinforcements.

In a booklet such as this, it is impossible to tell in full the history of each battalion, or to list the innumerable periods spent in the trenches or in billets out of the line; and so only the main battles are given, with a few of the subsidiary actions or smaller operations, in order to give an element of continuity. This inevitably results in some duplication where several battalions of the regiment served in the same operation, but it does make it possible to give a continuous, although sketchy, narrative for each battalion.

To find out details of battles, operations, or individual actions, and to find dates and places for periods spent in the trenches or in billets behind the lines, it is necessary to read sources such as battalion war diaries, individual accounts, and published histories of battalions and formations.

The casualty figures quoted are taken from the war diaries and, for simplicity, the figures given are normally the totals of those killed, wounded and missing. This may tend to exaggerate the scale of the losses, for the number killed were sometimes only a small proportion of the total, but it serves to illustrate the resilience with which battalions continued to fight, even when they were only able to muster a fraction of their original strength.

For example, when the 8th Seaforth lost 718 casualties at Loos, the total was made up of 49 killed, 371 wounded, and 298 missing. Many listed as missing were in fact prisoners of war or wounded.

2. THE BATTALIONS OF THE REGIMENTS IN WORLD WAR I

		Seaforth Highlanders	The Queen's Own Cameron Highlanders	10th (Scottish) Bn King's Liverpool Regt
REGULAR ARMY	Line Battalions	1st Seaforth 2nd Seaforth	1st Camerons 2nd Camerons	
	Special Reserve Battalions	3rd Seaforth	3rd Camerons	
TERRITORIAL FORCE	Field Units	1/4th Seaforth 1/5th Seaforth 1/6th Seaforth	1/4th Camerons 10th (Lovat Scouts) Bn	1/10th Liverpool Scottish 2/10th Liverpool Scottish (2nd Line Home Defence unit until 1917)
	2nd Line Home Defence Unit	2/4th Seaforth 2/5th Seaforth 2/6th Seaforth	2/4th Camerons	
	3rd Line Reserve Units	3/4th Seaforth 3/5th Seaforth 3/6th Seaforth 4th Reserve Training Bn	3/4th Camerons	3/10th Liverpool Scottish
	Volunteers		1st Volunteer Bn Camerons	
NEW ARMY	Service Battalions	7th Seaforth 8th Seaforth 9th Seaforth (Pioneers)	5th Camerons 6th Camerons 7th Camerons 11th Camerons	
	Reserve Battalions	10th Seaforth	8th Camerons	
	Garrison Battalion	1st Garrison Bn Seaforth		
	Labour Battalion		9th Camerons	

3. *THE DIVISIONS AND BRIGADES OF WORLD WAR I*

During the Great War, much emphasis was given to cultivating the identity and morale of the divisions and brigades in the fighting areas. The published histories of these formations are useful sources of information on the battalions which served in them.

The system of numbering, as far as it affected the regiment, was as follows:

The Regular Army

The Regular Army divisions which existed before war broke out in 1914 were numbered 1, 2, 3, 4, 5, 6. The Indian Army had its own similar system. After 1914 further Regular Army divisions were formed, including the 7, 8, 27, 28, 29 Divisions from battalions at home and in overseas garrisons.

The Territorial Force

The Territorial Force divisions, which existed before war broke out, were numbered in the order in which they went overseas. They were given numbers from 42 to 56, and also kept their territorial titles, e.g. the 51st (Highland) Division and 52nd (Lowland) Division.

Each division was composed of three brigades, also numbered, and so within the 51st (Highland) Division, for example, the brigades were numbered 152, 153 and 154.

The New Army

The New Army divisions formed in 1914 were numbered from 9 to 26, and those formed in 1915 were numbered from 30 to 41. The Scottish New Army divisions were the 9th (Scottish) Division, which was made up of 26 (Highland), 27 (Lowland), and 28 Brigade; and the 15th (Scottish) Division which had 44, 45 and 46 Brigades.

FORMATIONS IN WHICH BATTALIONS OF THE REGIMENT SERVED

Battalions of the regiment which took part in the fighting were grouped in the following formations.

Battalion		Brigade	Division
REGULAR ARMY			
1st Seaforth	(Aug 14-Nov 18)	Dehra Dun Brigade (19 Indian Brigade)	7th (Meerut) Division
2nd Seaforth	(Aug 14-Nov 18)	10 Brigade	4th Division
1st Camerons	(Aug-Sep 14)	—	(Army Troops)
	(Sep 14-Nov 18)	1 Brigade	1st Divison
2nd Camerons	(Nov 14-Nov 18)	81 Brigade	27th Division
TERRITORIAL FORCE			
1/4th Seaforth	(Aug-Nov 14)	Seaforth and Cameron Brigade	Highland Division
	(Nov 14-Nov 15)	Dehra Dun Brigade	7th (Meerut) Division
	(Jan 16-Nov 18)	154 Brigade	51st Highland Division
1/5th Seaforth	(Aug 14-Nov 18)	Seaforth and Cameron Brigade (152 Brigade from May 15)	Highland Division (51st Highland Division from May 15)
1/6th Seaforth	(Aug 14-Nov 18)	Seaforth and Cameron Brigade (152 Brigade from May 15)	Highland Division (51st Highland Division from May 15)
1/4th Cameron	(Aug 14-Feb 15)	Seaforth and Cameron Brigade	Highland Division
	(Feb 15-Apr 15)	24 Brigade	8th Division
	(Apr 15-Dec 15)	21 Brigade	7th Division
	(Dec 15-Jan 16)	91 Brigade	7th Division
	(Jan-Feb 16)	154 (Highland) Brigade	51st Highland Division
10th Camerons	(Oct 16-Jun 18)	82 Brigade	27th Division
	(Jul 18-Nov 18)	—	(Lines of Communication Troops)
1/10th Liverpool Scottish	(Aug-Nov 14)	South Lancs Brigade	West Lancs Division
	(Nov 14-Jan 16)	9 Brigade	3rd Divison
	(Jan 16-Nov 18)	166 Brigade	55th Division
2/10th Liverpool Scottish	(Feb 15-Apr 18)	172 Brigade	57th Division
NEW ARMY			
7th Seaforth	(Aug 14-Nov 18)	26 (Highland) Brigade	9th (Scottish) Division
8th Seaforth	(Sep 14-Nov 18)	44 (Highland) Brigade	15th (Scottish) Division
9th Seaforth	(Dec 14-Nov 18)	Divisional Pioneers	9th (Scottish) Division
1st Garrison Bn Seaforth Highlanders	(Mar 17-Sep 18)	228 Brigade	28th Division
5th Camerons	(Aug 14-Nov 18)	26 (Highland) Brigade	9th (Scottish) Division
6th Camerons	(Sep 14-Nov 18)	45 (Highland) Brigade	15th (Scottish) Division
7th Camerons	(Jan 15-Jun 18)	44 (Highland) Brigade	15th (Scottish) Division
9th Camerons	(Sep 16-Apr 17)	—	(Lines of Communication Troops)
11th Camerons	(Jun-Nov 18)	120 Brigade	40th Division

4. REGULAR ARMY BATTALIONS

1st BATTALION SEAFORTH HIGHLANDERS

The 1st Seaforth move to France   **1914**

When war broke out, the 1st Seaforth were stationed at Agra in India. The battalion moved to France with the Dehra Dun Brigade in the 7th (Meerut) Division of the Indian Expeditionary Force, arriving in October 1914.

La Bassée.   **Winter 1914-1915**

During the winter of 1914-1915 the 1st Seaforth held positions at Richebourg St Vaast, Neuve Chapelle and Festubert, north of La Bassée. They were heavily attacked at Givenchy in December 1914.

Neuve Chapelle   **March 1915**

On the 10th March 1915 the 1st Seaforth took part in the attack by the Indian Army Corps on the German positions at Neuve Chapelle. It was to set the pattern of operation where an intense artillery bombardment was followed by infantry attack, which was expected to sweep the stunned German defenders out of their positions.

Aubers Ridge   **May 1915**

On 9th May 1915 the 1st Seaforth suffered over 500 casualties in the unsuccessful attack on Aubers Ridge. The attack lacked fire support, and the infantry advance was decimated by machine gun fire. During the attack on Festubert the following week the Dehra Dun Brigade, having suffered such heavy casualties at Aubers Ridge, was held in reserve.

Loos   **September 1915**

In the attack on Loos, the Indian Corps had a diversionary task on the flank. Although it did not leave its trenches, the 1st Battalion suffered over 100 casualties.

The 1st Seaforth move to Mesopotamia   **1915**

In November 1915 the 7th (Meerut) Division, including the 1st Seaforth, sailed for Basra in the Persian Gulf. The task of the force was to relieve the garrison at Kut el Amara which was besieged by the Turks.

Sheikh Saad, Wadi, and Umm el Hannah   **January 1916**

The force, including the 7th (Meerut) Division, started the advance up the River Tigris in January 1916. The 1st Seaforth took part in three costly attacks on the Turkish positions at Sheikh Saad on 7th January, Wadi on 13th January, and Umm el Hannah on 21st-22nd January. These attacks across flat, open country, with no cover, reduced the 1st Seaforth to a strength of just over 100 men.

'The Highland Battalion' formed   **1916**

The 1st Seaforth and 2nd Black Watch had both suffered casualties on the same scale, and so on 4 February 1916 the two battalions were temporarily amalgamated to form 'The Highland Battalion'. The normal identities were resumed on 12 July 1916.

Sanniyat   **April 1916**

In early April the force advanced again, bypassing the Turkish position at Sanniyat. 'The Highland Battalion' managed to penetrate the Turkish position, but the ground was so waterlogged that they were forced to withdraw. The combined battalion lost 921 officers and men in three weeks bitter fighting.

Corporal Sydney Ware, VC, 1st Bn Seaforth Highlanders.

CORPORAL S. W. WARE WINS THE VICTORIA CROSS AT SANNIYAT   6th APRIL 1916

During the withdrawal after the attack on Sanniyat on 6th April 1916 Cpl Sydney Ware, one of the few left unwounded, picked up a casualty and carried him over 200 yards to cover. He then returned to fetch his other wounded men, and for two hours he continued to move under very heavy fire until they were all recovered. He was subsequently killed on 16th April 1916, but was awarded the VC.

Sanniyat   **February 191**

On 22nd February the 1st Seaforth took part in a further attack on the Turkish position at Sanniyat. This time the fire support was much more effective, and three lines of trenches were captured.

Sergeant Thomas Steele VC, 1st Bn Seaforth Highlanders.

L/Sgt THOMAS STEELE WINS THE VICTORIA CROSS
22 FEBRUARY 1917

During the fighting at Sanniyat on 22nd February 1917 the Turks counter attacked strongly and temporarily regained some of the captured trenches. Sgt Thomas Steele, the machine gun sergeant, doubled back with Pte Winder and seized a machine gun from some Indian troops who were withdrawing, and brought it into action just in time to stop the Turkish counter attack. Later on he was again responsible for rallying troops to defeat another counter attack. For his brave leadership he was awarded the VC.

The occupation of Baghdad   1917

The 1st Seaforth were with the force when, after 14 days hard marching, it captured Baghdad on 11th March 1917.

Moushahdieh, Beled and Istabulat   1917

The advance was continued beyond Baghdad, and in March-April 1917 the 1st Seaforth fought three actions at Moushahdieh, Beled, and Istabulat in which the railway system was secured.

The 1st Seaforth move to Egypt   1918

At the end of 1917 the 1st Seaforth moved back to Basra. They embarked for Egypt on 1st January 1918 and, after resting and refitting at Ismailia, they joined General Allenby's Force in Palestine.

Beit Lid   1918

As General Allenby's force pursued the retreating Turks, the 1st Seaforth took part in the capture of Beit Lid on 20th September 1918. It was the battalion's last action of World War I.

2nd BATTALION SEAFORTH HIGHLANDERS

The 2nd Seaforth move to France   1914

When war broke out, the 2nd Seaforth were stationed at Shorncliffe. They went to France with 10 Brigade of the 4th Division in the British Expeditionary Force.

Le Cateau, the Retreat from Mons, and the Marne   1914

The 2nd Seaforth were sent into the line at Le Cateau. They fought with 10 Brigade in the retreat from Mons, ending in the victory at the Battle of the River Marne which halted the German advance in early September 1914.

The Capture of Meteren   1914

The 2nd Seaforth took part in the attack on the German held village of Meteren on 10 October 1914. It was one of the last actions to be fought before the war developed into trench warfare.

The 2nd Battle of Ypres   April-May 1915

During April-May 1915 the 2nd Seaforth were heavily engaged in the defence of the Ypres salient against the German attacks. On 25th April they suffered their first major casualties when they took part in the costly attack on St Julien, losing 348 officers and men killed or wounded.

On 2nd May the battalion had its first experience of poison gas. At the time there was little protection against gas except for an ineffective respirator of impregnated cloth or even a handkerchief, and the battalion lost 24 dead from gas, with 324 sick.

The German attacks between 25th April-24th May 1915 cost the battalion over 1000 casualties.

Albert and Arras   1915-1916

After the crippling casualties suffered at Ypres, the 2nd Seaforth were transferred to the quiter sector of the 3rd Army front between Albert and Arras. Here they took part in minor operations but also had a chance to absorb reinforcements and carry out retraining between periods in the trenches.

The Battle of the Somme   July 1916

On 1st July 1916 the British offensive on the River Somme started, after an artillery bombardment of seven days. The objective of the 2nd Seaforth was the village of, Beaumont Hamel. By the end of the first day the British Army had lost 57,470 casualties, over 20,000 of whom were dead. The 2nd Seaforth alone lost over 500 killed and wounded.

The battle of the Somme lasted for four months and the total gain was three or four miles of enemy held ground. The 2nd Seaforth remained in and out of the front line for four months during the battle.

Lt DONALD MacKINTOSH WINS THE VICTORIA CROSS   11th APRIL 191

During the attack at Arras, on 11th April 1917, L[Donald MacKintosh was shot in the leg during the advance. Although he was crippled, he led his men on until they had captured an enemy trench, and then collected the survivors of other companies to drive back a counter attack. He was wounded again but still stayed in command. Although unable to stand he organized the remaining fifteen men to attack the final objective until he was wounded a third time. He was awarded a posthumous VC for his gallant leadership.

Drummer Walter Ritchie VC, 2nd Bn Seaforth Highlanders.

Lieutenant Donald MacKintosh VC, 2nd Seaforth Highlanders.

DRUMMER WALTER RITCHIE WINS THE VICTORIA CROSS   1st JULY 1916

During the battalion's attack on the first day of the Battle of the Somme, the 2nd Seaforth suffered appalling casualties in trying to secure the enemy positions. Drummer Walter Ritchie stood on the parapet, under heavy machine gun fire and bomb attacks, continually sounding the 'Charge' and rallying the attackers. He was awarded the VC for his initiative and gallantry. (After the war he was Drum Major of the 1st Seaforth).

Arras   1917

After a winter in the trenches, the 2nd Seaforth took part in the attacks at Arras in April-May 1917. In the first action on 9th April 1917 the 2nd Seaforth, in the attack by the 4th Division, had a successful advance to their objective four-and-a-half miles inside the German lines.

But on 11th April the attacks ran into the same deadly stalemate of trench warfare. Ordered to attack the chemical works at Roeux, the 2nd Seaforth suffered 526 casualties, which was 93% of the battalion. Three of the companies lost all their officers.

The Third Battle of Ypres   October 1917

In the further grim attempts to break the stalemate at Ypres, the 2nd Seaforth took part in the attack in October 1917 to drive the Germans off the Passchendaele ridge overlooking Ypres. The battalion suffered 457 casualties during the month.

The German Offensive   1918

After another winter in the trenches, the 2nd Seaforth were in the line at Arras when the Germans launched their final offensive on 21st March 1918. Arras lay between the two main German attacks and, as the Allied lines fell back on each side, it became a salient. When the German advance eventually ground to a halt, the 2nd Seaforth were sent to reinforce the front at La Bassee.

The Allied Offensive   1918

In the final Allied counter-offensive which began in early August 1918, the 2nd Seaforth advanced again. They took part in the fighting but with relatively few casualties. They ended the war near Valenciennes.

1st BATTALION THE QUEEN'S OWN CAMERON HIGHLANDERS

The 1st Bn The Queen's Own Cameron Highlanders march out of Edinburgh Castle for France, 12th August 1914.

The 1st Camerons move to France   1914

When war broke out on 4th August 1914 the 1st Camerons were stationed in Edinburgh Castle. Within a week they had been reinforced by 700 Army Reservists, and left for France on 12th August 1914.

The 1st Camerons at Mons and the Marne   1914

During the Retreat from Mons, the 1st Camerons were tasked as Army troops for the defence of the British Expeditionary Force Headquarters. Then they joined the 1st Division and remained in this formation for the rest of the war. They belonged to the 1st Brigade which, until the 2nd Guards Brigade was formed in 1915, included 1st Coldstream Guards, 1st Scots Guards and 1st Black Watch. In early September the 1st Camerons took part in the successful counter offensive on the River Marne.

The 1st Camerons at the Battle of the Aisne   1914

The battalion's first heavy engagement was at the battle of the Aisne, before the fighting had developed into the static operations of trench warfare. On 14th September 1914 the 1st Camerons attacked the German lines but came up against strongly prepared positions, and lost 151 casualties. On 25th September the battalion had a particular stroke of ill luck when battalion headquarters, which was sited in a cave in a quarry, was hit by a shell. The acting Commanding Officer Captain Miers, and almost the entire battalion HQ staff, were killed.

PRIVATE ROSS TOLLERTON WINS THE VICTORIA CROSS   14th SEPTEMBER 1914

During the 1st Camerons attack at the Aisne, Lieutenant Matheson was severely wounded. Pte Ross Tollerton managed to carry him to cover and later, when the battalion withdrew, Pte Tollerton, who had been twice wounded himself, stayed behind with Lt Matheson. He sheltered him for three days behind enemy lines, and managed to bring him to safety. He was awarded the VC for his bravery and initiative.

The First battle of Ypres,   October 1914

During October 1914 the 1st Camerons fought dogged defensive actions at Langemarck, Nonne Bosschen and Givenchy, which eventually brought the German advance to a halt outside Ypres.

Givenchy   December 1914

The 1st Division was sent to the Bethune area in December 1914 to strengthen the line. On 21st/22nd December the 1st Camerons took part in the attack by the 1st Division which made limited gains at Givenchy.

Aubers Ridge   May 1915

On May 9th May 1915 the 1st Camerons took part in the unsuccessful attack on Aubers Ridge, suffering 104 casualties from enemy machine guns which the artillery bombardment had failed to neutralize.

Pte Ross Tollerton VC, 1st Bn The Queen's Own Cameron Highlanders.

Loos September   1915

In the opening attack at the battle of Loos on 25th September 1915, the 1st Brigade was one of the few formations to break through the German lines. The 1st Camerons penetrated as far as the town of Hulloch, but the loss of 364 casualties reduced the battalion to a strength of only four officers and 200 soldiers. Later in the Loos campaign the 1st Camerons took part in the attack on the Hohenzollern Redoubt at Hulloch on 13th October 1915.

The Somme   1916

Three weeks after the opening of the Battle of the Somme, the 1st Camerons took part in the 1st Brigade's attack on Bazentin Ridge on 21st-23rd July 1916. It was at the stage when the trench warfare had reached a stalemate and the attack could make little progress against the elaborate German defences.

High Wood   September 1916

During September 1916 the 1st Camerons and the 1st Black Watch attacked the German positions in High Wood and, although they gained their objective, they suffered so many casualties that they could not hold them against the subsequent German counter attacks. One Company of the 1st Camerons was reduced to a strength of 12 soldiers.

The two regiments afterwards erected a St Andrew's Cross at High Wood as a memorial to this gallant but costly attack.

Passchendaele   1917

In November 1917 the 1st Camerons returned to Ypres and on 15th November they carried out a successful attack on Vocation Farm at Passchendaele, North East of Ypres.

The German Offensive   1918

When the Germans launched their final offensive in March 1918, the 1st Camerons were in the Bethune area which was not at first heavily attacked. On 18th April they fought a tough and successful defensive battle at Givenchy with over 100 casualties.

Epéhy September   1918

In September 1918 the 1st Camerons returned to the Somme. Between 18th-24th September 1918 they attacked successfully at Epéhy, capturing their objective and a large quantity of German weapons. The 1st Division took 1100 prisoners.

The Selle,   October-November 1918

On 17-18th October 1918 the 1st Division attacked through the mist, with enemy smoke and gas shells falling. The battalion captured its objective of La Vallée Mulâtre ridge. In the 1st Camerons final operation of the war they attacked across the Sambre and L'Oise Canal, capturing 500 prisoners and a large number of German machine guns and field artillery.

2nd BATTALION THE QUEEN'S OWN CAMERON HIGHLANDERS

The 2nd Camerons move to France   1914

When war broke out, the 2nd Camerons were stationed at Poona in India. In October 1914 they sailed for Great Britain, joining 81st Brigade in the 27th Division, which was formed from battalions returning from overseas. The 2nd Camerons arrived in France on 19th December 1914.

The Second Battle of Ypres   1915

The 2nd Camerons took over in the trenches south of Ypres in January 1915. The 27th Division was to bear the brunt of the German efforts to take Ypres, and their stolid defence brought the enemy advance to a halt. Holding positions in the Ypres Salient from 21-29 April 1915 the 2nd Camerons took part in the gallant defence of Hill 60 against determined German attacks.

At the end of April 1915 the 27th Division redeployed to new positions centred on Frezenberg village, a semi-circular defensive line about 2½ miles east of Ypres, with the 2nd Camerons holding positions astride the Menin road and in Sanctuary Wood.

The 2nd battle of Ypres prevented the Germans capturing the town, but the cost to the 2nd Camerons was 673 casualties during the month of fighting.

After Ypres, the 2nd Camerons held positions on the Somme during the summer of 1915.

The 2nd Camerons move to Macedonia 1915

In September 1915 Bulgaria entered the war as an ally of Austria-Hungary and Germany, and the Bulgarians invaded Serbia, reaching as far as Macedonia. A French and British force was sent to protect Greece, but was forced back by the Bulgarians.

In November 1915 the 27th Division was sent from France to Macedonia to reinforce the Allied army which was now holding positions known as the 'Birdcage' round the port of Salonika.

The Capture of Bala and Zir 1916

In May 1916 the Bulgarians advanced into Greece and the 27th Division left its positions to reinforce the line in the Struma Valley. From 30th September-3rd October the 2nd Camerons led the successful attack on the Bulgarians which captured the villages of Bala and Zir.

The Struma Valley 1916-1918

After the battle the 2nd Camerons held positions in the trenches in the Struma Valley for two years. Compared with the Western front, it was a low key campaign, most casualties being caused by malaria, against which no effective preventive medicine had yet been developed.

The Capture of Homondos 1917

On 13/14 October 1917 the 2nd Camerons and the Scottish Horse carried out a successful night attack on the Bulgarians at Homondos. Achieving surprise by a night march round the enemy position, they attacked from the flank, and the 2nd Camerons killed 120 and took 152 prisoners for the loss of 39 casualties.

Armistice with Bulgaria 1918

In September 1918 the Bulgarians were abandoned by their German allies, and the British advanced forward into Serbia and Bulgaria. An Armistice was agreed on 30th September 1918.

The 2nd Camerons in Trans Caucasia 1918

The final phase of the war for the 27th Division was to move by sea to Batum in Georgia, at the east end of the Black Sea, to expel the Germans from Trans-Caucasia. The 2nd Camerons returned to Great Britain from Georgia in May 1919.

5. SPECIAL RESERVE BATTALIONS AND DEPOTS

3rd (SPECIAL RESERVE) BATTALION SEAFORTH HIGHLANDERS

When war broke out on 4th August 1914, the 3rd (Special Reserve) Bn Seaforth Highlanders was mobilised at Fort George. It was moved by sea to Cromarty on 12th August 1914, and remained as the Cromarty Garrison until the end of the war. It formed an important element of the coastal defence plan around the Naval base of Invergordon.

It's wartime role was to provide drafts of reinforcements for the battalions in the front line and men for the newly formed service battalions. The men came both from the recruiting offices and from casualties who had returned from the front. Its strength varied from between 1150 to 2600.

At the end of the war the 3rd Seaforth moved from Cromarty to Glencorse, where it was disbanded in 1919.

3rd (SPECIAL RESERVE) BATTALION THE QUEEN'S OWN CAMERON HIGHLANDERS

When war broke out on 4th August 1914 the 3rd (Special Reserve) Bn The Queen's Own Cameron Highlanders mobilised at Inverness under Colonel D. W. Cameron of Locheil. On 13th August the 3rd Camerons moved to Invergordon, where they were responsible for the protection of the oil tanks at the Naval base. They remained at Invergordon until November 1917 when they moved to Ireland. The battalion was commanded for three years during the war by Colonel the MacKintosh of MacKintosh.

The battalion's role was to provide drafts of reinforcements for the battalions in the front line. The men came both from civilian life and from casualties who had been evacuated from France for treatment in Great Britain. During the war the battalion despatched 15,583 Cameron Highlanders to the front.

The 3rd Camerons returned from Ireland to Edinburgh where the battalion was put into 'suspended animation' in 1919. It was eventually disbanded in 1953.

DEPOT SEAFORTH HIGHLANDERS, FORT GEORGE

At the start of World War I the 3rd Seaforth were mobilised and moved to Cromarty, leaving the Depot Seaforth at Fort George as a holding unit. Its accommodation was extended by a large hutted camp. All recruits reported to the Depot for medical checks and issue of clothing, and were then drafted for training by the 3rd Seaforth.

DEPOT THE QUEEN'S OWN CAMERON HIGHLANDERS, CAMERON BARRACKS, INVERNESS

At the start of World War I, the 3rd Camerons mobilized and moved to Invergordon, leaving the Depot at Cameron Barracks as a holding unit. Recruits reported in to the Depot for inspection and kitting out, before being sent to the 3rd Camerons for training. During World War I the Tailors at Cameron Barracks turned out over 11,000 kilts for the regiment.

6. *TERRITORIAL FORCE BATTALIONS*

6th Bn Seaforth Highlanders clearing positions at Greenland Hill, Arras, 29th August 1918.

1/4th (ROSS-HIGHLAND) BATTALION SEAFORTH HIGHLANDERS TF

Mobilisation   **1914**

When war broke out on 4th August 1914 the 4th Battalion mobilized at Dingwall. Their first task was to prepare defences at Nigg to protect the Naval base in the Cromarty Firth.

Training at Bedford   **1914**

On 15th August the 4th Seaforth, who were in the Seaforth and Cameron Brigade of the Highland Territorial Division moved to Bedford, where they were brought up to strength by new recruits.

The 1/4th Seaforth move to France   **1914**

The 1/4th Seaforth were one of the first TF battalions to go to France, and arrived there on 6th November 1914. For the first few weeks they had to be kept in the rear area because of an epidemic of scarlet fever, but on 20th December they joined the 1st Seaforth in the Dehra Dun Brigade of the 7th (Meerut) Indian Division.

Neuve Chapelle   **March 191.**

The first major action for the 4th Seaforth was the attack on Neuve Chapelle on 10th March 1915. In an operation that achieved limited success, the 1/4th Seaforth attack was delayed until the evening. During the nights fighting they lost 168 casualties, but the battalion acquitted itself well beside the regular troops of the brigade.

Aubers Ridge   May 1915
In May 1915 the 1/4th Seaforth, still alongside the 1st Seaforth in the Dehra Dun Brigade, suffered over 200 casualties in the unsuccessful attack on Aubers Ridge.

Loos   September 1915
The 1/4th Seaforth did not take part in the main attack on Loos on 25th September 1915. But a party of 100 men had the task of protecting the cylinders of poison gas, which was used by the British for the first time.

The 1/4th Seaforth return to the Highland Division
In November 1915 the 7th (Meerut) Division left France for the Persian Gulf, and so the 1/4th Seaforth returned to the 51st Highland Division, joining 154 Highland Brigade in January 1916.

The Somme   1916
The 1/4th Seaforth had five hard days hard fighting in the attempts to capture High Wood, where the German and British lines nearly met. The thick trees and undergrowth made artillery support difficult, and the actions were mainly infantry attacks.

The Ancre   1916
The last phase of the Battle of the Somme was known as the Ancre, in which the 51st Highland Division captured Beaumont Hamel. The 1/4th Seaforth were in the line in the later stages of the operation.

Arras and the Scarpe   1917
On 9th April 1917 the 1/4th Seaforth were in the first attacking line of the 51st Highland Division in the attack at Arras. The battalion took its final objective successfully, capturing 167 prisoners although suffering over 200 casualties itself.

On 23rd April the 1/4th Seaforth succeeded in capturing the German positions in the Chemical Works at Roeux, beside the River Scarpe Canal, which had caused severe casualties in early attempts to take them. The battalion was hit by heavy artillery fire, including a misdirected British bombardment, but successfully resisted fierce German counter attacks.

The Third Battle of Ypres   1917
On 31st July 1917 the 1/4th Seaforth took part in the advance by the 51st Highland Division, which was the only division to achieve its objectives on the first day. It was the battalion's first encounter with enemy gas.

On 20th September the 51st Highland Division attacked again and the 1/4th Seaforth, in 154 Brigade, gained another 1000 yards at a cost of over 200 casualties.

Cambrai   1917
On 20th November 1917 the 1/4th Seaforth took part in the attack at Cambrai when seven divisions, with 324 tanks, achieved a major break through the German lines in the first massed tank attack in history. The attack cost the battalion over 300 casualties.

The German Offensive   1918
When the Germans launched their last major offensive on 21st March 1918 the 1/4th Seaforth were holding positions on the Beaumetz-Morchies line. Their stand, with the 7th Argylls, was considered to be one of the finest, though costliest, actions fought by the battalions of the 51st Highland Division.

The Counter-attack in Champagne   1918
In July the 51st Highland Division was withdrawn from the line and moved South to Epernay to support the French Army. It attacked in the close country of the River Ardre but ran into strong German opposition and suffered some of the worst fighting of the war.

Sgt Joh Meikle VC, 4th Bn Seaforth Highlanders TF.

Sgt JOHN MEIKLE WINS THE VICTORIA CROSS 20th JULY 1918
During the attack on Marfaux in the Ardre Valley, Sgt Meikle's company was held up by machine gunfire. He advanced alone, across 150 yards of open ground, killing the crew of one machine gun with his revolver, and putting the other out of action with a heavy stick. Then he waved the company on. He was subsequently killed attacking another machine gun post, and was awarded the VC for his gallantry.

The final Allied Offensive   1918
The 1/4th Seaforth returned with the 51st Highland Division to Cambrai in October 1918, and took part in the Division's final operation of the war, the advance towards Valenciennes. In a series of attacks the 1/4th Seaforth encountered fierce German resistance, and lost over 300 casualties. But when the Division was relieved in the line on 28th October, it had made substantial gains of ground.

1/5th (SUTHERLAND AND CAITHNESS) BATTALION SEAFORTH HIGHLANDERS TF

Mobilisation 1914
When war broke out on 4th August 1914, the 5th Seaforth mobilised at Golspie. Their first task was to construct the defences on the North Sutor at the entrance to the Cromarty Firth Naval base.

Training at Bedford 1914
The 1/5th Seaforth moved South with the Highland Territorial Division and spent eight months training at Bedford. They were one of the battalions in the Seaforth and Cameron Infantry Brigade.

The 1/5th Seaforth move to France 1915
The 1/5th Seaforth moved to France on 1st May 1915, and took over from 1/6th Seaforth in the trenches at Richebourg St Vaast, near La Bassee, on 22 May 1915.

Festubert 1915
The first major action of the 1/5th Seaforth was on 15th June 1915 when they joined an attack by 153 and 154 Brigades on the German positions at Festubert. It was the battalion's first time 'over the top' of the trenches.

Laventie, Albert, Arras, 1915-1916
During June-July 1915 the 1/5th Seaforth held sections of the line around Laventie, and from August to December in the Albert Sector. In March 1916 the 51st Highland Division took over 'the Labyrinth' North of Arras.

The Somme 1916
During the early stages of the Battle of the Somme, the 51st Highland Division held positions in the line on Vimy Ridge.

In late July 1916, after the first phase of the Somme offensive was over, the 1/5th Seaforth moved to the Somme and their duty included spells at High Wood and Mametz Wood.

Beaumont Hamel 1916
In October 1916 the 1/5th Seaforth took over in the line opposite the ruined village of Beaumont Hamel. On 13th November the 51st Highland Division launched an attack on the village, the 1/5th Seaforth leading the 152 Brigade advance. They took their objective, and captured over 600 prisoners, but suffered over 300 casualties.

Arras and the Scarpe 1917
On 9th April 1917 the 1/5th Seaforth took part in the attack of the three Scottish Divisions, the 9th, 15th and 51st Highland, at Arras. Advancing on the left front with 152 Brigade, the battalion took its objective but at a cost of over 300 casualties.

On 15-16th May the battalion held Roeux against a particularly fierce German attack.

The Third Battle of Ypres 1917
On 31st July 1917 the 1/5th Seaforth took part in the 51st Highland Division advance at Ypres, and successfully captured their objectives and took 700 German prisoners.

The battalion remained in the Ypres salient until 24th September 1917.

Cambrai 1917
On 20th November 1917 the 1/5th Seaforth took part in the first attack ever carried out with massed tanks. They quickly broke through the German lines and captured the village of Ribecourt, with 300 German prisoners. Next day they captured their objective of Flesquières.

After the battalion had been relieved on 24th November, events were less successful, for the Germans counter-attacked and recovered nearly all the ground which they had lost to the 51st Highland Division.

Lance Corporal R. MacBeath VC, 5th Bn Seaforth Highlanders TF.

L/Cpl R. MacBEATH WINS THE VICTORIA CROSS
20th NOVEMBER 1917
During the advance at Cambrai the 1/5th Seaforth were held up by a nest of machine guns at Ribecourt L/Cpl Robert MacBeath was sent out to reconnoitre and, with a Lewis gun and revolver, succeeded in putting five enemy machine guns out of action and capturing three officers and 30 men. He was awarded the VC for his gallantry.

The German Offensive 1918
When the Germans launched their last major offensive on 21st March 1918, the 1/5th Seaforth were in the line astride the Bapaume-Cambrai road. The German attack started with an intense bombardment of gas and shells, and the 1/5th Seaforth held their ground for six days until relieved. They sustained 377 casualties in the fighting.

On 4th April 1918 the 1/5th Seaforth returned to the line on the River Lawe Sector North of Bethune, and again held off a heavy attack on 11-12 April, at a further cost of over 200 casualties.

The Counter-Attack in Champagne   1918
In July 1918 the 51st Highland Division was moved South to the Epernay area to support the French Army. The 1/5th Seaforth were to experience their heaviest fighting in stopping the German break through on the Marne. From 21st-28th July, in the Valley of the River Arde, they lost 369 casualties, but this offensive action turned the tide of the German advance.

The Scarpe   1918
The 1/5th Seaforth returned in August 1918 to the area of Rouex on the River Scarpe, and took part in the recapture of the infamous chemical works and Rouex itself.

The Final Allied Offensive   1918
The 1/5th Seaforth moved back to the Cambrai area in October 1918. The 51st Highland Division advanced on 12-13th October and, although it took its objectives, it suffered heavy casualties. The 1/5th Seaforth were again in the line for the attack at Thun St Martin, their last battle of the war. The final 16 days fighting had cost the battalion over 400 casualties.

1/6th (MORAYSHIRE) BATTALION SEAFORTH HIGHLANDERS TF

Mobilisation   1914
When war broke out on 4th August 1914 the 6th Seaforth mobilized at Elgin.

Training at Bedford   1914
The 1/6th Seaforth moved with the Highland Territorial Division and spent eight months training at Bedford. They were one of the battalions in the Seaforth and Cameron Infantry Brigade.

The 1/6th Seaforth move to France   1915
The 1/6th Seaforth moved to France on 1st May 1915 and started their first spell of duty in the trenches at Richebourg St Vaast, North of La Bassée, on 19th May. They handed over to the 1/5th Seaforth three days later.

Festubert   1915
On 15th June 1915, 153 and 154 Brigades attacked at Festubert, and the task of the 1/6th Seaforth was to give covering small arms fire. The attack provoked heavy German counter bombardment, and in the packed trenches the battalion suffered 140 casualties from shell fire.

Laventie, Albert, Arras   1915-1916
In late June the 1/6th Seaforth took over in the trenches at Laventie, and from August to December in the Albert sector. In March 1916 the Highland Division took over 'the Labyrinth' sector from the French. The routine was that each battalion did six days in the line, then six days in the support trenches, a further six days in the line, and then six days rest in billets.

On 28th April the 1/6th Seaforth received an unpleasant shock when the Germans exploded seven large mines simultaneously under the forward company positions, and followed this with heavy artillery fire. The battalion lost 67 casualties, but by dogged resistance, managed to prevent a German breakthrough.

The Somme   1916
During the preparations for the offensive on the Somme, the 51st Highland Division took over positions on Vimy Ridge. In mid July, after the first phase of the battle of the Somme was over, the 1/6th Seaforth moved to take over the line at Mametz Wood and High Wood.

The 6th Bn Seaforth Highlanders in the trenches 1916.

Beaumont Hamel   1916

On 13th November the 51st Highland Division attacked the strong German positions in the ruined village of Beaumont Hamel which had for long resisted capture and which the Germans considered impregnable. The German tactic was to shelter in deep bunkers during the attack and then to emerge and attack the assaulting troops from the rear. The 1/6th Seaforth allotted a complete company to the task of countering this, and the battalion took its objectives at the cost of 277 casualties.

Arras and the Scarpe   1917

On 9th April 1917 the 1/6th Seaforth took part in one of the most successful actions of the war when the 51st Highland Division, together with the 9th and 15th Scottish Divisions, attacked the German positions at Arras. It was one of the rare occasions when the attack was entirely successful and drove the enemy back as much as four to five miles in places.

In late April and May the 1/6th Seaforth held the line against strong German counter attacks in the area of the Roeux chemical works.

The Third Battle of Ypres   1917

On 31st July 1917 the 1/6th Seaforth took part in the 51st Highland Division's advance at Ypres which achieved its objectives with considerable success.

Sgt ALEXANDER EDWARDS WINS THE VICTORIA CROSS   31st JULY/1st AUGUST 1917

During the advance of the 1/6th Seaforth at Ypres, C Company was held up by a German machine gun post. Sgt Alexander Edwards attacked the post, killed the gunners and captured the gun. Later, although wounded, he stalked and killed an enemy sniper, rescued a wounded officer under heavy fire, and led his men on to the objective with the greatest gallantry. He was awarded the VC. He was later killed near Arras on 24 March 1918.

Cambrai   1917

On 20th November 1917 the 1/6th Seaforth took part in the first attack ever made with massed tanks. 152 Brigade was allocated 36 of the 324 tanks in the attack. At battalion level the 1/6th Seaforth had only seven, because breakdowns were frequent. The battalion broke through the Hindenburg line and captured their objective, part of the village of Flesquières. The attack achieved a major breakthrough and, for the loss of 69 casualties, the battalion took 300 prisoners.

The German Offensive   1918

When the Germans launched their last major offensive on 21st March 1918, the 1/6th Seaforth were holding the line between Beaumetz and Morchies. For five days, in an engagement which cost it nearly 400 casualties, the battalion came under heavy artillery bombardment and infantry attack but held its ground. However the withdrawal of flanking units made it necessary for the 1/6th Seaforth to carry out an orderly withdrawal to a new position in order to stabilise the line.

On 9th April the 1/6th Seaforth returned to the line on the River Lawe North of Bethune, and held off a heavy German attack on 11-12 April 1918.

Sgt Alexander Edwards VC, 6th Bn Seaforth Highlanders.

The Counter-attack in Champagne   1918

In July 1918 the 51st Highland Division moved South to the Epernay area to support the French Army. The 1/6th Seaforth took part in the operations which halted the German advance on the Marne. The fighting was to cost some of the heaviest casualties of the war, the 1/6th Seaforth losing over 400 killed, wounded and missing. The battalion, organised as a composite company, took part in the counter-attack in the valley of the River Ardre which turned the tide of the German advance.

The Scarpe   1918

The 1/6th Seaforth returned in August 1918 to the Arras area, and took part in the attacks on Greenland Hill near Roeux, a feature which was vital for the final British offensive.

The Final Allied Offensive   1918

The 1/6th Seaforth moved back to the Cambrai area in October 1918. In its final operation of the war the 51st Highland Division advanced towards Valenciennes. The 1/6th Seaforth took part in a series of attacks by 152 Brigade and, when they reached their final positions before being relieved in the line on 28th October, they had lost over 300 casualties.

1/4th BN THE QUEEN'S OWN CAMERON HIGHLANDERS TF

Pipes and Drums of 4th Bn The Queen's Own Cameron Highlanders TF in France 1915.

Mobilisation   **1914**

When war broke out on 4th August 1914 the 4th Camerons mobilised at Inverness and moved to Cromarty for coastal defence duty, protecting the Invergordon Naval Base.

Training at Bedford   **1914**

The 4th Camerons moved to Bedford with the Seaforth and Cameron Brigade of the Highland Territorial Division, and were brought up to strength with extra recruits, many coming from the London Scottish.

The 1/4th Camerons move to France   **1915**

Because the 1/4th Camerons were up to strength, they were warned for an early move to France. But an epidemic of measles broke out, and it was February 1915 before the battalion was fit to move. It arrived in France on 20th February 1915, 960 strong, and joined 24 Brigade in the 8th Division. The 1/4th Camerons took over in the line on the Estaires-La Bassée road on 28th February 1915

Neuve Chapelle   **March 1915**

The first major action of the war for the 4th Camerons was the attack on Neuve Chapelle, north of La Bassée, during 10-17th March 1915. The 24th Brigade's task was to secure the flank against enemy counter attack. The 1/4th Camerons repulsed a strong counter attack on 12th March, capturing 300 Germans. The seven days fighting cost the battalion 140 casualties.

Festubert   **May 1915**

In April 1915 the 1/4th Camerons were transferred to 21 Brigade in the 78th Division, and in May the battalion played a gallant part in the attack at Festubert.

On 17th May the 1/4th Camerons attacked the German positions at night. It was pouring with rain and they had to cross 800 yards of ground, seamed with deep wide ditches of water. They took their objective, but the battalion on their flank failed to make progress and the 1/4th Camerons were left unsupported and had to withdraw. The battalion lost its Commanding Officer Lt Col A. Fraser, killed, and over 250 other casualties.

Givenchy   **1915**

On 15th-16th June 1915 the 4th Camerons took part in the attack by the 7th and 51st (Highland) Divisions at Givenchy, intended as a preliminary to the attack at Loos.

Loos   **September 1915**

On 25th September 1915 the 1/4th Camerons attacked with the 7th Division at St Elie, on the left of the main advance. Seven days of bitter and continuous fighting brought the 7th Division some gains, but cost the battalion nearly 200 casualties.

The 1/4th Camerons drafted   **1916**

After Loos, the 7th Division was reorganized and reinforced with New Army battalions, and in January 1916 the 1/4th Camerons returned to the 51st Highland Division. But the casualties at Festubert and Loos had reduced the 1/4th Camerons to below a strength of 500. Because the reinforcement system at home was concentrating on the New Army service battalions of the Camerons, there seemed to be no immediate prospect of bringing the battalion up to strength, and so it was broken up, the majority being drafted to the 1st Camerons, and 12 of the officers to the 1/Liverpool Scottish.

10th (LOVAT'S SCOUTS) BATTALION
THE QUEEN'S OWN CAMERON HIGHLANDERS TF

The Lovat Scouts were raised by Lord Lovat in 1900 for service in the South African War. Being a separate regiment, their history is not within the scope of this book, except for the period from 1916-1919 when they were designated as the 10th Camerons.

Formation of the 10th (Lovat's Scouts) Battalion

After taking part in the campaign in Gallipoli, the 1st and 2nd Regiments of Lovat's Scouts, which had served as dismounted Yeomanry in the Highland Mounted Brigade, were amalgamated to form an infantry battalion. The battalion was designated the 10th (Lovat's Scouts) Bn Cameron Highlanders. It continued to wear its own uniform and to be known as 'The Lovat Scouts'. The battalion was brought up to strength with a company from the 3rd Scottish Horse and was formed in Cairo on 27 September 1916.

Macedonia   1916-191

The 10th (Lovat's Scouts) Bn landed at Salonika on 20t October 1916 and joined 82 Brigade of the 27th Division The battalion's skill at observation and fieldcraft, and it aptitude for patrolling, made it most useful in th operations in the Struma Valley. In October 1917 the Lova Scouts carried out a particularly successful attack on th enemy held village of Salmah, where they surprised th Bulgarians, killing 70 and capturing over 100.

France   191?

In June 1918 the 10th (Lovat's Scouts) Bn left Macedoni and moved to France. For the last few months of the wa the Lovat Scouts retrained in observation and signallin; and were sent to join the Observer Groups of the Lova Scouts (Sharpshooters) which had been formed by Lor Lovat in 1916 for use on the Western front. The battalior was disbanded in April 1919.

1st (SCOTTISH) BATTALION THE KING'S (LIVERPOOL)
REGIMENT TF

Mobilization   1914

When war broke out in 1914 the Liverpool Scottish mobilized at Liverpool and moved to Edinburgh, where they formed part of the Forth defences.

Move to France   1914

On 2nd November 1914 the 1st Liverpool Scottish arrived at Le Havre on SS Maidan. They joined 9 Brigade in the 3rd Division of the Regular Army. Their first duty in the trenches was at Kemmel on 27th November 1914.

The Ypres Salient and the Battle of Hooge   1915

The 1st Liverpool Scottish held the line in the Ypres Salient during the winter 1914-1915. Their first major offensive operation, the Battle of Hooge (officially termed the First Action at Bellewaarde), was an attack by 9 Brigade to capture the German trenches North of the Menin road at Hooge, which overlooked Ypres. The attack succeeded, but at the cost for the 1st Liverpool Scottish of 402 casualties, or 74% of the battalion strength.

The Somme   1916

On the formation of the 55th (West Lancashire) Division, the 1st Liverpool Scottish were transferred to its 166th Infantry Brigade. After the Battle of Hooge, it was over a year before the battalion had been rebuilt to strength and retrained.

The Battle of the Somme started on 1st July 1916, anc from 9th-14th August the 1st Liverpool Scottish took par in the attempt to take the village of Guillemont, losing 28(casualties. In September they held the line at Delvillé Wood, extending the trenches in preparation for an attack.

Among the reinforcements after the Somme were twelvé officers from the 1/4th Camerons when that battalion hac to be drafted due to the heavy casualties sustained at Loos This did much to strengthen the affiliation between thé Liverpool Scottish and the Camerons.

CAPTAIN N. G. CHAVASSE WINS THE VICTORIA
CROSS ON   *9th AUGUST 1916*

During the attack on Guillemont Capt Noel Chavasse, the Medical Officer of the 1st Liverpool Scottish, carriec out most outstanding work in treating casualties anc recovering wounded under heavy fire. For his exceptiona bravery and devotion to duty he was awarded the VC.

The 3rd Battle of Ypres   1917

The 1st Liverpool Scottish took part in the successful attack by the 55th Division on 31st July 1917 which broke through the German lines, capturing 630 prisoners and taking all its objectives. Although the battalion lost 24(casualties, it had achieved a conspicuously successful attack which did much to restore confidence after the costly and frustrating operations in the Battle of the Somme.

Capt N. G. CHAVASSE WINS A BAR TO THE VICTORIA CROSS   31st JULY-2nd AUGUST 1917

During the attack at Ypres on 31st July 1917 Captain Noel Chavasse, VC, the Medical Officer of the 1st Liverpool Scottish, was severely wounded in the head while carrying a casualty to the dressing station. He was badly wounded again next day, but carried on recovering casualties and treating wounded for two days. On 2nd August he was mortally wounded when a shell hit the dressing station. He was awarded a bar to the VC for his determination and bravery during the third battle of Ypres.

He is one of only three men who have won a bar to the Victoria Cross.

Épéhy   1917

In September 1917 the 1st Liverpool Scottish moved from Ypres to a very lightly defended sector of the line at Épéhy near Cambrai. On 20th November the enemy attacked the 55th Division in great strength and almost overran it. The 1/5 South Lancashire Regiment, on the left of the Division, lost every single man as a casualty or prisoner. In the centre the 1st Liverpool Scottish fought a most determined defence, but lost two complete companies. Of their 622 casualties, over half were taken prisoner.

Givenchy   1918

After the Germans started their final offensive in March 1918, the 55th Division moved into the line at Givenchy. On 9th April 1918 the enemy attacked the division in great strength, and the 1st Liverpool Scottish fought another determined defensive battle. This time the 55th Division succeeded in holding its line intact and saving Bethune from capture.

The final Allied Offensive   1918

On 3rd October 1918 the 1st Liverpool Scottish started their final operation of the war when the 55th Division advanced from La Bassée and, by the time of the Armistice on 9th November, had advanced nearly 50 miles. The 1st Liverpool Scottish finished the war at Ath.

Capt Noel Chavasse, VC and Bar, MC, Medical Officer of the 1st Bn Liverpool Scottish TF.

2nd/10th (SCOTTISH) BATTALION THE KING'S (LIVERPOOL) REGIMENT TF

2nd Liverpool Scottish formed   1914

The 2nd Liverpool Scottish were formed at Liverpool as a second line battalion in September 1914. They were stationed at Blackpool in the South Lancashire Brigade until February 1915 when they moved to Tunbridge Wells. They remained in Kent, Surrey and Hampshire with the 57th Division, with the task of defending Great Britain against invasion, until 1917.

Move to France

In early 1917 the 57th Division was ordered to move to France, and the 2nd Liverpool Scottish arrived at Le Havre on 21st February 1917. The battalion took over a section of the trenches at Armentières on 26th February 1917.

The 2nd Liverpool Scottish remained there until October when they moved to Ypres, where they were in reserve for the Third Battle of Ypres.

Amalgamation with 1st Liverpool Scottish   1918

On 30th April 1918 the 2nd Liverpool Scottish were amalgamated with the 1st Liverpool Scottish whose losses in the fighting at Epéhy and Givenchy had reduced them to below effective fighting strength.

After the war a King's Colour was issued to the 2nd Liverpool Scottish in 1919.

THE 2nd AND 3rd LINE RESERVE BATTALIONS OF THE TERRITORIAL FORCE

Soon after the outbreak of war in 1914, when it became clear that the Territorial Force would be required to serve overseas, each TF battalion was given a 2nd and 3rd line reserve. When a 1st line battalion was sent overseas with the British Expeditionary Force, the 2nd line battalion took its place in the home defence of Great Britain, and the 3rd line battalion supplied men for the other two.

This resulted in the following battalions being formed.

2nd LINE BATTALIONS

2/4th (ROSS HIGHLAND) Bn SEAFORTH HIGHLANDERS TF

Formed at Dingwall in September 1914, it served at Fort George, Blair Atholl, Pitlochry and Stirling until 1916. It then served in Norfolk from 1916 until absorbed into the 4th Reserve battalion in April 1918.

2/5th (SUTHERLAND AND CAITHNESS) Bn SEAFORTH HIGHLANDERS TF

Formed at Golspie in September 1914, it served at Fort George and Blair Atholl. In 1915 it was absorbed by the 2/6th Battalion.

2/6th (MORAYSHIRE) Bn SEAFORTH HIGHLANDERS TF

Formed at Elgin in September 1914, it also served at Fort George, Blair Atholl and Crieff, and in November 1915 absorbed the 2/5th Battalion. It served in Norfolk from 1916 until disbanded in September 1917.

2/4th Bn THE QUEEN'S OWN CAMERON HIGHLANDERS TF

Formed at Inverness in September 1914, it served at Fort George, Blair Atholl, and Aberfeldy, until in 1916 it moved to Norfolk. It served there until disbanded in 1918. The battalion supplied 2077 men in drafts to the BEF.

3rd LINE BATTALIONS

3/4th (ROSS HIGHLAND) Bn SEAFORTH HIGHLANDERS TF

Formed at Dingwall in April 1915, it was stationed at Ardersier Camp and Ripon. It was amalgamated into the 4th Reserve Training Battalion in 1916.

3/5th (SUTHERLAND AND CAITHNESS) Bn SEAFORTH HIGHLANDERS TF

Formed in April 1915, it was stationed at Ardersier Camp and Ripon. It was amalgamated into the 4th Reserve Training Battalion in 1916.

3/6th (MORAYSHIRE) Bn SEAFORTH HIGHLANDERS TF

Formed in April 1915, it was stationed at Ardersier Camp and Ripon. It was amalgamated into the 4th Reserve Training Battalion in 1916.

4th RESERVE TRAINING Bn SEAFORTH HIGHLANDERS

In August 1916 the 4th Reserve Training Bn Seaforth Highlanders was formed at the 3rd Line Training Centre of the Highland Division at Ripon. The battalion was made up of the 3/4th, 3/5th and 3/6th Bns Seaforth Highlanders TA.

In May 1918 it moved to Glencorse, and was disbanded in 1919.

3/4th Bn THE QUEEN'S OWN CAMERON HIGHLANDERS TF

Formed at Inverness in April 1915, it moved to Ripon in November 1915. In September 1916 it was amalgamated into the 3rd (Special Reserve) Battalion at Invergordon.

3/10th (SCOTTISH) Bn THE KING'S (LIVERPOOL) REGIMENT TF

Formed at Liverpool in May 1915 as the draft-finding battalion for the 1st and 2nd Battalions, the 3rd Liverpool Scottish served at Blackpool and Oswestry. The battalion was disbanded in early 1919.

HOME DEFENCE VOLUNTEER BATTALION

1st VOLUNTEER BATTALION THE QUEEN'S OWN CAMERON HIGHLANDERS

A battalion of part time volunteers was raised in 1917 as the 1/1st Bn Northern Counties Highland Volunteer Regiment, and became the 1st Volunteer Bn Cameron Highlanders in 1918. It was raised from the counties of Inverness and Nairn, under arrangements of the Territorial Force Association. It was based in Inverness, and its four companies recruited from Inverness and Beauly, Nairn-shire, Badenoch and Lochaber. Its role was home defence and it was similar to the Home Guard of World War II.

The battalion was composed of men whose age, fitness or employment made them ineligible for normal military service except in an emergency. The battalion held a camp at Fort George in 1918. It was disbanded in February 1920.

7. THE 'NEW ARMY' BATTALIONS

On the outbreak of war in 1914, Lord Kitchener was appointed Secretary of State for War. Foreseeing a war of at least three years, he set about organizing a massive expansion of the Army. Instead of using the framework of the Territorial Force, as had been intended in Haldane's reorganisation of the Army in 1908, Kitchener decided to raise separate New Armies for service in the field.

The first service battalions were raised in August-September 1914 and were grouped into three new armies, K1, K2 and K3, each of six infantry divisions. In October 1914 a fourth Army, K4, was formed, but was subsequently broken up to reinforce the first three Armies.

Recruits for the Seaforth Highlanders under training in Edinburgh during World War I.

5th (Service) Bn The Queen's Own Cameron Highlanders parade in Cologne 1919.

7th (SERVICE) BATTALION SEAFORTH HIGHLANDERS

Formation of the 7th Seaforth   1914
The 7th Seaforth were formed at Fort George in August 1914 as part of Kitchener's First New Army, K1. They joined 26 (Highland) Brigade of the 9th (Scottish) Division, along with the 8th Black Watch, 8th Gordons, and 5th Camerons, at Aldershot. During the winter of 1914-1915 the battalion trained in the South of England and on Salisbury Plain.

Move to France   1915
The 9th Division was the first of the new Army Divisions to reach France. In May 1915 the 7th Seaforth landed at Boulogne, and on 1/2 July 1915 the 9th Division took over in the trenches near Festubert.

Loos   1915
The first major battle for the 7th Seaforth was the attack at Loos which started on 25th September 1915. It was the first occasion on which the British used poison gas. The 7th Seaforth and the 5th Camerons together attacked the strong German position on the Hohenzollern Redoubt. In a series of attacks over three days, the battalion took its objective at a cost of over 500 casualties.

The Ypres Salient   1915-1916
The 7th Seaforth spent October-December 1915 in the 'Salient' at Ypres, in the particularly bleak period of cold, muddy trench warfare where the British Corps clung grimly to the gains it had made in the battle of Ypres.

From January-May 1916 the 9th Division held the Ploegsteert (or 'Plugstreet') area where the trenches and billets were much better, and morale improved greatly.

The 7th (Service) Bn Seaforth Highlanders come out of action at the Somme on 19th July 1916, led by Piper 'Scott' MacKay.

The Somme   1916
On 1st July 1916 the battle of the Somme started, and on 14th July the 9th Division was sent in to attack the German positions at Longueval and Delville Wood. In a week of most severe fighting the 7th Seaforth carried out some successful attacks, but at the cost of over 450 casualties.

The Butte de Warlencourt   1916
The 9th Division battalions, including the 7th Seaforth, were now badly under strength, and so were withdrawn from the line on 23rd July 1916. The battalion held positions on Vimy Ridge during August-September. In October 1916, it returned to the Somme, and took part in the attacks in the area of the Butte de Warlencourt, which were made in the most unpleasant and difficult muddy conditions.

Arras   1916-1917
In December 1916 the 9th Division moved to a sector of the line near Arras. On 9th April 1917 the 7th Seaforth took part in the attack at Arras as the right leading battalion of 26 Brigade. The only serious resistance met was on the battalion's flank at the 'Island' near Blangy, which was stormed and captured. The six days fighting achieved considerable gains and the battalion's losses were 181 casualties.

Passchendaele   1917
The 7th Seaforth held positions at Cambrai in July 1917 and then in September moved to Ypres. On 12th October they took part in the attack on Passchendaele Ridge. In wet miserable conditions, in deep mud, the battalion suffered over 230 casualties in one of the grimmest and most thankless battles of the war.

The German Offensive   1918
When the Germans launched their last major offensive on 21st March 1918, the 7th Seaforth were holding positions on the Somme. This sector bore the full brunt of the German attack, and the 7th Seaforth carried out a tough withdrawal losing over 300 casualties.

The Final Allied Offensive   1918
In April the 7th Seaforth were moved North to Flanders and on 16th April 1918 they made a most successful attack which recovered the village of Wytschoete from the Germans.

In September 1918 the 7th Seaforth were in the line at Ypres. Between 28th September and 25th October the 9th Division advanced from its positions on the Frezenberg Ridge outside Ypres, and the 7th Seaforth took part in the series of attacks which carried the line forward over 20 miles to near Harlebecke. The final operation cost the 7th Seaforth 331 casualties.

The 7th Seaforth were presented with a King's Colour by General Sir Henry Plumer at Solingen, Germany, on 19th February 1919.

8th (SERVICE) BATTALION SEAFORTH HIGHLANDERS

Formation of the 8th Seaforth   1914
The 8th Seaforth were formed at Fort George in September 1914 as part of Kitchener's Second New Army, K2. They joined 44 Brigade of the 15th (Scottish) Division at Aldershot in September 1914, along with the 9th Black Watch, 10th Gordons and 7th Camerons.

Move to France   1915
The 8th Seaforth left for France in July 1915, landed at Boulogne, and concentrated at St Omer. The battalion took over a sector in the line at Loos on 6th August 1915.

Loos
The first major battle for the 8th Seaforth was the attack at Loos on 25th September 1915, which was preceded by the first British gas attack of the war. The 8th Seaforth, in the right hand brigade, had a hard fight through Loos village and, after house to house fighting, they broke through to attack Hill 70 beyond. The 44th Brigade took Hill 70, but the cost in casualties was so high that it had only a tenuous hold on its objective. When the 8th Seaforth were relieved that night, they had lost 718 out of the 776 who had started the day.
During the winter of 1915-1916 the 15th (Scottish) Division was given a chance to recover its strength. It was to take almost a year before the losses at Loos were made good. The 8th Seaforth were reinforced with drafts, and the battalion was retrained and reorganised, taking its turn in the trenches in the Loos Sector and the Hohenzollern Redoubt.

The Somme   1916
The battle of the Somme started on 1st July 1916, but the 15th (Scottish) Division was not committed until the third phase in August. The 8th Seaforth took part in raids on the enemy lines and held the captured Switch Line against heavy counter attacks on 17th-19th August 1916.

Arras   1917
In the attack on the German positions east of Arras, which started on 9th April 1917, the 8th Seaforth were in reserve, providing men for working parties and carrying ammunition. Then on 23rd April 1917 they attacked the German positions at Guemappe with some success, although with a loss of over 300 casualties.

The Third Battle of Ypres   1917
In July 1917 the 8th Seaforth took part in the attack on the German positions on Passchendaele Ridge overlooking Ypres. The attack by the 15th Division gained 2000 yards and did much to improve the security of the British lines at Ypres, but it cost the 8th Seaforth 203 casualties.
In early August the battalion was reinforced again, but there was hardly a chance to train the new drafts before the battalion was back in the line. On 22nd August 1917 the 8th Seaforth attacked again and gained more ground, but a further 393 casualties reduced the battalion to just over 200 strong.

Sgt J. B. McClurg (centre) with the RSM and CSM of 8th (Service) Bn Seaforth Highlanders in France.

The German Offensive   1918
During the winter of 1917-1918 the 8th Seaforth held the line in the Arras and Cambrai area, while new drafts arrived and the battalion was retrained.
When the German offensive started on 21st March 1918, the 8th Seaforth were at Monchy, West of Arras. The 15th (Scottish) Division had to give some ground, but it succeeded in saving Arras from being overrun.

The Marne   1918
In July 1918 the 15th (Scottish) Division was moved South to support the French in the Epernay Sector on the River Marne. On 28th July the 8th Seaforth took part in the 44 Brigade attack which captured the village of Buzancy.

The Final Allied Offensive   1918
In their last operation of the war, the 8th Seaforth returned to Loos. It was almost the same area where they had first gone into battle in 1915. In October, as the Germans withdrew, the 15th (Scottish) Division advanced. The 8th Seaforth ended the war at Huissignies.
The 8th Seaforth were presented with a King's Colour by Lieutenant General Sir Richard Butler at Nivelles, Belgium, on 10th February 1919.

9th (SERVICE) BATTALIONS SEAFORTH HIGHLANDERS (PIONEERS)

Formation of the 9th Seaforth   **1914**

The 9th Seaforth were formed at Fort George on 8th October 1914. They joined the 9th (Scottish) Division at Aldershot in December 1914 as the Pioneers of the 9th Division. It was the first Pioneer unit formed and the first to land in France. Many of its officers were qualified engineers, and the soldiers were mainly bricklayers, miners and labourers. They were trained in both infantry skills and simple engineering work. Their tasks included building roads, communication trenches, strong points, trench mortar emplacements, drainage and field tramways.

Move to France   **1915**

The 9th Seaforth moved to France 1915 and first went into the trenches at Bailleul.

Loos   **1915**

The first major operation for the 9th Seaforth was the battle of Loos which started on 25th September 1915. The battalion's task was to link up the captured trenches, and it dug two major communication trenches from the front line to the Hoherzollern Redoubt. The 9th Seaforth earned commendation for their excellent work under heavy fire, and they were often obliged to fight as infantrymen as well as pioneers.

The Somme   **1916**

During the battle of the Somme, the 9th Seaforth were split up in support of the Brigades of the 9th Scottish Division. They took part in the difficult fighting at Longueval and Delville Wood and in the attacks on Butte de Warlencourt. The tasks of the 9th Seaforth included keeping the roads in repair, often in the muddiest and most difficult conditions, consolidating captured positions, and constructing strongpoints. They often had to work under heavy fire.

Arras   **1917**

The 9th Seaforth took part in the 9th Division's attack at Arras in April 1917, when they had to cease their pioneer work and repel a German counter attack with their rifles.

On 5th June the 9th Seaforth carried out a particularly fine piece of pioneering work when it entrenched a newly captured piece of ground in the dark, under heavy fire, despite heavy casualties.

The German Offensive   **1918**

When the Germans launched their last major offensive on 21st March 1918, the 9th Seaforth were supporting the 9th Scottish Division in the positions on the Somme. The battalion was used in an infantry role, and fought a determined defensive engagement at St Pierre Vaast Wood, followed by a rearguard action through Rancourt and Combles. Two platoons protected a battery of Divisional Field Artillery as it withdrew, firing over open sights. It held a further position on the railway embankment between Albert and Dernancourt, where it had the misfortune to be shelled by allied artillery.

The final Allied Offensive   **1918**

In the final offensive in September-October 1918, the 9th Seaforth took part in the 9th Division's advance from Ypres to its final engagement of the war near Harlebecke.

The 9th Seaforth (Pioneers) were presented with a King's Colour by Brigadier General A. H. Marindin at Malmedy, Belgium, on 10th June 1919.

10th (RESERVE) BATTALION SEAFORTH HIGHLANDERS

Formation of the 10th Seaforth   **1914**

The 10th Seaforth were formed at Cromarty on 28th October 1914 as part of Kitchener's Fourth New Army, K4. The battalion was started with a nucleus of the 3rd (Special Reserve) Battalion, and many of the NCOs were in their 60s and even 70s.

Fort George and Tain   **1915**

In March 1915 the 10th Seaforth moved to Fort George and became a Reserve Battalion, instead of a Service Battalion. Its role was to train and despatch drafts for the front. It moved to Tain in May 1915.

Catterick 1915 and Dunfermline   **1916**

In October 1915 the 10th Seaforth sent a large number of reinforcements to the 8th Seaforth to make up the casualties suffered at Loos. It moved to Catterick in October 1915 and to Dunfermline in April 1916. It was redesignated No 39 Training Reserve Battalion in September 1916, but carried on wearing the uniform of the Seaforth Highlanders until it was disbanded in 1919. It supplied a total of 59 drafts to other Seaforth battalions.

A King's Colour was issued for the 10th Seaforth after the war.

1st GARRISON BATTALION SEAFORTH HIGHLANDERS

Formation of the 1st Garrison Bn Seaforth   **1916**

The 1st Garrison Bn was formed at Tillicoultry in July 1916. It was made up of men who were below the normal standard of fitness for fighting, including those who had been wounded or who were too old. The battalion wore the uniform of the Seaforth Highlanders.

Salonika   **1916-1918**

In August 1916 the 1st Garrison Bn moved to Salonika. Although intended for duty in the city, it was sent up to the Struma front and spent 18 months of duty in the trenches facing the Bulgarians.

Rumania, Turkey   **1918-1919**

After the Armistice with Bulgaria in October 1918, it served in Constanza, in other towns in Rumania, and finally in Constantinople. It was disbanded in June 1919.

THE 5th (SERVICE) BATTALION, THE QUEEN'S OWN CAMERON HIGHLANDERS

Formation of the 5th Camerons   1914

When Field Marshal Lord Kitchener appealed for 100,000 volunteers for his New Armies, he asked Lt Col D. W. Cameron of Lochiel to raise a battalion by direct appeal. Lochiel, who was commanding the 3rd (Special Reserve) Battalion at Invergordon, set about recruiting with the greatest energy. His appeal brought such an overwhelming response from all over Scotland, that the Camerons had enough recruits to form four service battalions.

The 5th 'Lochiels' Camerons were formed at Inverness on 1st September 1914 as part of Kitchener's First New Army, K1. They started with a nucleus of 200 officers and men from the 3rd Camerons, and the companies, which were recruited by districts, included D Company recruited from the Glasgow Stock Exchange. The battalion moved south to Aldershot where it assembled. During the winter 1914-1915 the 5th Camerons trained at Aldershot, Alresford and Bordon.

Move to France   1915

The 5th Camerons moved to France under Lochiel's command, arriving on 10 May 1915 at Boulogne. They were in 26 (Highland) Brigade of the 9th (Scottish) Division. On 30th June 1915 they took over in the trenches from the 4th Camerons at Locon near Festubert.

Loos September   1915

The first major battle for the 5th Camerons was the attack at Loos where the British used gas for the first time in the war. On 25th September 1915 the 5th Camerons and 7th Camerons together attacked the German positions on the Hohenzollern Redoubt. The first objective of the 5th Camerons, was a trench nicknamed 'Little Willie.' The 9th (Scottish) Division attack achieved surprise and made good ground, but on the left flank the artillery fire had failed to cut the German wire, and the 5th Camerons found themselves unsupported. When they were relieved after three days fighting the battalion had only two officers and 70 men left out of the 820 who had started the attack.

CORPORAL J. D. POLLOCK WINS THE VICTORIA CROSS AT LOOS,   27th SEPTEMBER 1915

When the 5th Camerons had captured 'Little Willie' trench in the Hohenzollern Redoubt, and were defending it against counter-attacks by German bombers, Corporal James Dalgleish Pollock left the cover of his trench and crossed open ground under heavy fire until he was able to outflank the German bombers. Then, standing on the parapet, he attacked them from above with bombs. He was twice wounded but saved the Redoubt from being recaptured. He was awarded the VC for his gallantry.

The Somme   1916

On 1st July 1916 the Battle of the Somme started, and on 14th July the 9th (Scottish) Division was committed. In a week of most severe fighting the 5th Camerons took part in the capture of Longueval, Delville Wood and Waterlot Farm at a cost of 446 casualties.

The Butte de Warlencourt   1916

During the summer of 1916, as the 5th Camerons were slowly brought up to strength again with drafts, they held positions on Vimy Ridge. In October the 9th (Scottish) Division returned to the Somme, and the 5th Camerons took part in the attacks on the Butte de Warlencourt, made in the most unpleasant and difficult muddy conditions.

Arras   1917

The 9th (Scottish) Division moved to Arras in December 1916, and on 9th April 1917 took part in the attack North of the River Scarpe. The flanking battalion, south of the river, was the 6th Camerons. The 9th (Scottish) Division attack was an unqualified success and made considerable gains of ground with relatively light casualties. But then on 1st May a further attack by the 5th Camerons on the Roeux chemical works had the misfortune to be heavily shelled by British artillery who, because of faulty maps, bombarded the attacking troops rather than the objective. The 5th Camerons lost over 300 casualties.

Passchendaele   1917

The 5th Camerons held positions near Cambrai in July and August 1917, and then in September moved to Ypres. On 12th October the 5th Camerons attacked at Passchendaele, but the assembly area was heavily shelled, and the advance was decimated by enfiladed machine guns. The 5th Camerons lost over 200 casualties.

Corporal James Pollock VC, 5th (Service) Bn The Queen's Own Cameron Highlanders.

The German Offensive   1918

When the Germans launched their last major offensive on 21st March 1918, the 5th Camerons were holding positions on the Somme. The sector bore the full brunt of the German attack and, as they withdrew to stabilize the line, the 5th Camerons had a loss of 400 casualties.

The Final Allied Offensive   1918

In April the 9th (Scottish) Division moved North to Flanders, and on 19th July it made a successful attack which captured the village of Meteren.

On 28th September the 5th Camerons took part in the final battle which captured the ridge of Passchendaele. During October, the 9th (Scottish) Division advanced from Ypres to the Scheldt, fighting a series of actions which pushed the line forward 26 miles. After the Armistice the 5th Camerons crossed the Rhine into Germany on 13th December and were billetted at Solingen. A King's Colour was presented to the battalion by Sir Herbert Plumer at Solingen in February 1919. The battalion was disbanded on 15th November 1919.

6th (SERVICE) BATTALION THE QUEEN'S OWN CAMERON HIGHLANDERS

Formation of the 6th Camerons   1914

When Colonel D. W. Cameron of Lochiel appealed in August 1914 for men to join the Cameron Highlanders, the response was so great that the 5th 'Lochiels' Camerons were complete within a few days. On 8th September 1914 a further battalion, the 6th Camerons, was formed. It moved out of the 5th Battalion lines at Aldershot into a camp at Rushmoor.

The 6th Camerons included a complete company of Glasgow University students and many volunteers from the Glasgow Stock Exchange. The battalion formed part of Kitchener's Second New Army, K2. It joined 45 Brigade in the 15th (Scottish) Division, along with the 13th Royal Scots, 7th Royal Scots Fusiliers, and 11th Argylls.

Move to France   1915

The 6th Camerons moved to France, arriving at Boulogne on 10th July 1915. They took over in the line near Loos on 22nd July 1915.

Loos 1915

The first major battle for the 6th Camerons was the attack at Loos on 25th September 1915 when, for the first time in the war, the British used gas. 45 Brigade, with the 6th Camerons, started the day as the reserve brigade of the 15th (Scottish) Division.

The 6th Camerons were called forward to defend the left flank of the attack, and advanced against heavy machine gun fire. On the second day the battalion led the 45 Brigade attack on Hill 70. In the face of intense rifle and machine gun fire the 6th Camerons attacked repeatedly, and suffered 387 casualties before Hill 70 was taken.

Lt Col A. F. DOUGLAS-HAMILTON WINS THE
VICTORIA CROSS   26 SEPTEMBER 1915

The 6th Camerons were commanded at Loos by Lt Col Angus Douglas-Hamilton. The repeated assaults on Hill 70 by the remains of the 6th Camerons were inspired by the indomitable leadership of their Commanding Officer. He led his battalion from the front with conspicuous gallantry until he was mortally wounded. He was awarded the VC posthumously.

The Somme   1916

The 6th Camerons spent the next three months rebuilding the battalion after the casualties at Loos. They held the line at Hulluch and in the Hohenzollern Sector as drafts were absorbed and the battalion rebuilt.

The battle of the Somme started on 1st July 1916, and the 15th (Scottish) Division was committed during the third phase in August. The 6th Camerons carried out a successful attack on the Switch Line on 12th August, and took part in the 45 Brigade attack on Martinpuich on 15th September which cost the battalion 240 casualties.

Arras   1917

In the attack on the German positions East of Arras which started on 9th April 1917, the 6th Camerons advanced after the opening attack and successfully exploited the objective. The next day, as they continued the advance to Monchy Le Preux, they came under enfiladed machine gun fire from Roeux, but managed to capture Monchy at a cost of 272 casualties.

On 23rd April the 6th Camerons took part in the operations to consolidate the gains of the opening advance, suffering a further 140 casualties at Cavalry Farm near Guemappe.

Lieutenant Colonel Angus Douglas-Hamilton VC, 6th (Service) Bn The Queen's Own Cameron Highlanders.

The Third Battle of Ypres   1917

On 31 July 1917 the 6th Camerons took part in the attack on the Passchendaele ridge which pushed the German lines back 2000 yards and improved the security of Ypres. The 6th Camerons lost their Commanding Officer, Colonel J. C. Russell, and 296 casualties in the severe fighting to achieve the objectives.

The German Offensive   1918

During the final German offensive in March 1918 the 6th Camerons were in the Arras sector. In the 15th (Scottish) Division's withdrawal the 6th Camerons suffered 287 casualties, but the operation checked the German advance and saved Arras from being overrun.

Amalgamation of 6th and 7th Camerons   1918

Because of the casualties at Arras, all the battalions in the division were short of men, and so each brigade was reduced from four battalions to three. The three surplus battalions were used to bring the remainder up to strength.

Under this reorganization the 6th and 7th Camerons were amalgamated at Arras on 10th June 1918.

The Marne   1918

In July 1918 the 15th (Scottish) Division was moved South to support the French in the Epernay sector on the River Marne. In the attack at Buzancy the 6th Camerons captured the Sucrerie at a cost of 286 casualties.

The Final Allied Offensive   1918

In their last operation of the war the 6th Camerons returned to Loos, to the same ground where they had first gone into battle in 1915. In October, as the Germans withdrew, the 15th (Scottish) Division advanced. The Armistice was announced as the 6th Camerons were on the march at St Anne.

The 6th Camerons were presented with a King's Colour by Sir Richard Butler at Braine-le-Comte on 21st January 1919. The battalion was disbanded on 25th June 1919.

2nd Lt David MacDonald with the King's Colour presented to the 6th (Service) Bn The Queen's Own Cameron Highlanders 1919.

7th (SERVICE) BATTALION THE QUEEN'S OWN CAMERON HIGHLANDERS

Formation of the 7th Camerons   **1914**

The 7th Camerons were formed from the men who answered Lochiel's appeal for volunteers to join the Cameron Highlanders. When the 5th and 6th Camerons were complete, the 7th Battalion was formed on 18th September 1914. Like the 5th and 6th Battalions, the 7th Camerons contained a high proportion of young professional men from Glasgow and Inverness who had answered Lochiel's appeal.

The 7th Camerons left Inverness on 30th November 1914 for Aldershot. They joined 44 Brigade of the 15th (Scottish) Division, along with the 9th Black Watch, 8th Seaforth, and 10th Gordons.

During the winter of 1914-15 the battalion trained at Liphook, Cirencester and Chiseldon.

Move to France   **1915**

The 7th Camerons moved to France, arriving at Boulogne on 9th July, 1915. They took over in the line at Houchin on 28th July.

Loos   **1915**

The first major battle for the 7th Camerons was the attack at Loos on 25th September 1915, which was preceded by the first British gas attack of the war.

The 7th Camerons started as the support battalion of 44 Brigade and, when the 8th Seaforth and 9th Black Watch had taken Loos, the 7th Camerons passed through them and attacked the half finished German Redoubt on Hill 70. The battalion secured Hill 70, the Commanding Officer Lt Col J. W. Sandilands rallying the survivors of nine battalions to hold it. The 7th Camerons lost 548 casualties in the attack.

During the winter 1915-1916, the 7th Camerons held the line in the Loos sector and in the Hohenzollern Redoubt. The 15th (Scottish) Division was given a chance to recover its strength. New drafts arrived and the battalion was reorganized and retrained.

The Somme   **1916**

The Battle of the Somme started on 1st July 1916, and the 15th (Scottish) Division was committed in the third phase. On 17th August the 7th Camerons successfully attacked the Switch Line of the German positions at Contalmaison, but lost 231 casualties.

Arras   **191?**

In the attack on the German positions East of Arras which started on 9th April 1917, the 7th Camerons took part in the attack by 44 Brigade which advanced 4000 yards and gained all its first objectives. Two days later the 7th Camerons attacked Monchy, suffering heavy casualties from enfilade machine gun fire. With the survivors o several other battalions they held Monchy against heavy German counter attacks.

On 23rd April the 7th Camerons took part in the operations to consolidate the gains of the opening attack. The two phases of the battle of Arras had cost the battalion 659 casualties, and for a time it was reduced to the effective strength of a company.

The Third Battle of Ypres   **1917**

In July 1917 the 7th Camerons moved to Ypres for the attack on the German positions on Passchendaele Ridge overlooking Ypres. They carried out a successful battalion raid on 28th July, and next day took part in the attack by 44 Brigade. The operations gained 2000 yards and did much to improve security of the British lines round Ypres, but cost the 7th Camerons a further 292 casualties.

The German Offensive   **1918**

During the winter of 1917-1918 the 7th Camerons held the line in the Arras and Cambrai area, and new drafts gradually built up numbers again.

When the German offensive started on 21st March 1918 the 7th Camerons were in the Arras sector. In the 15th (Scottish) Division's withdrawal, the 7th Camerons lost 388 casualties in the operation which managed to check the German advance and save Arras from being overrun.

Amalgamation with 6th Camerons   **1918**

Because of the casualties at Ypres and Arras all the battalions in the division were well below strength, and so each brigade was reduced from four battalions to three, the surplus battalions were used to bring the remainder up to strength. Under this reorganisation the 7th Camerons were amalgamated with the 6th Camerons at Arras on 10th June 1918.

After the war a King's Colour was presented to a representative party of the 7th Camerons by HRH The Duke of York at Inverness on 17th September 1920.

8th (RESERVE) BATTALION THE QUEEN'S OWN CAMERON HIGHLANDERS

Formation of the 8th Camerons   **1914**

The 8th Camerons were formed on 14th December 1914 at Inverness as part of Kitchener's Fourth New Army, K4. The battalion was started with a nucleus of the 3rd (Special Reserve) Bn and included a contingent from the Glasgow Stock Exchange who had joined the Camerons in answer to Lochiel's appeal for recruits for the regiment.

Inverness and Tain   **1914-1915**

The 8th Camerons moved from Inverness to Tain in May 1915. In July 1915 they became a Reserve battalion instead of a Service battalion.

Catterick 1915 and Stirling   **1916**

In October 1915 the 8th Camerons moved to Catterick and in April 1916 to Stirling. The battalion was redesignated the 40th Training Reserve Battalion in September 1916, but carried on wearing the uniform of the Cameron Highlanders until 1918.

Kent   **1917-1918**

In September 1917 the 40th Training Reserve Bn was moved to Kent and formed part of the coastal defences. Its designation was changed to 286 Infantry Battalion, and in October 1917 it was renamed the 52nd (Graduated) Bn Gordon Highlanders.

     1919-1920

After the Armistice in November 1918, the battalion moved to Germany as part of the Army of Occupation. It returned to Catterick in 1919, and then to Glencorse, where it was disbanded in March 1920.

9th (LABOUR) BATTALION THE QUEEN'S OWN CAMERON HIGHLANDERS

The 9th Camerons were raised at Blairgowrie in August 1916 for use on labouring tasks such as unloading stores in the docks and repairing roads.

The 9th Camerons moved to France in September 1916 and worked in the docks at Le Havre, Calais and other French ports. In May 1917 the Labour Corps was formed, and the 9th Camerons were transferred to it as No 7 and No 8 Labour Companies.

After the war a King's Colour was presented to a representative party of the 9th Camerons by HRH The Duke of York at Inverness on 17th September 1920.

11th (SERVICE) BATTALION THE QUEEN'S OWN CAMERON HIGHLANDERS

The 11th Camerons were formed at Etaples on 9th June 1918 as a Labour battalion from men drawn from Labour companies. The battalion joined 120 Brigade of the 40th Division. In July 1918 it was changed from a Labour to a Service battalion.

The 11th Camerons served in the trenches from August 1918 until the Armistice. They were finally disbanded on 1st June 1919.

A King's Colour was presented to the battalion by Sir Beavoir de Lisle at Roubaix on 20th January 1919.

M

CHAPTER IV THE REGIMENTS 1919-1939

1. REGULAR ARMY BATTALIONS

1st BATTALION SEAFORTH HIGHLANDERS

The 1st Seaforth in Scotland   1919-1922
After World War I a cadre of the 1st Seaforth returned from Egypt to Fort George in June 1919. It moved to Glencorse in July and joined up with a nucleus of the 3rd (Special Reserve) Bn, whose numbers brought it up to strength. The reformed 1st Seaforth returned to Fort George in November 1919 as the home service battalion of the regiment.

It provided the Royal Guard at Ballater in 1919. On 3rd December 1920 Colonel HRH The Prince of Wales was appointed Colonel in Chief.

During the coal strike of 1921 the 1st Seaforth were sent to Bridge of Allan and Cowdenbeath for strike duty.

The 1st Seaforth in Ireland   1921-1926
The 1st Seaforth left Fort George for Ireland in July 1921 and, after a short time in Dublin, moved to Belfast for duties in aid of the civil power. The battalion remained in Northern Ireland until 1926, at a very difficult period of political friction with the newly independent Irish Free State and of civil disorder in Ulster.

1st Bn Seaforth Highlanders in Cairo 1936.

The 1st Seaforth in Aldershot and Dover   1926-1933
In January 1926 the 1st Seaforth moved to Aldershot, and during the General Strike they provided escorts for food convoys across London. In November 1928 they moved to Dover where, on 29th June 1929, they trooped the Regimental Colour before HRH The Prince of Wales, the Colonel in Chief.

The 1st Seaforth in Palestine   1934
The 1st Seaforth sailed for Palestine at the start of a foreign tour, and arrived in Jerusalem in December 1934. By happy chance the 2nd Seaforth were stationed at Haifa, only 100 miles away, and the two Seaforth battalions spent four months in the same country, until the 2nd Seaforth left for Great Britain on the completion of their foreign tour. A series of social, ceremonial and sporting events was held to make the most of this unique occasion.

The 1st Seaforth in Egypt   1934-1936
In September 1934 the 1st Seaforth moved to Cairo. The following year there was a threat that the Italians, who had attacked Abyssinia, might also invade Egypt, and so the 1st Seaforth were sent for a month to protect the RAF airfield at Mersa Matruh in the Western Desert.

The 1st Seaforth in the Palestine troubles   1936

In response to the state of emergency declared in Palestine during the Arab revolt, the 1st Seaforth were sent back to Palestine from May to October 1936. To counter the widespread sabotage, cutting of telephone wires and oil pipe lines, ambushes on convoys, and guerilla attacks by organized gangs, the 1st Seaforth mounted an intensive programme of operations. They carried out night patrols, village searches and ambushes, picquetted roads by day, and operated a striking force of a company group supported by tanks, armoured cars and guns. The battalion returned to Cairo in October 1936.

The 1st Seaforth in Hong Kong   1937-1938

The 1st Seaforth left Cairo for Hong Kong in December 1936, having handed over to the 2nd Camerons. At the time, China and Japan were at war with each other, and the main task of the battalion was to prepare the defences of Hong Kong against invasion. In September 1937 a typhoon struck Hong Kong, with winds reaching an estimated 164 mph, and the 1st Seaforth did much useful work in clearing up the devasted colony.

The 1st Seaforth in Shanghai   1938-1940

In March 1938 the 1st Seaforth were sent from Hong Kong to Shanghai. Their task was to protect the British

1st Bn Seaforth Highlanders in Shanghai 1938.

Sector of the International Settlement against the truculent behaviour of the Japanese and against terrorist attacks.

At the time of the Munich crisis in September 1938 the 1st Seaforth were ordered back to Hong Kong. The battalion embarked on HMS Birmingham at four hours notice, and arrived at Kowloon next day, after a record voyage when the ship had sailed at her full speed of 29 knots. The battalion returned to Shanghai the following week and remained there until 1940.

2nd BATTALION SEAFORTH HIGHLANDERS

The 2nd Seaforth in India   1919-1932

After World War I the 2nd Seaforth returned for a short time to Fort George, and then went abroad to India as the foreign service battalion of the regiment, arriving in Meerut in November 1919. In November 1922 the battalion set out to march the 500 miles from Ambala to the North West Frontier Camp of Landi Kotal, taking nearly two months for the march. The 2nd Seaforth spent over a year on the frontier until moving to Nowshera in 1924. In 1927 they marched the 250 miles to their next station at Lahore.

The 2nd Seaforth on the North-West Frontier   1930-1931

Having moved to Jhansi in 1929, the 2nd Seaforth were sent up to the North-West Frontier in August 1930 for operations against the Afridi tribesmen. From a base at Miri Khel, west of Peshawar, the battalion helped to build roads and strongpoints to prevent infiltration by the Afridis, and it saw active service against the tribesmen.

2nd Bn Seaforth Highlanders during operations on the North West Frontier of India 1930-1931.

2nd Bn Seaforth Highlanders in India 1932.

2nd Bn Seaforth Highlanders in Palestine 1933.

The 2nd Seaforth in Palestine   1932-1933

The 2nd Seaforth left Jhansi in November 1932, and moved to Haifa in Palestine for the last part of their foreign service tour. At first all was peaceful and uneventful, but in late 1933 there were demonstrations and riots as Arab resentment of Jewish immigration increased.

In December 1933 the 1st Seaforth arrived in Palestine at the start of their foreign tour, and the two battalions of the regiment were stationed only 100 miles apart. It was un unprecedented chance for social and sporting meetings of which the 1st and 2nd Seaforth took full advantage.

The 2nd Seaforth in Dover   1934-1937

On their return to Great Britain the 2nd Seaforth were stationed at Dover Castle, taking over from the 1st Seaforth. On 5th July 1935 the battalion received its 8th Stand of Colours from the Colonel in Chief, HRH The Prince of Wales. By the time the 2nd Seaforth left Dover, the two battalions of Seaforth Highlanders had served continuously in Dover for nine years from 1928 to 1937.

The 2nd Seaforth in Glasgow   1937-1939

The 2nd Seaforth arrived in Glasgow in September 1937 and were stationed at Maryhill Barracks until the outbreak of war in 1939. The battalion furnished the Royal Guard at Ballater in 1938.

1st BATTALION THE QUEEN'S OWN CAMERON HIGHLANDERS

The 1st Camerons in Scotland   1919

After World War I the 1st Camerons remained in Germany while demobilization was carried out, and a cadre of the battalion returned to Inverness in April 1919. It moved to Invergordon and joined up with a nucleus from the 3rd (Special Reserve) Battalion. In July 1919 the 1st Camerons embarked for India for a tour as the foreign service battalion of the regiment.

The 1st Camerons in India   1919-1925

The 1st Camerons were stationed first at Rawalpindi, and from May to October 1920 were sent up to the Kurram valley to deter Afghan border raiders. In 1922 a detachment supported the police in dealing with riots in Rawalpindi.

In November 1922 the 1st Camerons moved to Calcutta where, on 9th January 1923, the battalion received its 6th Stand of Colours from General Sir Havelock Hudson, GOC in C Eastern Command.

A picquet of the 1st Bn The Queen's Own Cameron Highlanders in the Rangoon riots of 1930.

The 1st Camerons in Burma   1925-1930

In November 1925 the 1st Camerons moved to Burma. They were stationed at first in Maymyo, and from 1928 in Rangoon, with Company detachments at Mandalay and in the Andaman Islands. During the Rangoon riots of 1930 the 1st Camerons were called out to disperse rioters and to provide guards and picquets.

The 1st Camerons in India   1930-1934

The 1st Camerons returned to India in November 1930 and were stationed at Fyzabad. In 1931 the battalion route-marched through the Gonda district where they received a memorable welcome, being the first British troops to visit the district since 1861.

The 1st Camerons in Sudan   1934-1936

In December 1934 the 1st Camerons moved to the Sudan for the final part of their tour of foreign service, and were stationed in Khartoum until March 1936.

The 1st Camerons in Great Britain   1936-1939

On their return to Great Britain in 1936, the 1st Camerons were stationed at Catterick. In 1937 the battalion took part in the Coronation ceremonial of HM King George VI, the Colonel in Chief of the Regiment. In the Highland Brigade Gathering at Redford Barracks, Edinburgh, the first to be held in Great Britain, the 1st Camerons won first place.

The battalion moved to Aldershot in October 1938, and were stationed there when World War II broke out.

1st Bn The Queen's Own Cameron Highlanders march past HM King George VI after Church parade at Aldershot 1939.

2nd BATTALION THE QUEEN'S OWN CAMERON HIGHLANDERS

The 2nd Camerons in Great Britain   1919-1920

After World War I the 2nd Camerons remained at Tiflis in the Caucasus while demobilization was carried out, and then in May 1919 the cadre of the battalion returned to Inverness. It moved to Dreghorn Camp, Edinburgh where it joined up with a nucleus from the 3rd (Special Reserve) Battalion, and moved to Aldershot in September 1919.

The 2nd Camerons in Ireland   1920-1922

In May 1920 the 2nd Camerons moved to Ireland. They were stationed in Queenstown, with detachments in the small towns round Cork. It was to be a turbulent tour of duty in a part of Ireland reduced to anarchy by the events of the Sinn Fein rebellion. The battalion's task was to preserve order and protect loyalists, by patrolling the country and searching for illegal weapons.

The 2nd Camerons in Aldershot   1922-1923

In February 1922, after the Republic of Ireland was set up, the 2nd Camerons returned to Aldershot where they formed part of the 1st Guards Brigade.

The 2nd Camerons in Germany   1923-1926

In October 1923 the 2nd Camerons left Aldershot for Germany for service with the British Army of the Rhine. They were stationed at Mullheim, near Cologne, until December 1924, and then for a year in Wiesbaden.

The 2nd Camerons in Edinburgh   1926-1930

The 2nd Camerons returned from Germany to Redford Barracks, Edinburgh, in November 1926. When the Scottish National War Memorial at Edinburgh Castle was opened by The Prince of Wales on 14th July 1927, in the presence of King George V and Queen Mary, the 2nd

Camerons provided the Guard of Honour. In February 1928 the 2nd Camerons and the Scots Greys formed the ceremonial procession for the funeral of Field Marshal Earl Haig.

During June 1928 the 2nd Camerons carried out an interesting exercise when they embarked at Edinburgh on the battleship HMS Rodney and the battle cruisers HMS Renown and Repulse, and landed near Fort George. After tactical exercises with the 2nd Bn Black Watch, the 2nd Camerons route-marched to Lochaber where they paraded before Lochiel at Achnacarry and visited Erracht, the home of Sir Alan Cameron who had raised the 79th in 1793. By the time the battalion returned to Edinburgh it had marched 250 miles.

In 1929 the 2nd Camerons provided the ceremonial troops for the Reunion of the Church of Scotland and the United Free Church, for the 600th Anniversary of Edinburgh's Charter granted by King Robert the Bruce, for two levees held by HRH The Duke of York, and for many other public occasions.

presented the 2nd Camerons with their 3rd Stand c Colours at Aldershot. During 1934 the 2nd Cameror carried out public duties in London in August an September, mounting guard at St. James's Palace Buckingham Palace, and the Bank of England.

The 2nd Camerons in Palestine   1935-193

In November 1935 the 2nd Camerons left Aldershot fc Palestine at the start of a tour as the foreign servic battalion of the regiment. From April to October 1936 the were engaged on duties in aid of the civil power against th Arab Revolt, their tasks including patrols, convoy escort: riot control duties, cordon and searches, and guards agains terrorist attacks on vital installations.

The 2nd Camerons in Egypt   1936-193

The 2nd Camerons moved to Cairo in December 193€ and to Moascar on the Suez Canal in January 1938. Th

2nd Bn The Queen's Own Cameron Highlanders route marching in Scotland 1928.

The 2nd Camerons in Aldershot   1930-1935

The 2nd Camerons moved to Aldershot in October 1930. In 1933 the battalion won the Army Football Cup, and the trophy was presented by HM King George V, Colonel in Chief of the Regiment.

On 14th July 1933 HRH The Duke of York (later King George VI), Honorary Colonel of the 4th Camerons,

2nd Bn The Queen's Own Cameron Highlanders o anti-terrorist duty in Palestine 1936.

battalion carried out mobile desert training with its limitec motor transport, which was a useful foretaste of the deser warfare for which it was destined two years later.

The 2nd Camerons in India   1938-193<

In November 1938 the 2nd Camerons moved to India and were stationed at Ahmednagar until August 1939.

2. THE DEPOTS 1919-1939

DEPOT SEAFORTH HIGHLANDERS, FORT GEORGE

The Depot Seaforth Highlanders remained at Fort George, with the role of training recruits for the regular battalions of the regiment.

DEPOT THE QUEEN'S OWN CAMERON HIGHLANDERS, CAMERON BARRACKS, INVERNESS

The Depot Cameron Highlanders remained at Cameror Barracks, with the role of training recruits for the regula battalions of the regiment.

3. THE TERRITORIAL ARMY BATTALIONS 1920-1939

SEAFORTH HIGHLANDERS TA

The 4/5th and the 6th Battalions Seaforth Highlanders in camp at Fort George in 1930.

4th (ROSS-SHIRE) BATTALION SEAFORTH HIGHLANDERS TA   1920-1921

After World War I the 4th Seaforth were reconstituted as the Territorial Army battalion of Ross-shire.

5th (SUTHERLAND AND CAITHNESS) BATTALION SEAFORTH HIGHLANDERS TA   1920-1921

After World War I the 5th Seaforth were reconstituted as the Territorial Army battalion of Sutherland and Caithness.

4/5th (ROSS, SUTHERLAND AND CAITHNESS) BATTALION SEAFORTH HIGHLANDERS TA   1921-1939

In 1921 the Territorial Army was reduced in size and, among the amalgamations ordered, the 4th Seaforth and 5th Seaforth were joined to become the 4th/5th Seaforth. The battalion had two companies in Ross-shire dressed in the uniform of the Seaforth Highlanders, and two companies in Sutherland and Caithness dressed in the Sutherland kilt, badge and uniform.

The 4th and 5th Seaforth become separate battalions again — 1939

In 1939, when war was imminent, the Territorial Army was doubled, and the 4th and 5th Seaforth became separate battalions again.

6th (MORAYSHIRE) BATTALION SEAFORTH HIGHLANDERS TA   1920-1939

After World War I the 6th Seaforth were reconstituted as the Territorial Army battalion of Moray.

7th (MORAYSHIRE) BATTALION SEAFORTH HIGHLANDERS TA   1939

In 1939, when war was imminent, the Territorial Army was doubled, and the 6th Seaforth split into two battalions, the newly formed battalion becoming the 7th Seaforth.

THE QUEEN'S OWN CAMERON HIGHLANDERS TA

The contingent from 4th Bn The Queen's Own Cameron Highlanders TA commanded by Captain S. H. Hill, which took part in the Coronation Procession of King George VI in 1937.

4th BATTALION THE QUEEN'S OWN CAMERON HIGHLANDERS TA   1920-1939

After World War I the 4th Camerons were reformed with a Territorial area of Inverness-shire and Nairnshire.

5th BATTALION THE QUEEN'S OWN CAMERON HIGHLANDERS TA   1939

In 1939, when war was imminent and the Territorial Army was doubled, the 4th Camerons split into two battalions, the newly formed battalion becoming the 5th Camerons.

10th (LIVERPOOL SCOTTISH) BATTALION THE KING'S REGIMENT (LIVERPOOL) TA   1920-1937

After World War I the Liverpool Scottish were reformed in March 1920. In June 1922, under Army Order No. 481, they were affiliated to The Queen's Own Cameron Highlanders, although this was not shown in the Army List until June 1929.

The Liverpool Scottish at camp on the Isle of Man 1933.

1st BATTALION THE LIVERPOOL SCOTTISH, THE QUEEN'S OWN CAMERON HIGHLANDERS TA   1937-1939

In September 1937 the Liverpool Scottish were officially redisignated as a battalion of The Queen's Own Cameron Highlanders and ceased to be a battalion of The King's Regiment (Liverpool). In 1938 the Liverpool Scottish received new Colours from HM King George VI, Colonel in Chief of the Camerons, at Everton Football Club Ground.

2nd BATTALION THE LIVERPOOL SCOTTISH, THE QUEEN'S OWN CAMERON HIGHLANDERS TA   1939

In 1939, when war was imminent and the TA was doubled, the Liverpool Scottish split into 1st Battalion and 2nd Battalion The Liverpool Scottish, The Queen's Own Cameron Highlanders.

CHAPTER V THE REGIMENTS IN WORLD WAR II

1. INTRODUCTION

During the Second World War the regiments were again greatly expanded. By contrast to Kitchener's recruiting campaign of World War I, which ignored the Territorial system and formed a 'New Army', the expansion for World War II was achieved by doubling the existing Territorial Army.

Because the campaigns of World War II were widely dispersed over Europe, the Middle East, the Far East and other theatres, the stories of the individual battalions are, in general, more varied than in World War I, and the brief accounts in this booklet may give a misleading impression of the relative importance of a battalion's war history. A battalion which happened to serve, for example, in North Africa, Sicily, and North West Europe, tended to earn a greater share of the limelight than a battalion which served with equal distinction against the Japanese in the Far East, but which belonged to what was sometimes termed 'The Forgotten Army'. The length of a battalion's narrative is, therefore, no yardstick in assessing the merits of its fighting record.

2. THE BATTALIONS OF THE REGIMENTS IN WORLD WAR II

	Seaforth Highlanders	The Queen's Own Cameron Highlanders
REGULAR ARMY BATTALIONS	1st Seaforth 2nd Seaforth 2nd Seaforth (Reformed in 1940 after St. Valéry)	1st Camerons 2nd Camerons 2nd Camerons (Reformed in 1942 after Tobruk)
TERRITORIAL ARMY BATTALIONS	4th Seaforth 5th Seaforth 6th Seaforth 7th Seaforth	4th Camerons 4th Camerons (Reformed in 1940 after St. Valéry. Redesignated in 1942 as 2nd Camerons) 5th Camerons 1st Liverpool Scottish 2nd Liverpool Scottish
HOME DEFENCE BATTALIONS	8th Seaforth	6th Camerons
RESERVE BATTALIONS	9th Seaforth	7th Camerons (Redesignated 5th Scottish Parachute Battalion)

3. THE DIVISIONS AND BRIGADES OF WORLD WAR II

When World War II broke out, the Regular battalions in Great Britain were already formed into the traditional divisions and brigades of the Regular Army, and the numbering of the Territorial Army divisions and brigades had been retained from World War I. When the Territorial Army was doubled in 1939, some of the New Army divisions of World War I were reformed.

Battalion		Brigade	Division
REGULAR ARMY			
1st Seaforth	(Mar 42-Jun 45)	1 (Indian) Brigade	23rd (Indian) Division
2nd Seaforth	(Sep 39-Mar 40)	17 Brigade	5th Division
	(Mar -Jun 40)	152 Brigade	51st (Highland) Division
2nd Seaforth (Reformed)	(Jul 40-Jun 45)	152 Brigade	51st (Highland) Division
1st Camerons	(Sep 39-Jun 45)	5 Brigade	2nd Division
2nd Camerons	(Sep 39-Jun 42)	11 Indian Brigade	4th (Indian) Division
2nd Camerons (Reformed)			
	(Jan 44- Jun 45)	11 Indian Brigade	4th (Indian) Division
TERRITORIAL ARMY			
4th Seaforth	(Sep 39-Jun 40)	152 Brigade	51st (Highland) Division
5th Seaforth	(Sep 39-Jul 40)	26 Brigade	9th (Highland) Division
	(Jul 40-Jun 45)	152 Brigade	51st (Highland) Division
6th Seaforth	(Sep 39-Mar 40)	152 Brigade	51st (Highland) Division
	(Mar 40-Jun 45)	17 Brigade	5th Division
7th Seaforth	(Oct 41-Jun 45)	46 Brigade	15th (Scottish) Division
4th Camerons	(Sep 39-Jun 40)	152 Brigade	51st (Highland) Division
5th Camerons	(Sep 39-Jul 40)	26 Brigade	9th (Highland) Division
	(Jul 40-Jun 45)	152 Brigade	51st (Highland) Division

4.   THE REGULAR ARMY BATTALIONS IN WORLD WAR II

1st BATTALION SEAFORTH HIGHLANDERS

The 1st Seaforth in Malaya and India   1940-1942

The 1st Seaforth were in Shanghai when World War II broke out, and remained there until the British Garrison was withdrawn in August 1940. The battalion moved first to Singapore and then to Penang. In February 1941 it moved to Agra in India, and was stationed there when Japan entered the war in December 1941.

The 1st Seaforth in Assam and Burma   1942-1944

In March 1942 the 1st Seaforth mobilised and joined the 23rd Indian Division in Assam and operated in the Kohima and Imphal areas, carrying out long range patrolling into Burma as far as the River Chindwin while the Burma Army was withdrawn.

In 1943 the 1st Seaforth took part in the offensive patrolling operations on the Chindwin River in Burma designed to distract the Japanese from General Wingate's second expedition behind enemy lines.

During the Japanese attack on India, the 1st Seaforth patrolled deep into enemy-held territory. Their operations did much to disrupt the enemy plans to reach Imphal, and the battalion fought a particularly successful action when it attacked and captured Kasom. The 1st Seaforth continued fighting in the jungle until late 1944 when, after two-and-a-half years of active operations, they were withdrawn to India to train for the reconquest of Malaya.

2nd BATTALION SEAFORTH HIGHLANDERS

The 2nd Seaforth in France   1939-1940

When war broke out in 1939, the 2nd Seaforth mobilized at Maryhill Barracks, Glasgow, and moved to France with the British Expeditionary Force. They formed part of the 17th Infantry Brigade in the 5th Division. When in March 1940 the Territorial Army Divisions were strengthened by the inclusion of a Regular Army battalion in each brigade, the 2nd Seaforth moved to the 51st Highland Division as the regular battalion of 152 (Seaforth and Cameron) Brigade, the other battalions in the brigade being the 4th Seaforth TA and 4th Camerons TA.

2nd Bn Seaforth Highlanders, Motor transport at the outbreak of World War II.

The 2nd Seaforth at St Valéry-en-Caux   1940

When the Germans advanced in May 1940 the 51st Highland Division was detached to French command. The 2nd Seaforth were holding positions in the Maginot Line in the Saar district, from which they fought a withdrawal action until the 51st Highland Division was switched to hold positions North of Abbeville.

On 4th June 1940, the final day of the evacuation of the BEF at Dunkirk, the 51st Highland Division was still opposing the German bridgehead at Abbeville. But the overwhelming strength of the German advance forced the 51st Highland Division to withdraw South West down the French coast. At St Valéry-en-Caux the 51st Highland Division was cut off from its French Army allies and surrounded. The 2nd Seaforth, after a determined resistance, were forced to surrender on 11th June 1940.

The 2nd Seaforth reformed   1940

After the disaster of St Valéry the 51st Highland Division was reformed round a nucleus provided by the Territorial Army battalions of the 9th (Scottish) Division, and the Seaforth Highlanders re-raised their 2nd Battalion. The reconstituted 152 Highland Infantry Brigade was composed of the 2nd Seaforth, 5th Seaforth, and 5th Camerons.

The 2nd Seaforth at El Alamein   1942

On 14th August 1942 the 2nd Seaforth landed in Egypt with the 51st Highland Division. After six weeks intensive preparation they took part in the attack by the 8th Army at El Alamein, which began on 23rd October 1942.

The 2nd Seaforth started the battle in Corps reserve, and on 24th October they were called forward to attack a German strongpoint and to form a bridgehead through the minefield which was holding up the 2nd Armoured Brigade. The battalion suffered 100 casualties in successfully holding this bridgehead for 36 hours.

In the final phase of the battle, Operation 'Supercharge' 152 Brigade made the break through the enemy defences to allow the armour to operate beyond the minefields. The 2nd Seaforth had the task of mopping up and exploiting the objective.

The Prime Minister, Mr Winston Churchill, visits 152 Highland Brigade training in Egypt before the battle of El Alamein 1942.

The 2nd Seaforth in Tripoli 1943

On 20-21st January 1943 the 2nd Seaforth were attached to 154 Brigade for an attack at Corradini known as the 'Battle of the Hills'. On 23rd January 1943 the 51st Highland Division reached Tripoli, and the 2nd Seaforth took part in the Victory Parade on 4th February where the salute was taken by the Prime Minister, Mr Winston Churchill.

The 2nd Seaforth at Wadi Akarit 1943

In early April 1943 the advancing 8th Army reached a bottleneck, where the Germans held strong positions on the Djebel Roumana ridge and along the Wadi Akarit which connected it to the sea. When the 51st Highland Division attacked on 6th-7th April 1943, 152 Brigade's objective was the Djebel Roumana. The task of the 2nd Seaforth was to follow the 5th Seaforth and 5th Camerons on to the objective, mop up, and to link up with the brigade attacking the Wadi Akarit positions on the right flank. Although the 2nd Seaforth suffered heavy casualties, they successfully held the ridge against strong enemy counter attacks.

The campaign in North Africa had cost the 2nd Seaforth 483 casualties.

The 2nd Seaforth in Sicily 1943

After the battle of Wadi Akarit the 2nd Seaforth trained in Algeria for the invasion of Sicily. The 51st Highland Division concentrated at Sousse and embarked in landing craft, sailing via Malta for Sicily. During the landings on 10 July 1943, 152 Brigade was in reserve. After the beachhead was established, 152 Brigade advanced until, on 13th July 1943, the 5th Seaforth encountered stiff opposition from a German Parachute battalion at Francofonte. Next day the 2nd Seaforth carried out a successful battalion attack which wiped out half the German Parachute force.

The 2nd Seaforth had some hard fighting in the Plain of Catania, and in the attack on the Sferro Hills on 31st July-1st August 1943.

The campaign in Sicily had cost the 2nd Seaforth 194 casualties.

The 2nd Seaforth in Great Britain 1943-1944

When Sicily had been captured from the German and Italian forces, the 2nd Seaforth returned to Great Britain in November 1943. The 51st Highland Division was billetted in Hertfordshire, Essex, and Buckinghamshire while it prepared for the landings in Normandy.

The 2nd Seaforth in Normandy 1944

The 2nd Seaforth arrived in Normandy three days after D Day. They landed at Courseulles and took part in two months of difficult operations to hold the bridgehead over the River Orne against fierce German counter attacks. When the break-out began in August 1944, the 2nd Seaforth attacked and captured the strongly held German positions at Tilly-la-Campagne.

On 2nd September 1944 the 51st Highland Division liberated St Valery, and on 10th September the 2nd Seaforth took part in the 51st Highland Division attack on German positions holding Le Havre.

The 2nd Seaforth in Holland 1944

The 2nd Seaforth advanced through France and Belgium, and their next operation was the Battle of the Maas which was intended to clear South West Holland and open the port of Antwerp. On 23rd October 1944 the 2nd Seaforth attacked successfully across water obstacles at Schijndel. By 5th November the 51st Highland Division had cleared the country South of the River Maas, and on 14th November the 2nd Seaforth attacked across the Nederwert Canal, using assault boats and 'Buffaloes'.

On 17th November the 2nd Seaforth crossed the Zig (or Uitwaterings) Canal through a bridgehead established by the 5th Camerons, and took Beringen.

The 2nd Seaforth in the Ardennes 1945

In January 1945 the 51st Highland Division was sent to check the last desperate German counter attack of the war, the offensive in the Ardennes. The fighting was in bitter weather and in deep snow. On 11th January the 2nd Seaforth captured Ronchampey and next day occupied Laroche.

The 2nd Seaforth in the Reichswald 1945

On 9th February 1945 the 2nd Seaforth crossed the German frontier, and for a week were engaged in the fierce close-quarter fighting through the Reichswald Forest towards the German defences in the Siegfried Line. By 16th February the 2nd Seaforth were through the Reichswald and attacked towards Goch, where they forced a bridgehead over the anti-tank ditch. By early March the 2nd Seaforth were on the West bank of the Rhine. The three weeks fighting through the Reichswald and Siegfried Line had cost the battalion 120 casualties.

The 2nd Seaforth at the Rhine Crossing 1945

The 51st Highland Division was one of the assault divisions in the operation to cross the Rhine. The 2nd Seaforth were under command of 153 Brigade, and crossed the Rhine in assault boats on the night of 23rd-24th March 1945. On the East bank they exploited from Esserden and, having rejoined 152 Brigade, advanced over the Oudi Issel River using the remains of a bridge destroyed by the enemy.

The 2nd Seaforth in Germany 1945-1946

The 2nd Seaforth fought further actions at Adelheide and Ganderkesee, and took part in the capture of Bremervorde, two days before the German Army surrendered on 4th May 1945. The battalion took part in the Victory Parade at Bremerhaven on 12th May 1945.

The Massed Pipes and Drums of the 2nd, 5th, 6th, and 7th Battalions Seaforth Highlanders and the 1st Seaforth Highlanders of Canada, at the Seaforth Highlanders Gathering held at Cuxhaven in July 1945.

1st BATTALION THE QUEEN'S OWN CAMERON HIGHLANDERS

The 1st Camerons move to France   **1939**

When war broke out in 1939, the 1st Camerons mobilised at Aldershot and moved to France with the British Expeditionary Force, arriving at Cherbourg on 24th September 1939. They formed part of the 5th Infantry Brigade in the 2nd Division, and prepared positions at Aix. On 5th December 1939 the 1st Camerons were inspected in the field by HM King George VI, the Colonel in Chief of the Regiment, and from this occasion the introduction of the Royal Blue hackle originated.

The 1st Bn The Queen's Own Cameron Highlanders preparing defences in France in 1939.

The 1st Camerons at La Bassée   **1940**

When the Germans advanced into Belgium in May 1940, the 2nd Division moved forward to the River Dyle, east of Brussels. As the BEF withdrew, the 1st Camerons fought a counter-attack action on the River Escaut, and on 25th May 1940 held a defensive position on the La Bassée canal against an attack by about 300 German tanks, until they were ordered to withdraw to Dunkirk.

The 1st Camerons at Dunkirk   **1940**

On 31st May 1940 the 1st Camerons embarked at Dunkirk, seventy nine strong. They still wore the kilt, and were the last battalion to wear it in action.

The 1st Camerons in Great Britain   **1940-1942**

The 1st Camerons were reformed in Yorkshire, where drafts of Camerons, West Yorkshires, Green Howards and HLI brought the battalion up to strength. After training in Yorkshire and the South of England, the 1st Camerons embarked for India on 11th April 1942.

The 1st Camerons in India   **1942-1944**

The 1st Camerons spent two years in India, training for Combined operations and jungle warfare, and with an internal security role. In March 1944 the 2nd Division was ordered to move to Assam, where the Japanese had invaded India and had reached Kohima.

The 1st Bn The Queen's Own Cameron Highlanders cross the River Irrawaddy in Burma 1945.

The 1st Camerons at Kohima 1944

The 1st Camerons started patrolling towards Kohima and, on 14th April 1944, by a successful attack on the Japanese position at Zubza, opened the road for the relief of Kohima. In the operations to recapture Kohima the 1st Camerons penetrated the Japanese lines and, having achieved surprise, captured 'Point 5120', a hill on which was a Naga village. They then captured Aradura Spur which had been a bastion of the Japanese defence.

After the recapture of Kohima, the 1st Camerons advanced South, attacking the Japanese at Viswema, until by 22nd June 1944 the road from Kohima to Imphal was open. The battle for Kohima had cost the 1st Camerons 283 casualties.

The 1st Camerons at the Irrawaddy and Mandalay 1944-1945

In November 1944 the 2nd Division advanced out of Assam into Burma. On 23rd-24th December the 1st Camerons crossed the River Chindwin at Kalewa, and on 3rd-4th January 1945 established a bridgehead over the River Mu, despite Japanese opposition. The battalion cleared a series of villages and reached Shwebo on 11th January.

On 24-25th February 1945 the 1st Camerons succeeded in gaining a bridgehead over the Irrawaddy river from which the 2nd Division was able to advance on Mandalay. The 1st Camerons carried out battalion attacks on Kyauktalon and on Ava fort on the outskirts of Mandalay.

After the occupation of Mandalay on 18th March 1945, the 1st Camerons advanced South down the Irrawaddy valley, attacking the Japanese positions at Legyi, North of Mount Popa.

The 1st Camerons return to India 1945

In early May 1945 the 1st Camerons returned by air from Burma to India, where they were to prepare for a sea-borne assault on Rangoon. But, after the surrender of Japan on 14th August 1945 ('VJ' Day), the battalion remained in India until March 1946.

2nd BATTALION THE QUEEN'S OWN CAMERON HIGHLANDERS

The 2nd Camerons in Egypt 1939-1940

The 2nd Camerons mobilised in Ahmednagar in July 1939 and moved to Egypt with the 11th Indian Infantry Brigade of the 4th Indian Division. They trained in desert warfare until, in June 1940, the battalion joined General R. N. O'Connor's Western Desert Force. In June 1940 the Italians had entered the war, and so the 2nd Camerons first task was to prepare defensive positions against the threatened invasion by the Italians.

The 2nd Camerons at Sidi Barrani 1940

The Italian advance started in September 1940, and the first infantry action in the Western Desert was a raid by the 2nd Camerons on the Italian Camp at Maktila on 22nd-23rd October 1940. The battalion's first major action came on 9th December 1940, when it took part in the attack on Nibeiwa Camp, and next day in the capture of Sidi Barrani.

By speed and surprise, General O'Connor had achieved the first British victory of the war. His two divisions had destroyed an army five times their own strength.

The 2nd Camerons in Eritrea 1941

With Egypt safe from invasion for the moment, the 4th Indian Division was sent to attack the Italian Army in Eritrea. The 2nd Camerons sailed down the Red Sea, landing at Port Sudan in January 1941. After advancing through Kassala, the 2nd Camerons spearheaded the 5th Indian Brigade attack on the Italian positions at Agordat on 31st January 1941.

The 2nd Camerons at Keren 1941

As the Italians fell back towards the Red Sea, they occupied strong mountain top positions dominating the road to Keren, and blew down 200 yards of cliff to block the road where it passed through a gorge. On 3rd February the 2nd Camerons succeeded in securing a hill (later known as 'Cameron Ridge') from which the subsequent attacks were made. After over five weeks of heavy fighting the 4th and 5th Indian Divisions broke through the Italian positions, the assaults by the 2nd Camerons on the 8000 foot Mt Sanchil and Brig's Peak being probably the hardest fighting of the operation. The 2nd Camerons lost 209 casualties at Keren, 41% of their strength.

The 2nd Camerons in the Western Desert 1941-1942

In the Western Desert, Rommel's Afrika Corps had advanced to the Egyptian border, and so in April 1941 the 4th Indian Division returned from Eritrea to Egypt. In June the 2nd Camerons took part in the Battle of Halfaya Pass, and then in the defensive operations until General Sir Claude Auchinleck was ready to take the offensive with Operation 'Crusader'.

In the relief of the besieged garrison of Tobruk, the 2nd Camerons took part in the attack on El Gubi on 4th December 1941. When the Germans hit back in January 1942, the 4th Indian Division withdrew to Gazala, the 2nd Camerons fighting successful rearguard actions at Maraua, El Faida and Carmusa.

The 2nd Camerons at Tobruk   1942

In May 1942 the Germans attacked the Gazala defences, and the 5th Indian Infantry Brigade was ordered to defend Tobruk. Rommel's advance pushed the 8th Army back into Egypt, leaving Tobruk surrounded and isolated. On 19th June 1942 the Germans attacked in overwhelming strength, and the Fortress was forced to surrender. After the capitulation, the 2nd Camerons fought on. Then, 24 hours later, having made his own terms, the Commanding Officer marched his battalion out of Tobruk into a prisoner of war camp with the Pipes playing, having ordered every fit man to try to reach El Alamein, 500 miles away.

The 2nd Camerons reformed   1942

On 20th December 1942 the 2nd Camerons were reconstituted when the 4th Camerons were redesignated as the 2nd Battalion. The new 2nd Camerons were stationed in the Shetlands, and they sailed for Egypt in December 1943. They rejoined the 11th Indian Infantry Brigade in the 4th Indian Division.

The 2nd Bn The Queen's Own Cameron Highlanders in Italy 1944.

The 2nd Camerons in Italy   1944

The 2nd Camerons moved to Italy in February 1944 and took part in the battle of Cassino, losing 250 casualties in a month of hard fighting to break through the Gustav Line.

After the capture of Cassino, the 2nd Camerons moved North for the attack on the Germans next major defensive position, the Gothic Line. During August-September 1944 the 2nd Camerons fought a series of actions ending with the liberation of San Marino.

The 2nd Camerons in Greece   1944-1945

After the Germans had withdrawn from Greece, the British Government provided a military force to supervise democratic elections and the surrender of weapons by the left wing resistance movements. The 2nd Camerons moved to Greece in November 1944 with the 4th Indian Division. When the war ended, the 2nd Camerons were in the Struma Valley, by coincidence the same area as the 2nd Camerons had ended World War I.

5.   THE REGIMENTAL DEPOTS AND INFANTRY TRAINING CENTRES IN WORLD WAR II

The unpredictable perils of war.
The Pipes and Drums of the No. 34 ITC Cameron Highlanders welcome No. 40 Inverness Company ATS to Cameron Barracks in 1939.

At the beginning of World War II, the Depots were expanded to form Infantry Training Centres (ITCs) which trained the recruits, the rejoined reservists, and the men called up under the Conscription Act, who were termed 'Militiamen'.

In 1941 the Seaforth Highlanders ITC and No 34 Cameron Highlanders ITC were amalgamated at Fort George to form No 11 Seaforth and Cameron ITC. The combined ITC was composed of the Recruit Companies which trained new recruits, and the Depot Companies which retrained men and posted them to battalions. In 1942, because of shortage of accommodation, the Depot companies were moved to Edinburgh, where they formed part of No 1 Infantry Depot at Redford Barracks.

When the campaign in North West Europe started in 1944, the Depot Companies became so large that Holding Battalions were formed. The Seaforth and Cameron Depot Companies became No 11 (Seaforth and Cameron) Holding Battalion, which moved to Forres in November 1944, and to Strathpeffer in January 1945. At the end of the war the Depot Companies of the Highland Regiments were combined to form the Highland Infantry Training Centre at Redford Barracks, Edinburgh.

After the Depot Companies had been removed, No 11 Seaforth and Cameron ITC remained at Fort George until November 1943, when the Fort George training area was needed for practice for the 'D' Day landings. The ITC moved to Pinefield Camp, Elgin, until 1946, when it moved to Redford Barracks, Edinburgh, to join up with the other Highland Regimental ITCs, eventually becoming the Highland Brigade Training Centre.

6. THE TERRITORIAL ARMY BATTALIONS IN WORLD WAR II

4th (ROSS-SHIRE) BATTALIONS SEAFORTH HIGHLANDERS TA

The 4th Seaforth Mobilise and move to France   1939-1940

When war broke out on 3rd September 1939, the 4th Seaforth mobilised at Dingwall. The 51st Highland Division moved to the south of England where it was visited by HM King George VI at Aldershot on 18th January 1940, before leaving for France with the British Expeditionary Force on 26th January 1940. The 4th Seaforth moved into defensive positions in the Maginot Line in the Saar Valley.

The 4th Seaforth at St Valéry-en-Caux   1940

When the Germans advanced in May 1940, bypassing the Maginot Line, the 51st Highland Division was moved back from the Saar to a new position on the Somme at Abbeville. The 4th Seaforth withdrew in contact with the enemy on the Saar and on 4th June, the last day of the evacuation of the BEF further north of Dunkirk, the battalion, together with the 4th Camerons, attacked the German bridgehead over the Somme at Abbeville. But the strength of the German advance forced the 51st Highland Division to fall back to the town of St Valéry-en-Caux, where it was hoped to evacuate it. By now they were cut off from the French Army, and the Highland Division was surrounded by the German advance. After a fierce resistance, the 4th Seaforth were forced to surrender at St Valéry on 12th June 1940.

5th (CAITHNESS & SUTHERLAND) BATTALION SEAFORTH HIGHLANDERS TA

The 5th Seaforth in Great Britain   1939-1942

When war broke out on 3rd September 1939, the 5th Seaforth mobilised at Golspie. They formed part of the 9th (Highland) Division, the duplicate division of the 51st formed when the Territorial Army was doubled in 1939. When the 51st Highland Division was reformed after St Valéry, the 5th Seaforth formed part of the new 152 Highland Infantry Brigade, together with the 2nd Seaforth and 5th Camerons.

The 5th Seaforth at El Alamein   1942

On 14th August 1942 the 5th Seaforth landed in Egypt with the 51st Highland Division. After six weeks intensive preparation, they took part in the attack by the 8th Army at El Alamein which began on 23rd October 1942.

The first task of the 5th Seaforth was to secure the start line for the Highland Division. The battalion took over in the line on 27th October, and then on 1st-2nd November took part in Operation 'Supercharge', in which 152 Brigade broke through the enemy defences to allow the armour to exploit beyond the minefields. The 5th Seaforth were the right assault battalion of the brigade, with the 5th Camerons on their left. The battalion lost 177 casualties at El Alamein.

The 5th Seaforth in Tripoli   1943

On 21st January 1943 the 5th Seaforth made a frontal attack on the German positions at Corradini, while 154 Brigade outflanked the enemy. After the 51st Highland

The 5th Bn Seaforth Highlanders in the anti-tank ditch at Mareth 1943.

Division reached Tripoli, the 5th Seaforth took part in the Victory Parade on 4th February where the salute was taken by the Prime Minister, Mr Winston Churchill.

The 5th Seaforth at Mareth   1943

In February 1943 the 51st Highland Division reached Mareth, an enemy defensive line sited behind the tank obstacle of the Wadi Zigzau, which had been extended by an artificial anti-tank ditch. The task of the 51st Highland Division was to establish a firm base for an attack by the 50th Division. The 5th Seaforth occupied the tank ditch during the attempts to break through the Mareth line. Eventually the Mareth position was outflanked to the south.

The 5th Seaforth at Wadi Akarit   1943

In early 1943 the 8th Army reached the bottleneck where the Germans held a strong position on the Djebel Roumana ridge and along the Wadi Akarit which connected it to the sea. When the 51st Highland Division attacked on 6th-7th April 1943, 152 Brigade's objective was the Djebel Roumana. The 5th Seaforth were the right assault battalion, with the 5th Camerons on their left. They took their objective and withstood a heavy German counter attack.

The campaign in North Africa cost the 5th Seaforth 472 casualties.

The 5th Bn Seaforth Highlanders landing at Cape Passero, Sicily, July 1944   (Photo by Brig G. L. W. Andrews)

The 5th Seaforth in Sicily   1943

After the battle of Wadi Akarit, the 5th Seaforth trained in Algeria for the invasion of Sicily. The battalion embarked at Sousse and sailed via Malta for Sicily. During the landings on 10th July 1943, 152 Brigade was in reserve. After the beachhead was established, 152 Brigade advanced, and on 13th July the 5th Seaforth encountered a German parachute battalion in a strong position at Francofonte. After the 5th Seaforth had made repeated attacks, the position was eventually captured by the 2nd Seaforth on 14th July.

The 5th Seaforth had some hard fighting in the Plain of Catania and in the 152 Brigade attack on 31st July-1st August 1944 to capture the Sferro Hills.

The campaign in Sicily cost the 5th Seaforth 132 casualties.

The 5th Seaforth in Great Britain   1943-1944

After the capture of Sicily, the 51st Highland Division returned to Great Britain in November 1943 to prepare for the invasion of Normandy. The 5th Seaforth were billetted in Hertfordshire and Essex.

The 5th Seaforth in Normandy   1944

The 5th Seaforth landed at Coursuelles in Normandy between 7th-9th June 1944, and moved into the Orne bridgehead near Escoville. They had seven weeks of very hard fighting against strong German counter-attacks.

In Operation 'Totalise', the breakout from Caen on 7th-8th August 1944, the 5th Seaforth joined the 2nd Seaforth in the capture of the strongly held village of Tilly-le-Campagne.

On 2nd September 1944 the 51st Highland Division liberated St Valéry-en-Caux, the 5th Seaforth and the 5th Camerons being the first Highlanders to enter the town. The 51st Highland Division then took part in the attack on the German positions holding Le Havre, the 5th Seaforth and the 5th Camerons breaching the minefield for the divisional attack.

The 5th Seaforth in Belgium and Holland   1944

In October 1944 the 5th Seaforth advanced rapidly through France, Belgium and Holland, and on 4th November made an assault crossing over the Aftwaterings Canal, and cleared the country as far as the River Maas. On 14th November the battalion made a further assault crossing over the Nederwert Canal, and three days later captured Zelen.

The 5th Seaforth in the Ardennes   1945

When the Germans counter-attacked in the Ardennes, in a desperate attempt to recapture the Low countries, the 51st Highland Division took part in the counter offensive in January 1945. In deep snow and bitter cold the 5th Seaforth captured Genes and Mierchamps.

The 5th Bn Seaforth Highlanders in action in Holland 1945.

The 5th Seaforth in the Reichswald   1945

The 51st Highland Division took a prominent part in the operation to breach the Siegfried Line and to defeat the German forces west of the Rhine. From 9th February the 5th Seaforth had a week of difficult fighting through the Reichswald Forest. They continued beyond the Reichswald, capturing Asperden and attacking Siebengewald with the 2nd Seaforth on 27th-28th February.

The 5th Seaforth at the Rhine Crossing   1945

The 51st Highland Division was one of the assault divisions in the operation to cross the Rhine. The 5th Seaforth crossed on 24th March 1945 and, passing through the 2nd Seaforth in the bridgehead, captured the village of Groin. On 28th March the 5th Seaforth established a bridgehead over the River Astrang, through which the armour passed for the final advance into Germany.

The 5th Seaforth in Germany   1945-1946

The 5th Seaforth met only minor opposition in the final weeks of the war and, when the German Army surrendered on 4th May 1945, the battalion had reached Bremervorde.

The 5th Seaforth took part in the Victory Parade at Bremerhaven on 12th May 1945. For the rest of the summer they were billetted in the Cuxhaven peninsula, carrying out dock duties, and being responsible for internal security. During the winter of 1945-1946 they guarded the SS concentration camp at Sandbostel, moving to Hanover in February 1946. The 5th Seaforth were disbanded on 3rd September 1946.

The 5th Bn Seaforth Highlanders crossing the Rhine March 1945.

6th (MORAYSHIRE) BATTALION SEAFORTH HIGHLANDERS TA

The 6th Seaforth Mobilise and move to France   1939-1940

When war broke out on 3rd September 1939, the 6th Seaforth mobilized at Elgin. They moved to Aldershot in October 1940 and, after intensive training, went to France with the 51st Highland Division on 26th January 1940.

The 6th Seaforth in France   1940

In March 1940, when each Territorial Army Brigade was strengthened by a Regular Army battalion, the 6th Seaforth was replaced in 152 Brigade by the 2nd Seaforth, and joined the 17th Brigade of the 5th Division at Hallouin.

When the Germans advanced into Holland in May 1940, the 6th Seaforth held positions in Belgium, and then on the Scarpe near Arras. They moved to Ypres as the left hand battalion of the British line but, when the Belgian Army surrendered, they had to fall back to Dunkirk. After a long rearguard action, the battalion was evacuated from Dunkirk on 1st June 1940.

The 6th Seaforth in Madagascar   1942

After Dunkirk the 6th Seaforth were reformed at Turriff, and remained in Great Britain until March 1942. They embarked with 17 Brigade, and on 6th May took part in the capture of Madagascar which was intended to secure the convoy route round the Cape of Good Hope. After the landings 17 Brigade, with the 6th Seaforth, attacked and occupied Antsirane.

The 6th Seaforth in India   1942

On 10th June, after four weeks in Madagascar, the garrison was relieved by South African troops, and the 6th Seaforth re-embarked for India where they were intended to take part in the defence of India against the Japanese.

The 6th Seaforth in Iraq and Iran   1942-1943

In September 1942, the 6th Seaforth moved with the 5th Division to Basrah, and then to Kermanshaw and Qum in Iran, to counter the German threat from the Caucusus. The 6th Seaforth were on police duty in Teheran during the bread riots of winter 1942-1943.

The 6th Seaforth in Sicily   1943

The 6th Seaforth moved from Iran to Egypt in January 1943. On 10th July 1943 they were among the assault troops in the invasion of Sicily. The battalion took part in the capture of Syracuse and Augusta, in the operations on the Simeto River and the Catania Plain, and in the capture of Catania.

The 6th Seaforth in Italy   1943-1944

On 3rd September 1943 the 17th Brigade was the assault brigade when the 5th Division crossed the Straits of Messina and landed in Italy. During the landing and subsequent advance, the battalion met very little trouble, but in October-November it encountered stiff opposition from the German rearguards at Isernia. The 6th Seaforth moved in November to the Adriatic front near Ortona, returning on 2nd January 1944 to the West of Italy, where they took part in the crossing of the Garigliano River, the first assault on the Gustav Line.

In February 1944, after the Anzio landings, the 5th Division was sent to reinforce the Anzio beach-head. The 6th Seaforth took part in the defence of Anzio against heavy German counter-attacks, and then in the advance on Rome in June 1944.

The 6th Seaforth in North West Europe   194

After 12 months fighting, the 6th Seaforth returned to Egypt to rest and refit. In March 1945 the battalion landed at Marseilles and moved North to join the British forces in Belgium. In the 6th Seaforth's last operation of the war they advanced into Germany through the bridgehead over the River Elbe, and finished the war at Lubeck.

7th (MORAYSHIRE) BATTALION SEAFORTH HIGHLANDERS TA

The 7th Seaforth in Great Britain   1939-1944

When war broke out on 3rd September 1939, the 7th Seaforth were embodied at Elgin. They moved to Forres on 9th September. When the 51st Highland Division was reformed after St Valery the 7th Seaforth were in the division for a short time, but in July 1940 they were sent to garrison the Shetland Islands. In October 1941 the battalion moved to Northumberland and joined 46 (Highland) Infantry Brigade of the 15th (Scottish) Division, in which it was to remain for the rest of the war. The 15th (Scottish) Division remained in Great Britain until 1944, training for the invasion of Normandy.

The 7th Seaforth at the Odon   1944

The 7th Seaforth sailed for Normandy on 16th June 1944, 10 days after the initial landings. The first task for the 15th (Scottish) Division was Operation 'Epsom', the attack to seize crossings over the River Odon to clear the way for the advance south of Caen. The plan included two battalion attacks by the 7th Seaforth at Cheux and Le Valtru. Then, having crossed the Odon, the battalion cleared the area south of the river and attacked further positions on Eterville ridge. In some of the hardest fighting of the campaign, the 7th Seaforth lost over 300 casualties.

The 7th Seaforth at Caumont   1944

In July the 15th (Scottish) Division were moved to the American Sector and took part in Operation 'Bluecoat', the break-out at Caumont. In the successful opening stages the 7th Seaforth captured Quarry Hill, and then became the advance guard of the Division until they encountered strong opposition at Lassy.

The 7th Seaforth in the advance to the Rhine 1944-1945

The 7th Seaforth crossed the River Seine, South of Rouen. On 28th August 1944 the battalion led the 46 Brigade advance, taking the village of Grand Roncherolles by a night attack, and then occupying Les Andelys.

The battalion continued into Belgium and Holland, meeting enthusiastic welcomes from the liberated populations of Courtrai and Loos. On 21st September 1944 the 7th Seaforth established the bridgehead over the Wilhelmina Canal from which the 15 (Scottish) Division cleared the area of Best. One of the vital stages of two weeks heavy fighting was the 7th Seaforth attack on the cement factory at Best.

In a week of fighting to protect the Nijmegen corridor against a strong German counter attack, the 7th Seaforth had a hard fight in the 46 Brigade attack on 31st October 1944 which captured the villages of Liesel and Slot. Then after crossing the Deurne Canal, the battalion advanced to the River Maas. Under command of 44 Brigade, the 7th Seaforth took part in the assault on Blerick on 3rd December 1944.

During January 1944, the 7th Seaforth fought a series of actions at Hasselt, Schloss Moyland, and Schloss Kalbeck, as the 15th (Scottish) Division forced its way through the Seigfried Line defences up to the Rhine.

The 7th Seaforth at the Rhine Crossing   1945

After a period of training on the techniques for river crossings, the 7th Seaforth crossed the Rhine north of Xanten on 24th March 1944, and captured the village of Mehr. A strong counter attack by German paratroopers was only defeated by the CO of 7th Seaforth bringing down artillery fire in his own battalion positions in the village.

The 7th Seaforth in Germany   1945-1946

In the final advance into Germany, the 7th Seaforth crossed the Elbe on 29th April 1945. The 15th (Scottish) Division carried out its third major assault river crossing of the campaign, the only division cross by assault the Seine, the Rhine, and the Elbe. When the German Army surrendered on 4th May 1944, the 7th Seaforth had almost reached Lubeck. They were stationed at Keil until January 1946, when the battalion returned to Great Britain for disbandment.

4th BATTALION THE QUEEN'S OWN CAMERON HIGHLANDERS TA

The 4th Camerons mobilize and move to France   1939-1940
When war broke out on 3rd September 1939, the 4th Camerons mobilized at Inverness. The 51st Highland Division moved to the South of England where it was visited by HM King George VI, Colonel in Chief of the Regiment, at Aldershot on 18th January 1940. The 4th Camerons left for France with the British Expeditionary Force on 26th January 1940. After arriving at Le Havre, the battalion moved forward to defensive positions in the Maginot Line in the Saar Valley.

The 4th Camerons at St Valéry-en-Caux   1940
When the Germans advanced in May 1940, bypassing the Maginot Line, the 51st Highland Division withdrew from the Saar to a new line on the Somme at Abbeville. The 4th Camerons moved by train to Rouen, and then by busses to their new positions. On 4th June, the last day of the evacuation of the BEF, further North at Dunkirk, the 4th Camerons together with the 4th Seaforth attacked the German bridgehead over the Somme. But the strength of the German advance forced the 51st Highland Division to fall back to the fishing port of St Valéry-en-Caux, where it was hoped to evacuate it. Cut off from the French Army, and with no ships available, the 51st Highland Division was surrounded by the German advance. The 4th Camerons were forced to surrender at St Valéry on 12th June 1940.

The 4th Camerons reformed   1940-1942
In July 1940 the 4th Camerons were reconstituted in Inverness. The new battalion sailed for Aruba in the Dutch West Indies in August 1940. Its task was to guard the oil refineries in Aruba, and a detachment was based in Bermuda.

The 4th Camerons returned to Great Britain in February 1942 and formed part of 15th (Scottish) Division, until moving to the Shetlands.

The 4th Camerons redesignated as the 2nd Camerons   1942
After the capture of the 2nd Camerons at Tobruk in June 1942, the regiment obtained authority for the 4th Camerons to be redesignated as the 2nd Battalion on 2nd December 1942.

5th BATTALION THE QUEEN'S OWN CAMERON HIGHLANDERS TA

The 5th Camerons in Great Britain   1939-1942
When war broke out on 3rd September 1939, the 5th Camerons mobilized at Inverness. They moved to Tain as part of 26 Infantry Brigade in the 9th (Highland) Division, the duplicate division of the 51st, formed when the Territorial Army was doubled in 1939. When the 51st Highland Division was reformed after St Valéry, the 5th Camerons formed part of the new 152 Highland Infantry Brigade, together with the 2nd and 5th Seaforth.

The 5th Camerons at El Alamein   1942
On 11th August 1942 the 5th Camerons landed in Egypt with the 51st Highland Division. After six weeks of intensive preparation, they took part in the attack by the 8th Army at El Alamein which began on 23rd October 1942.

The 5th Camerons were split, in order to carry out two separate tasks. Two companies provided covering parties for the Royal Engineers who made vehicle breaches in the enemy minefields; and two companies assaulted under command of 154 Brigade. On 2nd November, 152 Brigade took part in Operation 'Supercharge', designed to break through the enemy defences to allow the armour to exploit beyond the minefields. The 5th Camerons were the left battalion of the brigade, with the 5th Seaforth on their right.

The 5th Camerons in Tripoli   1943
On 16th January 1943 the 5th Camerons were heavily shelled at Buerat, while moving in desert formation as the advanced guard of the division. After the 51st Highland Division reached Tripoli, the 5th Camerons took part in the Victory Parade where the salute was taken by the Prime Minister, Mr Winston Churchill.

The 5th Camerons at Mareth   1943
In February 1943 the 51st Highland Division reached Mareth, an enemy defensive line sited behind the tank obstacles of the Wadi Zigzau which had been extended by

The 8th Army Commander, Lieutenant General B. L. Montgomery, meets officers of the 5th Bn The Queen's Own Cameron Highlanders before the battle of El Alamein, September 1942. He is accompanied by Major General Douglas Wimberley, GOC, 51st Highland Division, and (right) Lieutenant Colonel R. D. M. C. Miers, CO, 5th Camerons.

an artificial anti-tank ditch. The task of the 51st Highland Division was to establish a firm base for an attack by the 50th Division. The 5th Camerons were ordered to advance through the 5th Seaforth, who were holding a section of the anti-tank ditch, and then to attack the enemy positions which were interfering with the advance. The 5th Camerons were heavily shelled, losing 121 casualties, before the Mareth position was eventually outflanked to the South.

Pipers of the 5th Bn The Queen's Own Cameron Highlanders play at St. Valery after its recapture by the 51st Highland Division in September 1944.

The 5th Camerons at Wadi Akarit   1943

In early 1943 the 8th Army reached the bottleneck where the Germans held a strong position on the Djebel Roumana ridge and along the Wadi Akarit, which connected it to the sea. When the 51st Highland Division attacked it on 6th-7th April 1943, 152 Brigade's objective was the Djebel Roumana. The 5th Camerons were the left assault battalion, with the 5th Seaforth on their right. They took the objective and then successfully withstood determined German counter attacks.

The campaign in North Africa cost the 5th Camerons 565 casualties.

The 5th Camerons in Sicily   1943

After the battle of Wadi Akarit, the 5th Camerons trained in Algeria for the invasion of Sicily. The battalion embarked at Sousse, and sailed via Malta for Sicily. During the landings on 10th July 1943, 152 Brigade was in reserve. After the beachhead was established, the Brigade advanced with the 5th Camerons as the advanced guard. The battalion cleared several small enemy positions. On 13th July the 5th Seaforth encountered a German parachute battalion in a strong position at Francofonte and, while the 2nd Seaforth assaulted the main position, the 5th Camerons carried out a successful flanking attack.

In their last battle of the Sicily campaign, the 5th Camerons were the leading battalion of the 152 Brigade's attack on the Sferro Hills. They took their objective against determined opposition, and were reinforced during the attack by two companies of the 2nd Seaforth.

The campaign in Sicily cost the 5th Camerons 68 casualties.

The 5th Camerons in Great Britain   1943-1944

After the capture of Sicily, the 51st Highland Division returned to Great Britain to prepare for the invasion of Normandy. The 5th Camerons were billeted in Hertford.

The 5th Camerons in Normandy   1944

The 5th Camerons landed at Courseulles in Normandy on 'D + 1' Day, 7th June 1944, and moved into the Orne bridgehead. They had seven weeks of very hard fighting against strong German counter attacks, before the break out from Normandy in early August 1944.

In Operation 'Totalise', the breakout from Caen on 7th-8th August 1944, the 5th Camerons advanced down the axis of the Falaise road to capture the village of Lorquichon and to occupy Poussy.

On 2nd September 1944 the 51st Highland Division liberated St Valéry-en-Caux, the 5th Camerons and 5th Seaforth being the first Highlanders to enter the town. The 51st Highland Division then took part in the attack on 11th September 1944 on the German positions holding Le Havre, the 5th Camerons and 5th Seaforth breaching the minefield for the divisional attack.

The 5th Camerons in Belgium and Holland   1944

In October 1944 the 5th Camerons advanced rapidly through France, Belgium and Holland. The battalion met tough opposition when it attacked the German positions at Schijndel and Vught. On 4th November the 5th Camerons made an assault crossing over the Aftervaterings Canal and cleared the country as far as the River Maas, and on 14th November made a further assault crossing over the Nederwert Canal. The crossing over the Zig Canal on 17th November 1944, where the 5th Camerons managed to cross a collapsed bridge and hold a bridgehead against a strong counter-attack until the 2nd Seaforth could pass through, was possibly their most successful action of the campaign.

The 5th Bn The Queen's Own Cameron Highlanders at Schijndel 1944.

The 5th Camerons in the Ardennes   1945

When the Germans counter attacked in the Ardennes, in a desperate attempt to recapture the Low countries, the 51st Highland Division took part in the counter offensive in January 1945. In deep snow and bitter cold the 5th Camerons carried out a series of attacks in the villages of the Ardennes.

The 5th Camerons in the Reichswald   1945

The 51st Highland Division took a prominent part in the operations to breach the Siegfried Line and to defeat the German forces West of the Rhine. The 5th Camerons entered the Reichswald forest on 9th February 1945 and, in a week of most difficult close quarter action, fought their way through the forest. They then continued beyond Reichswald forest, attacking Hervost and advancing to Asperden.

The 5th Camerons at the Rhine Crossing 1945

The 51st Highland Division was one of the assault divisions in the operation to cross the Rhine. The 5th Camerons crossed on 24th March 1945 and, passing through the 2nd Seaforth in the bridgehead, attacked and captured Mittleburg after a hard struggle.

The 5th Camerons in Germany 1945-1946

On 27th March the 5th Camerons went on to capture Isselburg. The final advance into Germany started on 7th April 1945 and included an attack at Adelheide. The last action of the war for the 5th Camerons was at Glinde.

The 5th Camerons took part in the Victory Parade at Bremerhaven on 12th May 1945. For the rest of the summer they were billetted at Cuxhaven, moving to Westertimke for the winter, where their duties included guarding the prisoner of war camps. In 1946 152 Brigade moved to Hanover with the role of maintaining law and order.

In October 1946 the 5th Camerons were disbanded in Inverness.

1st BATTALION THE LIVERPOOL SCOTTISH, THE QUEEN'S OWN CAMERON HIGHLANDERS TA

The 1st Liverpool Scottish in Great Britain 1939-1945

When war broke out in 1939, the 1st Liverpool Scottish were mobilized at Liverpool. They formed part of 165 Liverpool Infantry Brigade in the 55th (West Lancashire) Division.

The 1st Liverpool Scottish remained in Great Britain during the war, with the tasks of defence against invasion, and of training drafts for service overseas.

No 4 Independent Company in Norway 1940

When the Germans invaded Norway in 1940, the 1st Liverpool Scottish provided a platoon for an Independent Company of Volunteers for service in Norway. After the fall of Norway most of the volunteers served with the Commandos.

The 1st Liverpool Scottish in Gibraltar 1945-1947

At the end of the war, when the 55th Division was disbanded, the 1st Liverpool Scottish moved to Gibraltar. They remained there until disbanded in February 1947.

2nd BATTALION THE LIVERPOOL SCOTTISH, THE QUEEN'S OWN CAMERON IIIGHLANDERS TA

When war broke out in 1939 the 2nd Liverpool Scottish were mobilized in Liverpool. They formed part of 165 Liverpool Infantry Brigade in the 55th (West Lancashire) Division. At first the 2nd Liverpool Scottish were responsible for the security of the Merseyside Docks, and then from late 1939 they were given coast defence and anti-invasion roles.

In September 1942 the 2nd Liverpool Scottish were transferred to the 218th Independent Brigade, guarding vulnerable points in Yorkshire. On 1st November 1942 they were converted into the 89th Anti-Tank Regiment RA, and were eventually disbanded in 1946.

7. MISCELLANEOUS BATTALIONS

When war broke out in 1939, a number of National Defence Companies were formed of ex-soldiers enlisted for home service. Because recruiting was slow, the companies were given regimental identities, and many World War I soldiers were encouraged to join. The battalions were allotted tasks defending vital installations in their regimental areas.

8th (HOME DEFENCE) BATTALION SEAFORTH HIGHLANDERS

The 8th Seaforth were formed in November 1939 and were based at Golspie. In December 1941 the battalion became the 30th Bn Seaforth Highlanders, but continued to carry out Home Defence tasks.

9th BATTALION SEAFORTH HIGHLANDERS

The 9th Seaforth were formed in September 1940 at Market Harborough. The battalion was at first intended to be a Field Force battalion, but in November 1942 became a Reserve battalion and subsequently a Holding battalion.

6th (HOME DEFENCE) BATTALION THE QUEEN'S OWN CAMERON HIGHLANDERS

The 6th Camerons were formed from a National Defence Company and were based at Inverness. In 1942 the battalion became the 30th Bn The Queen's Own Cameron Highlanders, and was split up into independent companies in 1943.

7th BATTALION THE QUEEN'S OWN CAMERON HIGHLANDERS

In May 1940 the 50th Holding Battalion The Queen's Own Cameron Highlanders was formed from a cadre drawn from No 34 (Cameron Highlanders) Infantry Training Centre. It was renamed the 7th Camerons in October 1940, and had a coastal defence role. In November 1941 the 7th Camerons joined the 15th (Scottish) Division in Northumberland.

In August 1942 the 7th Camerons were given a new role and designation when they were redesignated the 5th (Scottish) Parachute Battalion, The Parachute Regiment. The regiment distinguished itself in action in North Africa, Italy, the South of France, and Greece.

CHAPTER VI   THE REGIMENT SINCE WORLD WAR II
1.   THE REGULAR ARMY BATTALIONS
1st BATTALION SEAFORTH HIGHLANDERS 1945-1961

The 1st Bn Seaforth Highlanders march through Dingwall after the Freedom had been granted to the Regiment in 1954.

The 1st Seaforth in Malaya   1945

At the end of the war the 1st Seaforth were in India, training for the reconquest of Malaya. After the Japanese surrender on 14th August 1945 the operation went ahead as planned, and the 1st Seaforth landed unopposed at Port Dickson in September 1945.

The 1st Seaforth in Java   1946

In 1946 the 1st Seaforth moved to Java, to preserve law and order in the island which the 78th Highlanders had captured from the Dutch in 1811. Soon after the battalion arrived there were violent riots, as Indonesian nationalists mounted their campaign to achieve independence from the Dutch.

The 1st Seaforth in Malaya   1946-1951

In October 1946 the 1st Seaforth moved to Ipoh in Malaya, and then to Singapore. When in early 1948 the communists launched their guerilla war aimed at taking over the Federation of Malaya, the 1st Seaforth began

three years of jungle operations. The battalion operated at first in Johore and later in East and Central Pahang, and accounted for nearly 100 terrorists.

The 1st Seaforth in Edinburgh   1951-1952

The 1st Seaforth left Malaya in 1951 and returned to Redford Barracks, Edinburgh. In 1951 the battalion provided the Royal Guard at Ballater, and provided Guards of Honour and ceremonial contingents for the Proclamation of HM Queen Elizabeth and the funeral of HM King George VI.

The 1st Seaforth in Germany   1952-1954

In April 1952 the 1st Seaforth left Edinburgh for the British Army of the Rhine and were stationed at Buxtehude, forming part of 31 Lorried Infantry Brigade in the 7th Armoured Division.

In June 1953 the 1st Seaforth sent a detachment to London to take part in the Coronation parade of HM Queen Elizabeth.

The Pipes and Drums of 1st Bn Seaforth Highlanders in Gibraltar 1956.

The 1st Seaforth in Elgin   1954

The 1st Seaforth returned briefly to Scotland in May 1954 spending six weeks at Pinefield Camp, Elgin before embarking for the Middle East. It was the first time that the 1st Seaforth had returned to Elgin since the Earl of Seaforth paraded his regiment for inspection at Elgin in 1778. On 15th May 1954 the Seaforth Highlanders received the Freedom of Dingwall, and the parade included detachments from the 1st Seaforth, the Depot, the 11th Seaforth TA, and the Seaforth Cadets.

The 1st Seaforth in Egypt   1954-1955

The 1st Seaforth joined the Middle East Land Forces in the Canal Zone in Egypt, where the British Army was in the process of moving its base in the Middle East from Egypt to Cyprus. The battalion's task was to protect British lives and property from the attacks of Egyptian terrorists.

The 1st Seaforth in Aden   1955

In June 1955 the 1st Seaforth were due to leave Egypt for Gibraltar, when they were sent at short notice to Aden to support the Aden Levies against dissident tribesmen. The battalion spent five months in the Western Aden Protectorate, before rejoining the Advance party which had moved direct from Egypt to Gibraltar.

The 1st Seaforth in Gibraltar   1955-1957

The 1st Seaforth were reunited in Gibraltar in November 1955, and spent two years as the garrison battalion. They were stood-by for the Suez landings, but were not required to embark.

The 1st Seaforth in Germany   1957-1961

In October 1957 the 1st Seaforth returned to the British Army of the Rhine where they were stationed in Munster, forming part of 6 Brigade in the 2nd Division.

On 14th August 1958 the 1st Seaforth received new

General Sir James Cassels, Colonel of the Regiment, inspects the 1st Bn Seaforth Highlanders in Munster on 25th November 1960 at the final parade before amalgamation.

Colours at Munster from Field Marshal Sir Gerald Templer, Chief of the Imperial General Staff. On 25th November 1960, before the amalgamation of Seaforth and Camerons, the 1st Seaforth held their farewell parade at Munster when the salute was taken by the Colonel of the Regiment, General Sir James Cassels.

In early 1961 the 1st Seaforth left Munster for Redford Barracks, Edinburgh where on 7th February 1961 the amalgamation of Seaforth and Camerons took place.

THE 2nd BATTALION SEAFORTH HIGHLANDERS 1945-1948

2nd Seaforth in Germany and Great Britain   1945-1948

The 2nd Seaforth remained in Germany for a year after the war, being responsible for law and order in Neustadt near Hanover. In 1946 the battalion returned to Great Britain, and was stationed at Knook Camp near Warminster and then at Bicester.

The 2nd Seaforth amalgamated   1948

In May 1948, as part of the reductions of the infantry, the 2nd Seaforth were reduced to cadre strength and amalgamated with the 1st Seaforth.

1st BATTALION THE QUEEN'S OWN CAMERON HIGHLANDERS 1946-1961

HM The Queen inspects 1st Bn The Queen's Own Cameron Highlanders at Balmoral when she presented new Colours to the battalion in 1955.

The 1st Camerons in Japan   1946-1947

The 1st Camerons left India in March 1946 for Japan, where they formed part of the British Occupational Force in Japan, and were stationed at Hiro on Shikoku Island. The battalion's task was to dismantle military installations and to suppress black market activities.

The 1st Camerons in Malaya   1947-1948

In February 1947 the 1st Camerons left Japan for Malaya and were stationed at Ipoh, with companies detached in other parts of Perak. The role of the battalion was internal security, in co-operation with the police force. Before the battalion returned to Great Britain it was reduced to cadre strength.

The 1st Camerons in Great Britain   1948-1949

The return of the 1st Camerons cadre in April 1948 coincided with the disbandment of the 2nd Battalion, and so the 1st Battalion was rebuilt to strength with Regular soldiers from both battalions. It was composed of two thirds Regular soldiers and a third of National Servicemen.

In October 1948 the 1st Camerons moved to Bulford as the nucleus of an operational brigade, ready for service overseas at short notice.

The 1st Camerons in Tripoli and Egypt   1949-1952

In February 1949 the 1st Camerons sailed for Tripoli where they joined the 1st Guards Brigade. The battalion was required to send drafts to other Highland regiments during the Malayan campaign and the Korean War.

Mortar platoon of 1st Bn The Queen's Own Cameron Highlanders training in Egypt 1951.

There had been increasing pressure from the Egyptians for the British to withdraw from Egypt, and in November 1951 the 1st Camerons moved at short notice to reinforce the Suez Canal Zone garrison. The battalion was based at Tel-el-Kebir, the Ordnance Depot for the strategic reserve of stores and equipment for the Middle East, and its task was to protect the base against sabotage, theft and sniping by Egyptian Terrorists. It was regularly involved in countering terrorist activity.

The 1st Camerons in Edinburgh   1952

The 1st Camerons left Port Said in April 1952 and returned to Edinburgh. During their short stay there, the 1st Camerons provided a Guard of Honour and Royal Guards at the Palace of Holyrood for the Queen's first visit to the Scottish capital after her accession.

The 1st Camerons in Austria   1952-1953

In August 1952 the 1st Camerons left Edinburgh for Spittal in Austria, where the battalion formed part of the occupation force of the British zone of Austria.

In June 1953 the 1st Camerons sent a detachment to London to take part in the Coronation parade of HM Queen Elizabeth.

The 1st Camerons in Germany   1953-1955

The 1st Camerons left Austria in November 1953 for Luneburg in West Germany, where they formed part of the 31st (Lorried) Infantry Brigade in the 7th Armoured Division. On 24th June 1954 HRH Prince Philip, Duke of Edinburgh, paid his first visit to the battalion since his appointment in 1953 as Colonel in Chief of the Regiment.

The 1st Camerons in Elgin   1955

In February 1955 the 1st Camerons left Luneburg for Elgin, where they were to prepare for service in Korea. On 30th May 1955 the battalion received its 7th Stand of Colours from HM The Queen at Balmoral Castle.

The 1st Camerons in Korea   1955-1956

After the war in Korea ended in 1953, a United Nations force remained in South Korea to maintain the security of the country. The 1st Camerons arrived in Korea in July 1955 and joined the 1st Commonwealth Division. The battalion was stationed by the Imjin river, and was ready to occupy defensive positions if hostilities broke out again. Its routine operational duties included the task of patrolling the De-militarized Zone. When the Commonwealth Division was disbanded, the 1st Camerons came under operational control of the 21st US Infantry Regiment.

The 1st Camerons in Aden   1956-1958

When the 1st Camerons left Korea in August 1956, they were under orders for Malaya. But, due to the impending crisis in Egypt, where President Nasser had nationalized the Suez Canal, the battalion was sent to Aden where the repercussions of Arab Nationalism were expected to threaten the internal security of the Colony.

The main role of the 1st Camerons in Aden was to support the Aden Protectorate Levies in operations to prevent incursions by Yemeni tribesmen. The battalion was based in Aden Colony, with companies detached to Dhala, Mukeiras and Beihan in the Protectorate, and at Little Aden guarding the BP oil refinery.

In 1957 the 1st Camerons won the Duke of Edinburgh's Trophy for shooting and physical fitness, while serving in Aden.

Medium Machine Gun of 1st Bn The Queen's Own Cameron Highlanders in Aden 1956.

The 1st Camerons in Dover   1958-1960

The 1st Camerons returned to Great Britain in March 1958, and were stationed in Dover, forming part of 19 Infantry Brigade. The battalion trained for its role in the strategic reserve, in which it was ready to move at short notice by air to any part of the world.

The 1st Camerons in Edinburgh   1960-1961

In early 1960 the 1st Camerons returned to Edinburgh. The year included many ceremonial events, including the laying up of the 6th Stand of Colours in Glasgow Cathedral, Guards of Honour for the General Assembly of the Church of Scotland, and providing the Royal Guard at Ballater.

On 25th November 1960, before the amalgamation of Seaforth and Camerons, the 1st Camerons held their farewell parade at Redford Barracks, when the salute was taken by Major General Douglas Wimberley, Colonel of the Regiment.

On 7th February 1961 the amalgamation of Seaforth and Camerons took place at Redford Barracks, Edinburgh.

The final parade before amalgamation of 1st Bn The Queen's Own Cameron Highlanders for Major General D. N. Wimberley, Colonel of the Regiment, 25th November 1960.

2nd BATTALION THE QUEEN'S OWN CAMERON HIGHLANDERS 1945-1948

The 2nd Camerons in Austria, Italy and Great Britain   **1945-1948**

In July 1945 the 2nd Camerons left Greece for Austria, moving to Italy in September 1945, and to Trieste in August 1946. In September 1947 they returned to Great Britain, and were stationed at Didcot until moving to Inverness in February 1948.

The 2nd Camerons disbanded   **1948**

On 30th June 1948, as part of the reductions in the infantry, the 2nd Camerons were disbanded at Inverness.

The 1st Bn Seaforth Highlanders arrive at Redford Barracks, Edinburgh for amalgamation with 1st Bn The Queen's Own Cameron Highlanders, 1961.

1st BATTALION QUEEN'S OWN HIGHLANDERS SINCE 1961

The 1st Queen's Own Highlanders in Edinburgh   1961

The amalgamation of the Seaforth Highlanders and The Queen's Own Cameron Highlanders was marked by a ceremony held at Redford Barracks, Edinburgh on 7th February 1961. The officers and sergeants assembled in the officers mess, where the two stands of Colours were set side by side, and a toast was drunk to the new regiment.

The same morning, at Edinburgh Castle, the last guard mounted by the 1st Camerons was relieved by the first guard mounted by the 1st Queen's Own Highlanders.

In March 1961 a detachment of the 1st Battalion visited the regimental area, with the Colours, Pipes and Drums, and Regimental Band. The detachment paraded on 4th March 1961 when the Regiment was presented with the Freedom of Inverness, and on 11th March for the Freedom of Dingwall. The detachment also marched through Kingussie, Fort William, Nairn, Grantown-on-Spey, Forres, Elgin, Dornoch, Wick and Thurso.

On 24th March 1961 HRH Prince Philip, Duke of Edinburgh, Colonel in Chief of the Queen's Own Highlanders, visited the 1st Battalion for the first time at Edinburgh.

The first guard found by 1st Bn Queen's Own Highlanders mounts at Edinburgh Castle on Amalgamation Day, 7th February 1961.

Detachment of 1st Battalion Queen's Own Highlanders marches through Inverness, March 1961.

The 1st Queen's Own Highlanders in the Far East 1961-1964

On 8th April 1961 the 1st Queen's Own Highlanders sailed for the Far East. They were stationed in Singapore as the British battalion in 99 Gurkha Infantry Brigade, in the 17th Gurkha Division.

On 6th February 1962 the battalion trooped the Regimental Colours of the 1st Seaforth and 1st Camerons in Singapore.

The 1st Queen's Own Highlanders in the Brunei Rebellion 1962-1963

As well as its internal security duties in Singapore, the 1st Battalion trained in the British dependencies in North Borneo, helping the police to prevent piracy, and deterring the Indonesians from interference in the North Borneo Territories. On 8th December 1962 there was a revolt in the Sultanate of Brunei where Azahari's rebels attacked the Sultan's palace, police stations, and installations throughout Brunei. The rebels took hostages and seized the Shell oilfield at Seria.

1st Bn Queen's Own Highlanders house clearing in Seria, Brunei 1962.

Patrol of A Company 1st Bn Queen's Own Highlanders in Seria, Brunei 1962.

1st Bn Queen's Own Highlanders round up rebels in Seria, Brunei 1962.

Battalion HQ and 'A' Company of the 1st Queen's Own Highlanders moved at very short notice from Singapore to Brunei by air, while 'B' Company sailed at full speed on the destroyer HMS Cavalier. 'A' Company carried out an air assault on the Seria oil field, and the battalion cleared Seria of rebels and released 46 European hostages. The battalion withdrew to Singapore in February 1963 after its first active service since the amalgamation of the regiment.

The 1st Queen's Own Highlanders in Brunei and North Borneo   1963
When the 1st Battalion returned to Borneo in May 1963, its duties included long range patrolling of the Indonesian border, and the training of local tribesmen as Border Scouts.

The 1st Queen's Own Highlanders in Edinburgh   1964
In March 1964 the 1st Queen's Own Highlanders returned to Edinburgh and were billetted at Milton Bridge camp. On 21st May 1964 the battalion received its first Stand of Colours from HRH Prince Philip, Duke of Edinburgh, the Colonel in Chief of the Regiment, at the Palace of Holyroodhouse.

The 1st Queen's Own Highlanders in West Germany
1964-1966
In June 1964 the 1st Queen's Own Highlanders moved to Osnabruck to join the British Army of the Rhine. They became an Armoured Personnel Carrier (APC) battalion in the 12th Infantry Brigade of the 2nd Division, being equipped at first with wheeled one ton Humber APCs, until these were replaced, in late 1965, by tracked AFV 432 APCs. The 1st Battalion won the Army Championship for shooting at Bisley in 1965 and 1966.

HRH Prince Philip, Duke of Edinburgh inspects the 1st Bn Queen's Own Highlanders before presenting Colours to the Battalion at Holyroodhouse 1964. He is accompanied by Lt Col W. G. McHardy, the Commanding Officer.

The old Colours ot the 1st Seaforth and 1st Camerons are marched off parade at the presentation of new Colours at Holyroodhouse, 1964.

1st Bn Queen's Own Highlanders on parade at Edinburgh Castle, December 1970, Lt Col A. S. Duncan Commanding

The 1st Queen's Own Highlanders in Berlin   1966-1968

The 1st Queen's Own Highlanders moved to Berlin in August 1966, where they joined the Berlin Infantry Brigade as part of the four power occupation force, with the USA, Russians and French. The Battalion again won the Army Championship for Shooting at Bisley in 1967.

The 1st Bn Queen's Own Highlanders on guard at Spandau Prison, Berlin, 1966.

The 1st Queen's Own Highlanders in Edinburgh   1968-197

The 1st Queen's Own Highlanders returned t Edinburgh in September 1968. Their three year tour i Great Britain was broken by a nine month tour in th Middle East.

The 1st Queen's Own Highlanders in Sharjah   1969-197

As part of Great Britain's treaty obligations to prote the Trucial States, and to help maintain the stability of th oil-producing countries of the Middle East, the 1st Queen Own Highlanders spent a nine month tour in the Trucia States, from May 1969 to February 1970, being based i Sharjah. The battalion trained in desert and mountai operations in the Trucial States and Oman.

The 1st Queen's Own Highlanders in Edinburgh   1970-197

On its return to Great Britain in 1970, the battalio provided the ceremonial and administrative duties for th Commonwealth Games held in Edinburgh, includin Guards of Honour for HM The Queen and HRH Princ Philip, Duke of Edinburgh.

The 1st Queen's Own Highlanders in West Germany
1971-197

The 1st Queen's Own Highlanders rejoined the Britis Army of the Rhine in April 1971, returning to Osnabruc where they formed part of 12 Mechanized Brigade in th 2nd Division. They were equipped with AFV 43 Armoured Personnel Carriers.

In 1971 the 1st Queen's Own Highlanders represente

Great Britain in the CENTO Small Arms Competition (NISHAN VII) and won first place, the only British Regiment to have won this distinction.

The 1st Queen's Own Highlanders in Northern Ireland 1971-1972

The 1st Battalion's first tour of duty in Northern Ireland since the troubles started again in 1969, was from November 1971 to March 1972. The 1st Queen's Own Highlanders were deployed in East Belfast, with Battalion Tactical Headquarters, B and D Companies in the Ballymacarret, and A, Support, and HQ Companies as the Brigade and Battalion reserve at Sydenham Royal Naval Aircraft Yard.

The 1st Queen's Own Highlanders in Northern Ireland 1972

In July 1972, when it was decided to restablish the Government's control over the so called 'No Go' areas of Belfast by an operation codenamed 'Motorman', the 1st Queen's Own Highlanders were flown to Northern Ireland at less than a week's notice, and remained there until November. The battalion was deployed with Tactical HQ and A Company at Dungannon, B Company with the Life Guards in Belfast, D Company with the 1st Gordons in Armagh and Lurgan, and Support Company with the Welsh Guards in Belfast.

The 1st Queen's Own Highlanders in Northern Ireland 1973-1974

In December 1973 the 1st Queen's Own Highlanders moved to Ireland for their third tour of duty. The battalion's area of responsibility was the Lower Falls in Belfast. Battalion Tactical HQ was in the Hastings Street Mill, A Company in the Reservation, B and D Companies in the Albert Street Mill, and Support Company at Broadway. The battalion returned to Osnabruck in April 1974.

The 1st Queen's Own Highlanders in West Germany 1974-1976

After returning from Northern Ireland, the 1st Queen's Own Highlanders trooped their Regimental Colour on 21st

An Armoured Personnel Carrier of 1st Bn Queen's Own Highlanders in Germany 1976.

July 1974 before the Colonel of the Regiment, General Sir Peter Hunt, in Osnabruck.

In November 1974 the battalion battle group carried out mechanised training and field firing, with armour and artillery, at Suffield in Canada. In 1975 the battalion won the Army Shooting Championship at Bisley.

On 26th April 1976 the 1st Battalion sent a detachment to Great Britain which, with a detachment of the TAVR, represented the regiment when it received the Freedom of Tain.

The 1st Queen's Own Highlanders in Edinburgh 1976-1980

In June 1976 the 1st Queen's Own Highlanders returned to Great Britain and were stationed at Kirknewton, near Edinburgh. The 1st Battalion celebrated its return to Scotland by trooping its Regimental Colour in the Northern Meeting Park at Inverness on 21st July 1976.

During nearly four years based at Kirknewton, the battalion spent six months in Belize, and two, four month tours in Northern Ireland.

The 1st Queen's Own Highlanders in Belize 1976-1977

In August 1976 the 1st Queen's Own Highlanders flew to the colony of Belize in Central America. The battalion formed part of the British Force whose task was to defend Belize against invasion by Guatemala. The battalion was deployed with Headquarters and one company at Belize Airport, and with company groups in Cayo and Toledo Districts. The battalion was supported by an Armoured Recce Squadron of the Life Guards, a Light Battery of 3rd Regiment Royal Horse Artillery, RAF Puma helicopters and Harriers.

1st Bn Queen's Own Highlanders Troop the Colour in Osnabruck 1974.

B Company group 1st Bn Queen's Own Highlanders, including an armoured recce troop of the Life Guards and a troop of 47 Light Regiment RA, Commanded by Major D. N. A. Blair, in Belize 1976.

The 1st Queen's Own Highlanders in Edinburgh
1977-1978

The 1st Queen's Own Highlanders returned to Edinburgh in February 1977, and the battalion provided the Royal Guard at Ballater during the summer. When on 15 October 1977 the Regiment received the Freedom of the District of Sutherland, a detachment of the 1st Queen's Own Highlanders paraded at Golspie. During the firemen's strike in November-December 1977, the battalion was employed on fire fighting duties in Edinburgh, and tackled 257 fires.

The 1st Queen's Own Highlanders in Northern Ireland 1978

The 1st Queen's Own Highlanders carried out a tour of duty in North Armagh from April-August 1978. Battalion HQ with Support and HQ Companies were based at Armagh, A Company were at Cookstown, B Company at Dungannon, and D Company at Middletown.

Guard of 1st Bn Queen's Own Highlanders commanded by Captain C. E. Gilmour on parade at Golspie when the regiment received the Freedom of Sutherland in 1977.

1st Bn Queen's Own Highlanders march through Elgin after the Regiment received the Freedom of Moray in 1978.

The 1st Queen's Own Highlanders in Edinburgh 1978-1979

At the time of the bicentenary of the Regiment on 15th May 1978, 200 years after the Earl of Seaforth's Highland Regiment was raised, the 1st Queen's Own Highlanders were on operational duty in Northern Ireland. The Bicentenary celebrations were delayed until after their return to Edinburgh when, on 14th October 1978, the Regiment was granted the Freedom of Moray District. The 1st Queen's Own Highlanders, with detachments of the 51st Highland Volunteers, the Camerons of Ottawa, the Camerons of Canada, and the Seaforth of Canada, paraded at Elgin where the original 78th had been inspected and passed fit for service in 1778.

In December 1978 the 1st Queen's Own Highlanders spent a short period training in Gibraltar.

A Patrol of 1st Bn Queen's Own Highlanders emplanes in a Wessex helicopter in South Armagh 1979.

The Prime Minister, Mrs Margaret Thatcher, visits D Company 1st Bn Queen's Own Highlanders at Crossmaglen in 1979. She is met by Major N. J. Ridley, the Company Commander.

The 1st Queen's Own Highlanders in Northern Ireland 1979

From July to October 1979 the 1st Queen's Own Highlanders carried out their most testing tour of duty in Northern Ireland when they were responsible for the difficult border country of South Armagh. Battalion HQ with Support Company were based at Bessbrook in a linen mill, A Company was at Forkhill, B Company at Newtonhamilton, and D Company at Crossmaglen. The battalion had the great misfortune to lose its Commanding Officer, Lt Col D. N. A. Blair, and his signaller, killed in an IRA bomb attack at Warren Point, when 16 other British soldiers died; and it also lost three other soldiers during the tour of duty. But the battalion had the satisfaction of achieving outstanding success in its anti-terrorist operations.

1st Bn Queen's Own Highlanders on operations in Northern Ireland 1979.

A patrol of 1st Bn Queen's Own Highlanders in South Armagh 1979.

Private MacKenzie on the alert in South Armagh.

The 1st Queen's Own Highlanders in Hong Kong 1980-1981

In March 1980 the 1st Queen's Own Highlanders moved to Hong Kong where they were stationed at Stanley Fort. The battalion's main operations role was the prevention of illegal immigration from China. During its tour in Hong Kong the battalion arrested over 9000 immigrants, by using foot patrols, ambushes, boats, helicopters and ponies. Companies also trained in Brunei and New Zealand.

A brick using a night viewing device to locate illegal immigrants in Hong Kong 1981.

L/Cpl Milne and CSM Duffus on patrol in South Armagh 1979.

A Company 1st Bn Queen's Own Highlanders training with a helicopter in Brunei 1981.

The Recce Platoon 1st Bn Queen's Own Highlanders training in Brunei jungle 1981.

The 1st Queen's Own Highlanders at Tidworth   1981—
The 1st Queen's Own Highlanders left Hong Kong in December 1981 and returned to Great Britain, forming part of 1 Infantry Brigade in the United Kingdom Mobile Force (Land).

The 1st Queen's Own Highlanders in the Falklands   1982
When Argentina invaded the Falkland Islands in April 1982, the 1st Queen's Own Highlanders were twice warned to be ready to take part in the recapture of the Islands. In the event the battalion moved to the Falklands at the end of the fighting, and had the role of clearing up Port Stanley and the settlements where fighting had taken place, and of restoring the civil community to normal. It returned to Tidworth in December 1982.

1st Bn Queen's Own Highlanders in the Falkland Islands 1982.

2. THE DEPOTS AND REGIMENTAL HEADQUARTERS SINCE WORLD WAR II

Primary Training Centres and Depots   1946-1948
In 1946 No 72 Primary Training Centre and Depot was established at Fort George, and No 79 PTC and Depot at Cameron Barracks. The job of the PTCs and Depots was to train all regular recruits and National Servicemen for six weeks before they were sent to the Highland ITC at Edinburgh, or to Corps ITCs for further training and drafting.

Regimental Depots   1948-1951
In April 1948 the PTCs were disbanded and the Regimental Depots re-established, the Depot Seaforth at Fort George, and the Depot Camerons at Cameron Barracks. Their roles were to act as Headquarters for the regiments, to assist the Territorial Army and Army Cadet Force, and to act as holding units for officers and soldiers awaiting release from the army or posting.

The training of all Highland Brigade recruits was taken over by the Highland Brigade Training Centre at Fort George, which in 1948 was formed by the 1st Bn Highland Light Infantry.

Regimental Depots   1951-1960
In 1951 the establishments of the Depot Seaforth and Depot Camerons were increased to allow them to run their own recruit training. Recruits trained for six weeks, followed by four weeks continuation training. at the the

Highland Brigade Depot, which was combined with the Depot Seaforth at Fort George.

Highland Brigade Depots   1960-1968
As part of the plans to reduce the infantry and to rationalize the system of training, the infantry regimental depots were combined into brigade depots. The site chosen for the Highland Brigade Depot was Aberdeen. In 1960 the Depots of the Seaforth, Camerons and Gordons were combined at Fort George, and the Depots of the Black Watch and the Argyll and Sutherland Highlanders at Stirling. The barracks at Bridge of Don were enlarged and modernised to accommodate the combined Highland Brigade Depot which was formed at Fort George in January 1964, and was fully established at Bridge of Don by May 1964.

Scottish Infantry Depots since   1968
On 1st July 1968, the regiments of the Highland and Lowland Brigades were combined to form the Scottish Division. The Highland Brigade Depot at Aberdeen became the Scottish Infantry Depot for training junior soldiers, and the Lowland Brigade Depot at Glencorse became the Scottish Infantry Depot for training adult recruits.

Headquarters of the Scottish Division were established at Edinburgh Castle.

REGIMENTAL HEADQUARTERS QUEEN'S OWN HIGHLANDERS

Regimental Headquarters was formed in 1960, shortly before the amalgamation of the Seaforth and Camerons. Its main duty is to be the Colonel of the Regiment's staff for running the affairs of the Regiment. The range of its activities includes the regimental museum, historical records and research, recruiting officers and soldiers for the regiment, the regimental trust funds, the Regimental Association, the welfare of serving and retired members of

the regiment, production of the regimental journal 'The Queen's Own Highlander', and numerous other activities.

The Regimental Headquarters offices are sited in Cameron Barracks, Inverness, the former Depot of The Queen's Own Cameron Highlanders, and the Regimental Museum is at Fort George, the former Depot of the Seaforth Highlanders.

3.   THE TERRITORIAL ARMY BATTALIONS SINCE 1947

11th BATTALION SEAFORTH HIGHLANDERS TA 1947-1967

The contingent from 11th Bn Seaforth Highlanders TA, commanded by Major G. H. Green, in the TA Review 1958.

When the TA was reformed in 1947 the 11th Seaforth were raised. The battalion's area included the combined territorial areas of the pre-war 4/5th and 6th battalions.

The lay out of the 11th Seaforth was:

Battalion HQ	Dingwall
A Company	Ross-shire
B Company	Morayshire
C Company	Caithness
D Company	Sutherland
S Company	Morayshire

The 11th Seaforth formed part of 152 (Highland) Infantry Brigade in the 51st Highland Division. In 1953 a detachment of the 11th Seaforth took part in the Coronation procession of HM Queen Elizabeth. On 14th July 1966 the 11th Seaforth received new Colours at Fort George from General Sir James Cassels, Colonel of the Regiment. On 31st March 1967 the 11th Seaforth were disbanded as part of the reorganization of the Territorial Army. The battalion was reformed as B and C Companies of the 3rd Bn Queen's Own Highlanders (Territorial).

4th/5th BATTALION THE QUEEN'S OWN CAMERON HIGHLANDERS TA 1947-1967

The 4th/5th Bn TA and Depot The Queen's Own Cameron Highlanders provide a Guard of Honour for HM Queen Elizabeth the Queen Mother, when the Freedom of Inverness was conferred on Her Majesty and on the Cameron Highlanders on 6th August 1953.

When the TA was reformed in 1947, the 4th/5th Camerons were raised. The battalion's area was the same as the pre-war territorial area of the 4th Camerons, and the lay out of the battalion in 1947 was:

Battalion HQ	Inverness
A Company	Badenoch
B Company	Lochaber and Skye (Skye was later transferred to C (Islands) Company)
C Company	Western Isles
D Company	Nairn

S Company	Inverness
HQ Company	Inverness

The 4th/5th Camerons formed part of 152 (Highland) Infantry Brigade in the 51st Highland Division.

In 1953 a detachment of the 4th/5th Camerons took part in the Coronation procession of HM Queen Elizabeth. On 31st March 1967 the 4th/5th Camerons were disbanded as part of the reorganization of the Territorial Army. The battalion was reformed as D (Cameron) Company 3rd Bn Queen's Own Highlanders (Territorial).

1st BATTALION THE LIVERPOOL SCOTTISH, THE QUEEN'S OWN CAMERON HIGHLANDERS TA 1947-1967

When the TA was reformed in 1947, the 1st Liverpool Scottish were re-raised in their old Headquarters at Fraser Street, Liverpool. The battalion became a motor battalion in the 23rd Armoured Brigade.

In 1953 a detachment of the 1st Liverpool Scottish took part in the Coronation procession of HM Queen Elizabeth.

In 1956 the battalion reverted to an infantry role and joined the 125th Infantry Brigade in the 42nd (South Lancashire) Division.

In 1957 and 1960 the 1st Liverpool Scottish won the Territorial Army Shield of the Duke of Edinburgh's Trophy Competition.

On 31st March 1967 the 1st Liverpool Scottish were disbanded as part of the reorganization of the Territorial Army. The Liverpool Scottish was reformed as 'V' (The Liverpool Scottish) Company 51st Highland Volunteers TAVR. Part of the battalion was also formed into 'R' (King's/Liverpool Scottish) Battery The West Lancashire Regiment Royal Artillery (Territorial).

3rd (TERRITORIAL) BATTALION QUEEN'S OWN HIGHLANDERS 1967-1969

On 1st April 1967, as part of the reorganization of the Territorial Army, the 3rd Queen's Own Highlanders were formed. The battalion had a Home Defence role in the Territorial and Army Volunteer Reserve III.

The composition of the battalion was:

Battalion HQ	Inverness
A (Lovat Scouts) Company	Inverness
B (Seaforth) Company	Ross-shire
C (Seaforth) Company	Morayshire
D (Cameron) Company	Fort William, Skye, Uist

Under a further reorganisation of the Territorial Army, the 3rd Queen's Own Highlanders were reduced to cadre strength in December 1968, and were finally disbanded on 31st March 1969.

THE 51st HIGHLAND VOLUNTEERS SINCE 1967

On 1st April 1967 the 51st Highland Volunteers TAVR were formed, with companies raised from the former Highland TA battalions. The 51st Highland Volunteers had the role of providing a reserve for the Regular Army in NATO as T&AVR II. The headquarters of the 51st Highland Volunteers were at Perth, and the battalion included:

B (Seaforth) Company	Wick
C (Cameron) Company	Inverness
V (Liverpool Scottish) Company	Liverpool

In 1969 No 2 (Queen's Own Highlanders) Company was raised.

Pipers and Drummers of 'V' (Liverpool Scottish) Company, 1st Bn 51st Highland Volunteers TA.

1st Bn 51st HIGHLAND VOLUNTEERS

On 1st April 1971 the 51st Highland Volunteers split into two battalions, the headquarters of the 1st Battalion remaining in Perth. The 1st Battalion included the Black Watch, Argyll and Sutherland Highlanders, London Scottish and Liverpool Scottish Companies.

2nd Bn 51st HIGHLAND VOLUNTEERS

On 1st April 1971 the 2nd Bn 51st Highland Volunteers was formed with its Headquarters in Elgin.

The composition of the 2nd Battalion was:

Battalion Headquarters	Elgin
A (Lovat Scouts) Company	Orkney and Shetland
B (Queens Own Highlanders) Company	Wick
C (Queen's Own Highlanders) Company	Inverness, Dingwall, Fort William
D (Gordons) Company	Aberdeen, Laurence-kirk
E (Queen's Own Highlanders) Company	Stornoway and Skye
G (Gordons) Company	Peterhead
HQ (Queen's Own Highlanders/ Gordons) Company	Elgin

When the 3rd 51st Highland Volunteers were formed in 1975, B and G Companies were transferred to the 3rd Battalion, and E Company was merged with C Company.

Reorganisation — 1980

In 1980 the structure of the three battalions was rationalised to improve command and communications. The 2nd 51st Highland Volunteers were reorganized as follows:

Battalion Headquarters	Elgin
A (Queen's Own Highlanders/ Lovat Scouts) Company	Wick, Thurso, Brora, Orkney
B (Gordons) Company	Peterhead, Keith
C (Queen's Own Highlanders) Company	Inverness, Stornoway, Fort William, Dingwall
D (Gordons/Lovat Scouts) Company	Aberdeen, Laurencekirk Shetland

3rd BN 51st HIGHLAND VOLUNTEERS

On 1st April 1975 the 3rd Bn 51st Highland Volunteers was formed with its Headquarters at Peterhead. The battalion had a home defence role, and its companies were thus widely dispersed.

Battalion HQ	Peterhead
B (Queen's Own Highlanders) Company	Wick
C (Argyll and Sutherland Highlanders) Company	Grangemouth
D (Argyll and Sutherland Highlanders) Company	Dumbarton
HQ (Gordons) Company	Peterhead

Reorganisation 1980

In 1980 the structure of the battalion was changed, and battalion Headquarters was moved to Stirling. B (Queen's Own Highlanders) Company reverted to the 2nd Battalion.

4. *THE REGIMENTAL CADETS*

THE QUEEN'S OWN HIGHLANDERS CADETS

Although the Army Cadet Force dates back to 1860, there were no Cadets in the Regimental Area until 1942, when the War Office expanded the cadet force. Each county had its own Cadet establishment, badged as Seaforth or Camerons, until 1961, when all the Cadet battalions of the regimental area of the Queen's Own Highlanders were combined into the 'Northern Counties ACF'.

In 1967 they were redesignated the 'North Highland Cadets', composed of county companies.

1 (Caithness) Company
2 (Inverness and Nairn) Company
3 (Western Isles) Company
4 (Moray) Company
5 (Ross) Company
6 (Sutherland) Company

In 1975 they were designated the '1st Cadet Battalion Queen's Own Highlanders (Seaforth and Camerons) ACF', but this was shortened in 1982 to 'Queen's Own Highlanders Battalion ACF'.

THE LIVERPOOL SCOTTISH CADETS

The Liverpool Scottish Cadets were formed between the wars. They have two companies and are closely associated with their parent Territorial Army unit, 'V' (Liverpool Scottish) Company, 51st Highland Volunteers TA.

CHAPTER VII ALLIED AND AFFILIATED REGIMENTS

1. ALLIED REGIMENTS OF CANADA

The Canadian regiments allied to the Queen's Own Highlanders are given in their order of precedence in the Canadian Reserve Army, which is based on the dates when they were raised.

THE CAMERON HIGHLANDERS OF OTTAWA

The origins of the Regiment

The Cameron Highlanders of Ottawa trace their origin to three militia companies raised in 1861 for garrison duty during the American Civil War, which in 1866 became the 43rd Carleton Battalion of Infantry, nicknamed the 'Carleton Blazers'. Their official date of formation as a regiment was 1881 when they became the 43rd Ottawa and Carleton Rifles, with the motto of the city of Ottawa, 'Advance'. After the Duke of Cornwall (later King George V) had inspected the regiment in 1901, it was redesignated the 43rd Duke of Cornwall's Own Rifles.

The Regiment in World War I

During World War I the regiment provided the 38th Battalion of the Canadian Expeditionary Force. It was awarded 16 Battle Honours.

CAPTAIN T. W. MacDOWELL WINS THE VICTORIA CROSS AT VIMY RIDGE, 1917

While serving with the 38th Bn Canadian, Expeditionary Force, Lieutenant Thain Wendell MacDowell was awarded the Victoria Cross for his gallantry during the fighting on Vimy Ridge from 9-13 April 1917 when, in the face of heavy machine gun and shell fire, he captured a strongly held enemy machine gun post, taking 77 prisoners and two machine guns, and then held the position until relieved by his battalion.

Captain T. W. MacDowell, VC

PRIVATE C. J. P. NUNNEY WINS THE VICTORIA CROSS AT DROCOURT-QUEANT, 1918

While serving with the 38th Bn Canadian Expeditionary Force, Private Claude Joseph Patrick Nunney was awarded the Victoria Cross for his conspicuous bravery during the fighting at Drocourt-Queant on 1-2 September 1918. During a heavy enemy barrage and counter attack he went round the outpost lines to encourage them and *subsequently inspired a successful company attack. He was also awarded the DCM and MM during the war, but died of wounds received in the action when he won the VC.*

Private C. J. P. Nunney, VC.

The Ottawa Highlanders

After World War I the regiment was reorganised as the Ottawa Regiment. In 1922 it was redesignated as The Ottawa Highlanders, and on 28 February 1923 was allied to The Queen's Own Cameron Highlanders.

The Cameron Highlanders of Ottawa

In 1933 the Ottawa Highlanders were redesignated The Cameron Highlanders of Ottawa.

The Camerons of Ottawa were presented with new Colours by Lord Tweedsmuir, Governor General of Canada, at Ottawa in 1936.

The Cameron Highlanders of Ottawa in World War II

When World War II broke out, the Camerons of Ottawa mobilised and were stationed in Iceland during 1940-1941. A 2nd (Reserve) Battalion was formed in Canada in 1940, and a 3rd Battalion was later formed in Holland in 1945 for service with the Canadian Occupation Forces.

The 1st Battalion landed in Normandy on 'D' Day, 6th June 1944, and took part in the campaign in North West Europe. It was awarded 20 Battle Honours.

The Cameron Highlanders of Ottawa since 1945

After the 1st Battalion was demobilized in 1945, the 2nd Battalion was reorganized as an infantry rifle battalion. On the amalgamation in 1961 of the Seaforth and Camerons, the alliance was renewed with the Queen's Own Highlanders. In 1967 HRH Prince Philip, Duke of Edinburgh, was appointed Colonel in Chief of the Cameron Highlanders of Ottawa, and in the same year the Regiment received new Colours from HM Queen Elizabeth at Ottawa.

THE QUEEN'S OWN CAMERON HIGHLANDERS OF CANADA

The raising of the 79th Cameron Highlanders of Canada

The regiment was raised in Winnipeg, Manitoba, in 1910 as a militia regiment. It was allowed to adopt the same uniform as The Queen's Own Cameron Highlanders, with variations in its badges. The regiment was allied to the Camerons, and the alliance was cemented when it sent a contingent to the Coronation of King George V in 1911, and the contingent was attached to the 1st Camerons in Aldershot. The 79th Cameron Highlanders of Canada received their first stand of Colours in Winnipeg in 1910, presented by Mrs D. C. Cameron, wife of the Lieutenant Governor of Manitoba.

The 79th Cameron Highlanders of Canada in World War I

In the Canadian Expeditionary Force which went to France in World War I, the regiment formed the 43rd, 174th and 179th Battalions, and part of the 16th and 27th Battalions. The 79th Cameron Highlanders of Canada were awarded 18 Battle Honours.

LIEUTENANT ROBERT SHANKLAND WINS THE VICTORIA CROSS 1917

On 26th October 1917, during the fighting on Passchendaele ridge near Ypres, Lieutenant Robert Shankland was awarded the Victoria Cross for conspicuous bravery and leadership.

The regiment between the Wars

The 79th Cameron Highlanders of Canada were reorganized in 1920 as the 1st Bn Cameron Highlanders of Canada, with 2nd and 3rd Reserve Battalions. In 1923 the regiment was redesignated 'The Queen's Own Cameron Highlanders of Canada'.

The Queen's Own Cameron Highlanders of Canada in World War II

When World War II broke out, the Camerons of Canada moved to Great Britain in 1940. A 2nd Reserve Battalion

Lieutenant Robert Shankland, VC

was formed in Canada to train reinforcements. The 1st Battalion took part in the Dieppe raid in 1942 and, having landed in Normandy in 1944, fought in the campaign in North West Europe. The Camerons of Canada were awarded 19 Battle Honours.

The Queen's Own Cameron Highlanders of Canada since 1945

After World War II the 1st Battalion of the Camerons of Canada was demobilised, and the 2nd Reserve Battalion was redesignated as The Queen's Own Cameron Highlanders of Canada. In 1955 the Headquarters of the regiment were moved from 202 Main Street Winnipeg to the Minto Armouries.

In 1961, on the amalgamation of Seaforth and Camerons, the alliance was renewed with the Queen's Own Highlanders. On 18th November 1961 the Camerons of Canada received new Colours at Winnipeg from The Hon Errick F. Willis QC, Lieutenant Governor of Manitoba. HRH Prince Philip, Duke of Edinburgh, was appointed Colonel in Chief of The Queen's Own Cameron Highlanders of Canada in 1967.

THE SEAFORTH HIGHLANDERS OF CANADA

The raising of the 72nd Highlanders of Canada

The regiment was raised in Vancouver, British Columbia, in 1911 as the 72nd Highlanders of Canada, a militia regiment. It was allowed to adopt the same uniform as the Seaforth Highlanders, with a cougar collar badge. In 1912 it was allied to the Seaforth Highlanders and was redesignated The 72nd Regiment, Seaforth Highlanders of Canada. The regiment received its first stand of Colours from HRH The Duke of Connaught in 1912.

The 72nd Seaforth Highlanders of Canada in World War I

In the Canadian Expeditionary Force which went to France during World War I, the regiment formed a large proportion of the 16th Battalion CEF and the whole of the 72nd and 231st Battalions. The 16 World War I battle honours of the 72nd Regiment, Seaforth Highlanders of Canada, include those gained by the three battalions.

The regiment between the Wars

The regiment received its second stand of Colours from Lt Gen Sir Arthur Currie on 1st April 1919.

The 72nd Regiment, Seaforth Highlanders of Canada were reorganized in 1920 as the Seaforth Highlanders of Canada, with a 1st Battalion and a 2nd (Reserve) Battalion. In 1925 HRH The Prince of Wales was appointed Colonel in Chief of the Regiment. The Seaforth Armoury in Vancouver, was opened as the home of the regiment in 1936.

The Seaforth of Canada in World War II

When World War II broke out the Seaforth of Canada moved to Great Britain in 1939. From 1943 they took part in the campaigns in Sicily, Italy, and the later stages of the campaign in North West Europe, and were awarded 25 Battle Honours.

PRIVATE E. A. SMITH WINS THE VICTORIA CROSS
1944

During the fighting in the Po Valley in 1944, Private Ernest A ('Smokey') Smith was awarded the Victoria Cross for his gallantry in destroying a Panther tank with a PIAT, and routing ten German infantrymen who jumped off the tank and attacked him.

The Seaforth of Canada since **1945**

The Seaforth of Canada were reformed after World War II as a militia battalion. On the amalgamation of the Seaforth and Camerons in 1961, the alliance was renewed with the Queen's Own Highlanders. On 3rd June 1962 the Seaforth Highlanders of Canada received new Colours from HRH Prince Philip, Duke of Edinburgh, and in 1967 HRH Prince Philip was appointed Colonel in Chief of the Seaforth Highlanders of Canada.

Private Ernest A. Smith, VC.

THE PICTOU HIGHLANDERS

The Pictou Highlanders, which were first raised in 1871, were also allied to the Seaforth Highlanders. In the reorganization of the Canadian Reserve Army in 1954 they were amalgamated with other units to form the Nova Scotia Highlanders, and the alliance ceased.

2. *ALLIED REGIMENTS OF AUSTRALIA*
THE ROYAL WESTERN AUSTRALIA REGIMENT

The alliance with the Cameron Highlanders of Western Australia **1938**

Although the regiment can trace its descent, through a series of disbandments, amalgamations and reorganisations, from the local forces raised to keep order during the gold rush of 1899, the alliance between the Queen's Own Highlanders and the RWAR dates effectively to 1936, when the 16th Bn (The Cameron Highlanders of Western Australia) Australian Military Forces was raised at Perth, Western Australia. The alliance with The Queen's Own Cameron Highlanders was officially authorized in February 1938, and the Cameron Highlanders of Western Australia adopted the uniform and badge of the Camerons.

The Cameron Highlanders of Western Australia in World War II

During World War II a 2nd Battalion was formed. The 1st Battalion fought against the Japanese in New Britain from 1944-1945. The 2nd Battalion served in the Western Desert, Syria and New Guinea. The regiment was disbanded in 1946.

The Cameron Highlanders of Western Australia 1948-1960

In 1948 the Cameron Highlanders of Western Australia were reformed, and in 1952 split into two battalions. During further reorganisations in 1960, the regiment was amalgamated with others to form the 16th Bn The Royal Western Australian Regiment. The Cameron Highlanders continued to form a company of the amalgamated regiment.

The Royal Western Australian Regiment **Since 1960**

After the amalgamation of Seaforth and Camerons in 1961, the alliance was renewed with the Queen's Own Highlanders. The 16th Bn Royal Western Australian Regiment received new Colours in 1962 from HRH Prince Philip, Duke of Edinburgh, at Perth.

THE ROYAL SOUTH AUSTRALIAN REGIMENT

The alliance with the South Australian Scottish Regiment 1952

Although the regiment can trace its descent, through a series of disbandments, amalgamations and reorganisations, from the Militia and Volunteer units of the 19th Century, the alliance with the Queen's Own Highlanders dates effectively from 1952, when the 27th Bn Royal South Australian Regiment was allied to the Seaforth Highlanders.

The regiment had earlier adopted the MacKenzie kilt in 1938 when it became the 27th South Australian Scottish Regiment. During World War II the 1st Battalion South Australian Scottish fought against the Japanese in New Guinea and the 2nd Battalion fought in the Middle East and the South West Pacific.

The South Australian Scottish Regiment was reformed after World War II, and the alliance with the Seaforth Highlanders was approved in 1952

The Royal South Australian Regiment **Since 1960**

Under the reorganisation of the Australian Citizens Military Forces in 1960, the South Australian Scottish were amalgamated with the 10th Battalion (Adelaide Rifles) and the 43rd Battalion (Bushmen's Rifles) to form the Royal South Australian Regiment. After the amalgamation of Seaforth and Camerons in 1961, the alliance was renewed with the Queen's Own Highlanders.

OTHER BATTALIONS OF THE AUSTRALIAN MILITARY FORCES

Other battalions of the Australian Military Forces which have been allied to the regiment, but which are now disbanded, include the 37th, 39th, 52nd Battalions AMF, and the Queensland Cameron Highlanders, 61st Battalion AMF.

3.   ALLIED REGIMENTS OF NEW ZEALAND

4th (OTAGO AND SOUTHLAND) BATTALION ROYAL NEW ZEALAND INFANTRY REGIMENT

The alliance with the Otago and Southland Regiment   1948

Although the regiment can trace its descent from the Dunedin and Invercargill Militia of 1860, the alliance with the Queen's Own Highlanders dates from 9th March 1948 when the 1st Battalion The Southland Regiment was allied to The Queen's Own Cameron Highlanders. In 1950 the Southland Regiment was amalgamated with the Otago Regiment, and a new alliance was formed with the Otago and Southland Regiment.

On the amalgamation of Seaforth and Camerons in 1961, a new alliance was formed with the Queen's Own Highlanders.

4th (Otago and Southland) Bn Royal New Zealand Infantry Regiment

In 1964, under a reorganisation of the New Zealand Territorial Regiments, the regiment was redesignated as the 4th (Otago and Southland) Battalion, Royal New Zealand Infantry Regiment. The regiment received new Colours from the Governor General of New Zealand on 15th February 1975.

7th (WELLINGTON AND HAWKES BAY) BATTALION ROYAL NEW ZEALAND INFANTRY REGIMENT

The alliance with the Wellington Regiment   1950

The regiment can trace its descent from the Maori Wars of the 1860s. When it was reformed as the Wellington Regiment in 1911, its Highland Rifles Company wore the uniform of the Seaforth Highlanders.

The alliance with the Queen's Own Highlanders dates from 1950, when the Wellington Regiment was allied to the Seaforth Highlanders, thus cementing the friendship that developed when the 2nd and 5th Seaforth fought alongside the 2nd New Zealand Division in the Western Desert in 1942-1943

On the amalgamation of Seaforth and Camerons in 1961, a new alliance was formed with the Queen's Own Highlanders.

7th (Wellington and Hawkes Bay) Bn, Royal New Zealand Infantry Regiment

In 1964, under a reorganisation of the New Zealand Territorial Regiments, the regiment was redesignated as the 7th (Wellington and Hawkes Bay) Battalion, Royal New Zealand Infantry Regiment. The regiment received new Colours from the Governor General of New Zealand on 23rd February 1979.

4.   AFFILIATED REGIMENT

7th DUKE OF EDINBURGH'S OWN GURKHA RIFLES

The 7th Gurkhas were formed in Burma in 1902. After World War II they were affiliated to the Cameronians (Scottish Rifles) but, when the Cameronians were disbanded in 1968, a new affiliation was approved with the Queen's Own Highlanders.

The 2nd Bn 7th Gurkhas had a particularly close association with the 2nd Camerons during World War II, when the two battalions fought alongside each other in the Western Desert and Italy, in the 4th Indian Division.

The 7th Gurkhas and 1st Battalion Queen's Own Highlanders served together in Hong Kong in 1980.

CHAPTER VIII   ANNEXES

1. THE REGIMENT AND THE ROYAL FAMILY

HRH Prince Frederick Augustus, Duke of York and Albany (1763-1827)

The 72nd Duke of Albany's Own Highlanders took their title, granted in 1823, from HRH Prince Frederick, Duke of York and Albany, second son of King George III. His Cypher 'F' with ducal coronet is one of the devices borne on the Regimental Colour of the Queen's Own Highlanders.

HM Queen Victoria (1819-1901)

The 79th Queen's Own Cameron Highlanders were granted the title 'The Queen's Own' by HM Queen Victoria on 10th July 1873 as a personal favour. The Cypher of Queen Victoria was granted as an additional badge to The Queen's Own Cameron Highlanders by HM King George V in 1921, and is borne on the Regimental Colour of the Queen's Own Highlanders.

HM King Edward VII (1841-1910)

In September 1866 HRH The Prince of Wales reviewed the Sutherland Rifle Volunteers at Dunrobin, and was appointed their Honorary Colonel. He held the appointment until 1908 when, as King Edward VII, he relinquished it on the formation of the Territorial Army, when the Sutherland Rifle Volunteers became the 5th Territorial Bn Seaforth Highlanders.

HRH Prince Leopold, Duke of Albany (1853-1884)

On 4th March 1882 HRH Prince Leopold, fourth son of Queen Victoria, was appointed Honorary Colonel of 3rd Militia Battalion Seaforth Highlanders. After his death in 1884 his Cypher 'L' with ducal coronet was added to the Seaforth Highlanders officers badge at Queen Victoria's request.

HRH Prince Albert, Duke of Clarence and Avondale (1864-1892)

On 19 July 1890 HRH Prince Albert, Duke of Clarence and Avondale, eldest son of the Prince of Wales (later King Edward VII) was appointed Honorary Colonel of 1st Volunteer Battalion The Queen's Own Cameron Highlanders. He died in 1892, while Honorary Colonel.

HM King George V (1865-1936)

On 12 November 1902 HRH The Prince of Wales wa appointed Colonel in Chief of The Queen's Own Camero Highlanders. He succeeded to the throne in 1910 as Kin George V, and remained Colonel in Chief of The Camero Highlanders until his death.

HRH Prince Leopold, Duke of Albany and Saxe-Coburg-Gotha (1884-1953)

On 19th July 1905 HRH Prince Leopold, Duke of Albany, grandson of Queen Victoria, was appointed Colonel in Chief of the Seaforth Highlanders. His appointment ceased in 1914 when he elected to remain in Germany after the outbreak of war.

HM King Edward VIII (1894-1972)

On 3rd December 1920 HRH The Prince of Wales wa appointed Colonel in Chief of the Seaforth Highlanders He succeeded to the throne in 1936 as King Edward VII and remained Colonel in Chief until his abdication.

HM King George VI (1895-1952)

On 1st July 1920 HRH Prince Albert, Duke of York, Earl of Inverness, was appointed Honorary Colonel of 4th (Territorial) Battalion The Queen's Own Cameron Highlanders. On his succession to the throne on 10 December 1936 as King George VI he became Colonel in Chief of The Queen's Own Cameron Highlanders and held the appointment until his death.

HRH Prince Philip, Duke of Edinburgh

On 2nd June 1953 HRH Prince Philip, Duke of Edinburgh, was appointed Colonel in Chief of The Queen's Own Cameron Highlanders. On the amalgamation of the Seaforth Highlanders and The Queen's Own Cameron Highlanders on 7 February 1961, he was appointed Colonel in Chief of the Queen's Own Highlanders, Seaforth and Camerons.

2. COLONELS OF THE REGIMENT

(Note: Former Colonels are shown with the highest rank held)

78th Regiment of (Highland) Foot

1777-1781 Lt Col Kenneth, Earl of Seaforth (Lt Col Comdt)

1782-1783 Col Thomas F. MacKenzie Humberston (Lt Col Comdt)

1783-1794 Lt Gen James Murray (Lt Col Comdt until 1786, then Colonel)

From 1786, 72nd (Highland) Regiment of Foot

1794-1798 Lt Gen Sir Adam Williamson, KB

1798-1815 Gen James Stuart

1815-1817 Lt Gen Lord Hill, GCB

1817-1823 Lt Gen Sir George Murray, GCB GCH

1823-1836 Lt Gen Sir John Hope, GCH

From 1823, 72nd (or The Duke of Albany's Own Highlanders) Regiment of Foot

1836-1847 Lt Gen Sir Colin Campbell, KCB

1847-1851 Lt Gen Sir Neil Douglas, KCB, KCH

1851-1870 Gen Sir John Aitchison, GCB

1870-1870 Gen Charles G. J. Arbuthnott

1870-1881 Gen Charles Gascoyne

1881-1885 Gen Sir Edward Selby Smyth, KCMG

78th (Highland) Regiment of Foot

1793-1796 Lt Gen Francis Humberston MacKenzie, Lord Seaforth (Lt Col Comdt)

From 1795, 78th (Highland) Regiment of Foot (or the Ross-shire Buffs)

1796-1809 Lt Gen Alexander MacKenzie Fraser

1809-1812 Gen Sir James Henry Craig, KB

1812-1822 Maj Gen Sir Samuel Auchmuty, GCB

1822-1834 Lt Gen Sir Edward Barnes, GCB

1834-1837 Lt Gen Sir Lionel Smith, KCB KCH

1837-1851 Lt Gen Sir Paul Anderson, CB KC

1851-1853 Lt Gen Sir Neil Douglas, KCB KCH

1853-1860 Lt Gen Sir William Chalmers, CB KCH

1860-1863 Gen Roderick Macneil

1863-1885 F M Sir Patrick Grant, GCB GCMG

79th Cameronian Volunteers

1793-1828 Lt Gen Sir Alan Cameron, KCB, of Erracht (Maj Comdt to 1794, Lt Col Comdt to 1805)

From 1804, 79th Cameronian Highlanders

From 1806, 79th Cameron Highlanders

1828-1841 Gen Sir Ronald C Ferguson GCB, of Raith and Novar

1841-1842 Lt Gen Hon John Ramsay, of Kelly

1842-1849 Lt Gen Sir James MacDonell, KCB KCH

1849-1854 Lt Gen James Hay, CB

1854-1862 Gen Sir William Henry Sewell, KCB

1862-1868 Gen Hon Sir Hugh Arbuthnott, KCB

1868-1870 Lt Gen John Francis Glencairn Campbell, CB

1870-1876 Gen Henry Cooper

From 1873, 79th Queen's Own Cameron Highlanders

1876-1879 Gen Sir Alfred Hastings Horsford, GCB

1879-1887 Gen Sir John Douglas, GCB, of

From 1881, 1st Bn Seaforth Highlanders

From 1881, 2nd Bn Seaforth Highlanders

From 1881, The Queen's Own Cameron Highlanders

Seaforth Highlanders (Ross-shire Buffs, The Duke of Albany's)

1885-1893 Gen Sir Edward Selby Smyth, KCMG

1893-1897 Gen Sir William Parke, KCB

1897-1907 Gen Sir Archibald Alison Bt, GCB

1907-1911 Lt Gen Sir Mostyn de la Poer Beresford

1911-1914 Gen Sir George Digby Barker, KCB

1914-1924 Maj Gen Robert Hunter Murray, CB CMG

1924-1931 Maj Gen Sir Colin J. Mackenzie, KCB

1931-1939 Maj Gen Sir Archibald B. Ritchie, KBE CB CMG

1939-1947 Lt Gen Sir William M. Thomson, KCMG CB MC

1947-1957 Maj Gen Sir John E. Laurie Bt, CBE DSO

1957-1961 F M Sir A. James H. Cassels, GCB KBE DSO

1887-1904 Gen Sir Richard Chambre Hayes Taylor GCB

1904-1914 Gen Sir Ian Standish Monteith Hamilton, GCB, GCMG, DSO, TD.

1914-1929 Lt Gen Sir John Spencer Ewart, KCB

1929-1943 Maj Gen Neville John Gordon Cameron, CB, CMG

1943-1951 Maj Gen Sir James Syme Drew, KBE, DSO, CB, MC

1951-1961 Maj Gen Douglas Neil Wimberley, CB, DSO, MC, LLD, DL

From 1961, Queen's Own Highlanders, (Seaforth and Camerons)

From 1961, Queen's Own Highlanders, (Seaforth& Camerons)

Queen's Own Highlanders (Seaforth & Camerons)

1961-1965 F M Sir A. James H. Cassels, GCB, KBE, DSO

1965-1976 Gen Sir Peter M. Hunt, GCB DSO OBE

1976-1982 Lt Gen Sir Chandos Blair, KCVO, OBE, MC

1982- Maj Gen John C. O. R. Hopkinson

COLONELS OF THE QUEEN'S OWN HIGHLANDERS

Field Marshal Sir James Cassels, GCB, KBE, DSO, Colonel of the Queen's Own Highlanders 1961-1966. (From the painting by Major A. C. Davidson-Houston)

General Sir Peter Hunt, GCB, DSO, OBE, Colonel of the Queen's Own Highlanders 1966-1975. (From the painting by Howard Barron)

Lieutenant General Sir Chandos Blair, KCVO, OBE, MC, Colonel of the Queen's Own Highlanders 1975-1983.

Major General John C. O. R. Hopkinson, Colonel of the Queen's Own Highlanders 1983.

3. BATTLE HONOURS

BATTLE HONOURS COMMEMORATING BATTLES BEFORE THE ARMY REFORMS OF 1881

72nd DUKE OF ALBANY'S OWN HIGHLANDERS		78th HIGHLANDERS, ROSS-SHIRE BUFFS		79th CAMERON HIGHLANDERS	
CARNATIC	1782-96	ASSAYE with ELEPHANT	1803	EGMONT OP ZEE	1799
HINDOOSTAN	1782-96	MAIDA (2nd/78th)	1806	EGYPT and SPHINX	1801
MYSORE	1782-96	JAVA	1811	CORUNNA	1809
CAPE OF GOOD HOPE	1806	KOOSH AB	1857	BUSACO	1810
SOUTH AFRICA	1835	PERSIA	1857	FUENTES D'ONOR	1811
SEVASTOPOL	1855	LUCKNOW	1858	SALAMANCA	1812
CENTRAL INDIA	1858	AFGHANISTAN	1879-80	PYRENEES	1813
PEIWAR KOTAL	1878			NIVELLE	1813
CHARASIAH	1879			NIVE	1813
KABUL	1879			TOULOUSE	1814
KANDAHAR	1880			PENINSULA	1809-14
AFGHANISTAN	1878-80			WATERLOO	1815
				ALMA	1854
				SEVASTOPOL	1855
				LUCKNOW	1858

BATTLE HONOURS 1881-1914

1st BN SEAFORTH HIGHLANDERS		2nd BN SEAFORTH HIGHLANDERS		1st BN THE QUEEN'S OWN CAMERON HIGHLANDERS	
TEL EL KEBIR	1882	CHITRAL	1895	TEL EL KEBIR	1882
EGYPT	1882	PAARDEBERG	1899	EGYPT	1882
ATBARA	1898	SOUTH AFRICA	1899-1902	NILE	1884-85
KHARTOUM	1898			ATBARA	1898
				KHARTOUM	1898
				SOUTH AFRICA	1900-02

BATTLE HONOURS AWARDED TO VOLUNTEER BATTALIONS WHICH SENT VOLUNTEERS AS REINFORCEMENTS TO SOUTH AFRICA

1st (ROSS-HIGHLAND) BN SEAFORTH HIGHLANDERS	1st SUTHERLAND-HIGHLAND RIFLE VOLUNTEERS	3rd (MORAYSHIRE) BN SEAFORTH HIGHLANDERS	1st (INVERNESS-HIGHLAND) BN CAMERON HIGHLANDERS	8th (SCOTTISH) BN KING'S LIVERPOOL REGIMENT
SOUTH AFRICA 1900-02	SOUTH AFRICA 1900-02	SOUTH AFRICA 1900-02	SOUTH AFRICA 1900-02	SOUTH AFRICA 1902

HONOUR AWARDED TO MILITIA BATTALION FOR GARRISON DUTY OVERSEAS DURING THE SOUTH AFRICAN WAR

3rd (MILITIA) BN SEAFORTH HIGHLANDERS	
MEDITERRANEAN	1900-01

T

BATTLE HONOURS — WORLD WAR I

After World War I, the Army Council appointed the Battles Nomenclature Committee to define the time and place of each action of the war. In 1920 the committee published their report 'The Official Names of the Battles and other Engagements fought by the Military Forces of the British Empire during the Great War 1914-1919'.

Regimental committees then worked out to which Battle Honours their regiments were entitled. To qualify for Battle Honour a battalion had to have had its HQ and 50 of its strength within the boundaries of a battle within the dates specified in the report.

The complete list of Battle Honours was published Army Orders in February 1925. Ten honours were selected to be borne on the King's Colour.

SEAFORTH HIGHLANDERS

(Note — Those shown in capitals were selected to be borne on the King's Colour)

Le Cateau		Flers-Courcelette		Hazebrouck	
Retreat from Mons		Le Transloy		Bailleul	
MARNE	1914, 18	Ancre Heights		Kemmel	
Aisne	1914	Ancre	1916	Béthune	
La Bassée	1914	ARRAS	1917, 18	Soissonais-Ourcq	
Armentières	1914	VIMY	1917	Tardenois	
Festubert	1914, 15	Scarpe	1917, 18	Drocourt-Quéant	
Givenchy	1914	Arleux		Hindenburg Line	
Neuve Chapelle		Pilckem		Courtrai	
YPRES	1915, 17, 18	Menin Road		Selle	
St Julien		Polygon Wood		VALENCIENNES	
Frezenberg		Broodseinde		France and Flanders	1914-18
Bellewaarde		Poelcappelle		Macedonia	1917-18
Aubers		Passchendaele		Megiddo	
LOOS		CAMBRAI	1917, 18	Sharon	
SOMME	1916, 18	St Quentin		PALESTINE	1918
Albert	1916	Bapaume	1918	Tigris	1916
Bazentin		Lys		Kut el Amara	1917
Delville Wood		Estaires		BAGHDAD	
Pozières		Messines	1918	Mesopotamia	1915-18

THE QUEEN'S OWN CAMERON HIGHLANDERS

(Note — Those shown in capitals were selected to be borne on the King's Colour)

Retreat from Mons		Albert	1916	Bapaume	1918
MARNE	1914, 18	Bazentine		Lys	
AISNE	1914			Estaires	
YPRES	1914, 15, 17, 18	DELVILLE WOOD		Messines	1918
Langemarck	1914	Pozières		Kemmel	
Gheluvelt		Flers-Courcelette		Béthune	
Nonne Bosschen		Morval		Soissonais-Ourcq	
Givenchy	1914	Le Transloy		Drocourt-Quéant	
NEUVE CHAPELLE		Ancre Heights		Hindenburg Line	
Hill 60		ARRAS	1917, 18	Epéhy	
Gravenstafel		Scarpe	1917	St Quentin Canal	
St Julien		Arleux		Courtrai	
Frezenberg		Pilckem		Selle	
Bellewaarde		Menin Road		SAMBRE	
Aubers		Polygon Wood		France and Flanders	1914-18
Festubert	1915	Poelcappelle		Struma	
LOOS		Passchendaele		MACEDONIA	1915-18
SOMME	1916, 18	St Quentin			

THE LIVERPOOL SCOTTISH

(Note — Those shown in capitals were selected to be borne on the King's Colour)

BELLEWAARDE		*YPRES*	*1917*	*CAMBRAI*	*1917*
SOMME	*1916*	*PILCKEM*		*LYS*	
Ginchy		*MENIN ROAD*		*ESTAIRES*	
Morval		*PASSCHENDAELE*		*FRANCE AND FLANDERS*	*1914-18*

BATTLE HONOURS — WORLD WAR II

SEAFORTH HIGHLANDERS

(Note — Those shown in capitals were selected to be borne on the King's Colour)

Ypres-Comines Canal		*Lower Maas*		*North Africa*	*1942, 43*
Somme	*1940*	*Meijel*		*Landing in Sicily*	
Withdrawal to Seine		*Venlo Pocket*		*Augusta*	
ST VALERY-EN-CAUX		*Ourthe*		*Francofonte*	
Odon		*RHINELAND*		*Adrano*	
Cheux		*Reichswald*		*Sferro Hills*	
CAEN		*Goch*		*SICILY*	*1943*
Troarn		*Moyland*		*Garigliano Crossing*	
Mont Pincon		*Rhine*		*ANZIO*	
Quarry Hill		*Uelzen*		*Italy*	*1943-44*
Falaise		*Artlenberg*		*MADAGASCAR*	
Falaise Road		*North West Europe*	*1940, 44-45*	*Middle East*	*1942*
Dives Crossing		*EL ALAMEIN*		*IMPHAL*	
La Vie Crossing		*Advance on Tripoli*		*Shenam Pass*	
Lisieux		*Mareth*		*Litan*	
Nederrijn		*Wadi Zigzaou*		*Tengnoupal*	
Best		*AKARIT*		*BURMA*	*1942, 44*
La Havre		*Djebel Roumana*			

THE QUEEN'S OWN CAMERON HIGHLANDERS

(Note — Those shown in capitals were selected to be borne on the King's Colour)

Defence of Escaut		*SIDI BARRANI*		*Tavoleto*	
ST OMER — LA BASSEE		*Tobruk 1941, 42*		*Coriano*	
Somme	*1940*	*Gubi II*		*Pian di Castello*	
St Valery-En-Caux		*Carmusa*		*Monte Reggiano*	
Falaise		*Gazala*		*Rimini Line*	
Falaise Road		*EL ALAMEIN*		*San Marino*	
La Vie Crossing		*Mareth*		*Italy*	*1944*
La Havre		*Wadi Zigzaou*		*KOHIMA*	
Lower Maas		*AKARIT*		*Relief of Kohima*	
Venlo Pocket		*Djebel Roumana*		*Naga Village*	
Rhineland		*North Africa*	*1940-43*	*Aradura*	
REICHSWALD		*Francofonte*		*Shwebo*	
Goch		*Adrano*		*MANDALAY*	
RHINE		*Sferro Hills*		*Ava*	
North West Europe	*1940, 44-45*	*Sicily*	*1943*	*Irrawaddy*	
Agordat		*Cassino I*		*Mt Popa*	
KEREN		*Poggio Del Grillo*		*Burma*	*1944-45*
Abyssinia	*1941*	*GOTHIC LINE*			

4. THE COLOURS

The Regimental Colour of 1st Bn Queen's Own Highlanders at Elgin 1978, on the occasion of the Bicentenary of the raising of the 78th Regiment of (Highland) Foot.

The Colours of the regiment are its most treasured and respected possession. They bear the battle honours of the regiment, and the various badges and devices which have been granted to mark particular associations or honours.

When the 72nd, 78th and 79th Highlanders were raised in the 18th Century, the colours were bigger than those in use today. They were 6' x 6' 6" and the pikes were 9' 10" long. Todays colours are 3' 9" x 3' and the pikes, including the Royal Crest, are 8' 7½".

Until 1857 they were provided by the Colonel of the Regiment at his own expense, but thereafter they were issued at Government expense.

The Queen's Colour

The Queen's Colour (termed the 'King's Colour' if the monarch is a King) is the Union Flag. After both World Wars I and II each regiment was allowed to add 10 selected battle honours to the King's Colour. The Queen's Colour of the Queen's Own Highlanders has a total of 33 battle honours from the two World Wars, being the combined battle honours of the Seaforth and Camerons.

The Regimental Colour

The Regimental Colour of the Queen's Own Highlanders is buff with a blue fringe, from the facings colours of the regiment. It has the regimental badge in the centre surrounded by the name of the regiment, and this is encircled by the standard wreath of thistles, roses and shamrocks, with the regimental motto 'Cuidich n' Righ' at the foot.

The Regimental Colour also bears:

The Cypher of HM Queen Victoria within the Garter. This was granted to The Queen's Own Cameron Highlanders by HM King George V in 1921.

The Cypher and Coronet of HRH Prince Philip, Duke of Edinburgh. Colonel in Chief of the Queen's Own Highlanders from 1961.

The Cypher and Coronet of Frederick Duke of York and Albany, brother of King George IV, from whom the 72nd Duke of Albany's Own Highlanders derived their title in 1823.

The Sphinx superscribed 'EGYPT'. The Battle Honour was granted to the 79th Cameron Highlanders for the regiment's part in the campaign in Egypt in 1801.

An Elephant superscribed 'ASSAYE'. The Battle Honour was granted to the 78th Highlanders (Ross-shire Buffs) for the regiment's part in the Battle of Assaye in 1803.

The last occasion on which the Colours of the regiment were carried in action was in the campaign in Afghanistan 1878-1880, when the 72nd Duke of Albany's Own Highlanders carried their Colours at the battle of Charasiah on 6th October 1879.

THE COLOURS OF THE REGIMENT

COLOURS OF THE 1st BN SEAFORTH HIGHLANDERS AND ITS PREDECESSORS

Stand	Date Presented		Present Location
		78th (later 72nd) Highlanders	
1st	1778	Provided by Lt Col The Earl of Seaforth and taken into service at Edinburgh.	Not known
		72nd Highlanders	
2nd	1787	Provided by Maj Gen James Murray and taken into service in India.	Not known
3rd	1800	Provided by Lt Gen James Stuart and taken into service at Perth.	Not known
		72nd Duke of Albany's Own Highlanders	
4th	1825	Provided by Lt Gen Sir John Hope and presented by Lady Hope at Bruntsfield Links, Edinburgh.	SUSM Edinburgh Castle
5th	1842	Provided by Lt Gen Sir Colin Campbell and presented by FM The Duke of Wellington at Windsor Castle.	Fort George
6th	1857	Presented to HRH The Duke of Cambridge at Shorncliffe.	Fort George
		1st Bn Seaforth Highlanders	
7th	1884	Presented by HM Queen Victoria at Osborne.	Scottish National War Memorial, Edinburgh Castle
8th	1911	Presented by HM King George V at Delhi.	St. Giles Church, Elgin
9th	1958	Presented by FM Sir Gerald Templer at Munster, West Germany. Carried from 1961 to 1964 by 1st Bn Queen's Own Highlanders.	Fort George
		2nd Bn 72nd Highlanders	
—	1805	Supplied by Lt Gen James Stuart and taken into service from 1805 to 1815.	SUSM, Edinburgh Castle

COLOURS OF 2nd BN SEAFORTH HIGHLANDERS AND ITS PREDECESSORS

		78th Highlanders (Ross-shire Buffs)	
1st	1793	Provided by Lt Col F. H. MacKenzie of Seaforth and taken into service at Fort George.	Fort George
2nd	C.1801	Provided by Maj Gen A MacKenzie-Fraser and taken into service in India.	Not known
3rd	1818	Provided by Maj Gen Sir Samuel Auchmuchty and taken into service in Ireland.	Not known
4th	1839	Provided by Lt Gen Paul Anderson and taken into service in Scotland.	St. Giles Cathedral, Edinburgh until 1982
5th	1854	Provided by the estate of the late Gen Paul Anderson	SUSM, Edinburgh Castle
6th	1868	Presented by Lady Windham, wife of the Governor General, in Canada.	Balmoral Castle
		2nd Bn Seaforth Highlanders	
7th	1899	Presented by HM Queen Victoria at Balmoral Castle.	Fort George
8th	1935	Presented by HRH The Prince of Wales at Dover. Carried until amalgamation of 1st and 2nd Battalions in 1948, and thereafter by 1st Battalion, together with its own 8th stand, until 1958.	Fort George
		2nd Bn 78th Highlanders	
1st	1794	Supplied by Lt Col F. H. MacKenzie of Seaforth and taken into service from 1794-1797.	Fort George
2nd	1804	Supplied by Col A. MacKenzie-Fraser and taken into service from 1804-1816.	SUSM, Edinburgh Castle
		Assaye Colour of 78th Highlanders	
—	1803	Granted by the Government of India as an Honorary Colour to commemorate the battle of Assaye.	Not known
—	1889	Replica bought by Officers of 2nd Bn Seaforth Highlanders.	Fort George

COLOURS OF MILITIA, TERRITORIAL AND SERVICE BATTALIONS
SEAFORTH HIGHLANDERS

Stand	Date Presented		Present Location
—	1885	**3rd (Militia) Bn Seaforth Highlanders** Presented by HRH The Duchess of Albany at Ballater.	Fort George
—	1909	**4th (Territorial) Bn Seaforth Highlanders** Presented by HM King Edward VII at Windsor. From 1920 carried by 4/5th Bn and from 1947 to 1966 by 11th Bn.	St. Clement's Church, Dingwall
—	1909	**6th (Territorial) Bn Seaforth Highlanders** Gifted by Sir George Cooper and presented by The Duke of Richmond and Gordon at Elgin. Carried by 11th Bn from 1947 to 1966.	St. Giles Church, Elgin
—	1919	**7th (Service) Bn Seaforth Highlanders** King's Colour presented by General Sir Herbert Plumer at Solingen, Germany.	Fort George
—	1919	**8th (Service) Bn Seaforth Highlanders** King's Colour presented by Lt Gen Sir Richard Butler at Nivelles, Belgium.	Fort George
—	1919	**9th (Service) Bn Seaforth Highlanders (Pioneers)** King's Colour presented by Brig Gen A. H. Marindin at Malmedy, Belgium.	Fort George
—	1919	**10th (Service) Bn Seaforth Highlanders** King's Colour issued, although 10th Bn had been redesignated in 1916. Not formally presented.	Fort George
—	1966	**11th Bn Seaforth Highlanders TA** Presented by Gen Sir James Cassels at Fort George.	Still carried (1982) by 2nd Bn 51st Highland Volunteers TA.

COLOURS OF 1st BN THE QUEEN'S OWN CAMERON HIGHLANDERS
AND ITS PREDECESSORS

1st	1794	**79th Cameronian Volunteers** Provided by Maj Alan Cameron of Erracht and taken into service at Stirling.	(Remnants) Fort George
2nd	1815	**79th Cameron Highlanders** Provided by Maj Gen Alan Cameron of Erracht and taken into service at Paris.	Fort George
3rd	1828	Provided by Lt Gen Sir Ronald Ferguson and presented by Lady Neil Douglas in Canada.	St. Giles Cathedral, Edinburgh (Until 1982)
4th	1854	Provided by the Colonel of the Regiment and presented by Mrs J. Elliot at Portsmouth.	Balmoral Castle
5th	1873	Presented by HM Queen Victoria at Parkhurst.	Scottish National War Memorial, Edinburgh Castle
		(The Green Colour was replaced by a Blue Colour on change of facing colour when the 79th became 'Queen's Own' in 1873).	(Green Colour at Fort George)
6th	1923	Presented by Gen Sir Havelock Hudson at Calcutta.	Glasgow Cathedral
7th	1955	Presented by HM Queen Elizabeth at Balmoral. Carried from 1961-1964 by 1st Bn Queen's Own Highlanders.	Fort George

COLOURS OF 2nd BN THE QUEEN'S OWN CAMERON HIGHLANDERS
AND ITS PREDECESSORS

1st	1804	**2nd Bn 79th Cameron Highlanders** Provided by Col Sir Alan Cameron of Erracht and taken into service at Stirling.	Fort George
2nd	1898	**2nd Bn The Queen's Own Cameron Highlanders** Presented by HM Queen Victoria at Balmoral.	Scottish National War Memorial, Edinburgh Castle
3rd	1933	Presented by HRH The Duke of York at Aldershot.	Inverness Town Hall

COLOURS OF MILITIA, TERRITORIAL AND SERVICE BNS
THE QUEEN'S OWN CAMERON HIGHLANDERS

		Inverness, Banff, Moray, Nairn Militia	
1st	1803	Taken into service at Inverness.	Fort George
		3rd Militia Bn The Queen's Own Cameron Highlanders	
2nd	1909	Presented by the MacKintosh of MacKintosh at Fort George.	Old High Church, Inverness
		4th Territorial Bn The Queen's Own Cameron Highlanders	
—	1909	Gifted by Maj Gen Sir Spencer Ewart. Presented by HM King Edward VII at Windsor. Carried from 1947-1967 by 4/5th Bn.	Still carried (1982) by 2nd Bn 51st Highland Volunteers TA.
		5th (Service) Bn The Queen's Own Cameron Highlanders	
—	1919	King's Colour presented by Gen Sir Henry Plumer at Solingen, Germany.	Destroyed when Fort William Town Hall was burnt down.
		6th (Service) Bn The Queen's Own Cameron Highlanders	
—	1919	King's Colour presented by Lt Gen Sir Richard Butler at Braine-le-Comte.	Old High Church, Inverness
		7th (Service) Bn The Queen's Own Cameron Highlanders	
—	1919	King's Colour presented by HRH The Duke of York at Cameron Barracks, Inverness.	Old High Church, Inverness
		9th (Service) Bn The Queen's Own Cameron Highlanders	
—	1919	King's Colour presented by HRH The Duke of York at Cameron Barracks, Inverness.	Scottish National War Memorial, Edinburgh Castle
		11th (Service) Bn The Queen's Own Cameron Highlanders	
—	1919	Presented by Sir Beauvoir de Lisle at Roubaix.	Scottish National War Memorial, Edinburgh Castle
		1st/10th (Scottish) Bn King's (Liverpool) Regiment TF	
1st	1909	Presented by King Edward VII at Knowsley.	Liverpool Cathedral
		1st Bn The Liverpool Scottish (The Queen's Own Cameron Highlanders) TA	
2nd	1938	Presented by HM King George VI at Liverpool.	Still carried (1982) by 51st Highland Volunteers TA
		2nd/10th (Scottish) Bn King's (Liverpool) Regiment TF	
—		King's Colour issued 1919. Not formally presented.	Scottish National War Memorial, Edinburgh Castle

COLOURS OF THE QUEEN'S OWN HIGHLANDERS

		1st Bn Queen's Own Highlanders (SEAFORTH and CAMERONS)	
1st	1964	Presented by HRH Prince Philip, Duke of Edinburgh, at the Palace of Holyrood, Edinburgh.	

The Colours of 1st Battalion Queen's Own Highlanders (Seaforth and Camerons).

5.　THE REGIMENT'S VICTORIA CROSS WINNERS

The Victoria Cross was instituted by Royal Warrant on 29th January 1856 and the first Army VCs were awarded for gallantry during the Crimean War.

The cross is made of bronze from the metal of cannons captured at Sevastopol.

The VC has been awarded to 27 members of the regiment and its Allied battalions. They are shown in chronological order.

1.	Lt A. C. Bogle	78th Highlanders (Ross-shire Buffs)	29 July 1857	Oonao (Indian Mutiny)
2.	Lt J. P. H. Crowe	78th Highlanders (Ross-shire Buffs)	12 August 1857	Boorbia (Indian Mutiny)
3.	Lt H. T. MacPherson	78th Highlanders (Ross-shire Buffs)	25 September 1857	Lucknow (Indian Mutiny)
4.	Surgeon J. Jee	78th Highlanders (Ross-shire Buffs)	25/26 September 1857	Lucknow (Indian Mutiny)
5.	Asst Surgeon V. M. McMaster	78th Highlanders (Ross-shire Buffs)	25 September 1857	Lucknow (Indian Mutiny)
6.	C/Sgt S. MacPherson	78th Highlanders (Ross-shire Buffs)	26 September 1857	Lucknow (Indian Mutiny)
7.	Pte H. Ward	78th Highlanders (Ross-shire Buffs)	25/26 September 1857	Lucknow (Indian Mutiny)
8.	Pte J. Hollowell	78th Highlanders (Ross-shire Buffs)	26 September 1857	Lucknow (Indian Mutiny)
9.	Lt A. S. Cameron	72nd Duke of Albany's Own Highlanders	30 March 1858	Kotah (Indian Mutiny)
10.	L/Cpl G. Sellar	72nd Duke of Albany's Own Highlanders	14 December 1879	Kabul (Afghanistan)
11.	Sgt J. MacKenzie	Seaforth Highlanders attached W.A.F.F.	6 June 1900	Doompassi (Ashanti)
12.	Sgt D. D. Farmer	1st Bn The Queen's Own Cameron Highlanders	13 December 1900	Nooitgedacht (South Africa)
13.	Pte R. Tollerton	1st Bn The Queen's Own Cameron Highlanders	14 September 1914	Aisne (WW I)
14.	Lt Col A. F. Douglas-Hamilton	6th Bn The Queen's Own Cameron Highlanders	25/26 September 1915	Loos (WW I)
15.	Cpl J. D. Pollock	5th Bn The Queen's Own Cameron Highlanders	27 September 1915	Loos (WW I)
16.	Cpl S. W. Ware	1st Bn Seaforth Highlanders	6 April 1916	Mesopotamia (WW I)
17.	Dmr W. Ritchie	2nd Bn Seaforth Highlanders	1 July 1916	Beaumont Hamel (WW I)
18.	Capt N. G. Chavasse	1/10 King's Liverpool (Scottish) Regiment	9 August 1916	Somme (WW I)
	Capt N. G. Chavasse	1/10 King's Liverpool (Scottish) Regiment (bar)	31 July/2 August 1917	Ypres (WW I)
19.	L/Sgt T. Steele	1st Bn Seaforth Highlanders	22 February 1917	Mesopotamia (WW I)
20.	Lt D. MacKintosh	2nd Bn Seaforth Highlanders	11 April 1917	Arras (WW I)
21.	Sgt A. E. Edwards	6th Bn Seaforth Highlanders	31 July 1917	Ypres (WW I)
22.	L/Cpl R. McBeath	5th Bn Seaforth Highlanders	20 November 1917	Cambrai (WW I)
23.	Sgt J. M. Meikle	4th Bn Seaforth Highlanders	20 July 1918	Marfaux (WW I)

ALLIED REGIMENTS

24.	Capt T. W. MacDowell	38th Ottawa Bn CEF	9-13 April 1917	Vimy Ridge (WW I)
25.	Lt R. Shankland	The Cameron Highlanders of Canada	26 October 1917	Ypres (WW I)
26.	Pte C. J. P. Nunney	38th Ottawa Bn CEF	1-2 September 1918	Drocourt Quéant (WW I)
27.	Pte E. A. Smith	Seaforth Highlanders of Canada	22 October 1944	Italy (WW II)

6. MEDALS

CAMPAIGN MEDALS AWARDED BEFORE THE ARMY REFORMS OF 1881

Medal	Bars	72nd Duke of Albany's Own Highlanders	78th Highlanders Ross-shire Buffs	79th Cameron Highlanders
Military General Service Medal 1793-1814	Egypt Maida Corunna Talavera Busaco Fuentes d'Onor Java Salamanca Pyrenees Nivelle Nive Toulouse		1806 (2nd/78th) 1811	1801 1809 1809 1810 1811 1812 1813 1813 1813 1814
Army of India Medal 1799-1826	Assaye Argaum Gawilghur		1803 1803 1803	
Waterloo Medal 1815				1815
South Africa Medal 1834-1853		1835		
Crimea War Medal 1854-1856	Alma Balaclava Sevastopol	1855		1854 1854 1854-55
Turkish Crimea Medal 1855		1855		1855
Indian General Service Medal 1854-1895	Persia North West Frontier		1856-57	1863, 1868
Indian Mutiny Medal 1857-1858	Defence of Lucknow Lucknow Central India	1858	1857 1857-58	1858
Ashantee War Medal 1873-1874	Coomassie			1874 (Draft of 79th) served with 42nd
2nd Afghan War Medal 1878-1880	Peiwar Kotal Charasiah Kabul Kandahar	1878 1879 1879 1880	1879-80	
Kabul to Kandahar Star 1880		1880		

CAMPAIGN MEDALS AWARDED TO REGULAR ARMY BATTALIONS SINCE 1881

Medal	Bars	1st Battalion Seaforth Highlanders (Amal. 1961)	2nd Battalion Seaforth Highlanders (Amal. 1947)	1st Battalion The Queen's Own Cameron Highlanders (Amal. 1961)	2nd Battalion The Queen's Own Cameron Highlanders (Re-raised 1897 Disbanded 1948)	1st Battalion Queen's Own Highlanders (Seaforth & Camerons) (Formed by Amal. 1961)
Egyptian Medal 1882-1889	Tel-el-Kebir	1882	1882 (2 Coys with 1st Bn)	1882		
	Nile 1884-1885			1884-85		
Khedives Egyptian Star 1882-1891		1882	1882 (2 Coys with 1st Bn)	1882-86		
Indian General Service Medal 1854-1895	Hazara 1888		1888			
	Hazara 1891		1891			
Indian General Service Medal 1895-1902	Relief of Chitral 1895		1895			
Queen's Sudan Medal 1896-1897		1898		1898		
Khedive's Sudan Medal 1896-1908	The Atbara	1898		1898		
	Khartoum	1898		1898		
Queen's South Africa Medal 1899-1902	Cape Colony		1899-1902	1900-1902		
	Paardeberg		1900			
	Orange Free State		1900-1902	1900-1902		
	Driefontein		1900			
	Transvaal		1900-1902	1900-1902		
	Johannesburg			1900		
	Diamond Hill			1900		
	Wittebergen		1900	1900		
	South Africa 1901**		1901	1901		
	South Africa 1902**		1902	1902		
King's South Africa Medal 1901-1902	South Africa 1901**		1901	1901		
	South Africa 1902**		1902	1902		
Indian General Service Medal 1908-1935	North West Frontier 1908		1908			
	North West Frontier 1930-31		1930-31			
1914 Star	5 Aug-22 Nov 1914	*1914	*1914	*1914		
1914-1915 Star		*1914-15	*1914-15	*1914-15	1914-15	
British War Medal 1914-1920		1914-18	1914-18	1914-18	1914-18	

CAMPAIGN MEDALS AWARDED TO REGULAR ARMY BATTALIONS SINCE 1881

Medal	Bars	1st Battalion Seaforth Highlanders (Amal. 1961)	2nd Battalion Seaforth Highlanders (Amal. 1947)	1st Battalion The Queen's Own Cameron Highlanders (Amal. 1961)	2nd Battalion The Queen's Own Cameron Highlanders (Re-raised 1897 Disbanded 1948)	1st Battalion Queen's Own Highlanders (Seaforth & Camerons) (Formed by Amal. 1961)
Victory Medal 1914-1918		1914-18	1914-18	1914-18	1914-18	
General Service Medal 1918-1962	Palestine	1936			1936	
	Malaya	1948-51				
	Arabian Peninsula			1957-58		
	Brunei					1962
1939-1945 Star		1939-45	1939-45	1939-45	1939-45	
Africa Star 1940-1943					1940-42	
	8th Army		1942-43			
Burma Star 1941-1945		1942-44		1944-45		
Italy Star 1943-1945			1943		1943-45	
France & Germany Star 1944-1945			1944-45			
Defence Medal 1939-1945		1939-45	1939-45	1939-45	1939-45	
War Medal 1939-45		1939-45	1939-45	1939-45	1939-45	
General Service Medal 1962-	Borneo					1962-63
	Northern Ireland					1971-

Note — Bars marked either ** or * were awarded to individuals depending on qualification.

CAMPAIGN AND WAR MEDALS AWARDED TO MILITIA, VOLUNTEER, TERRITORIAL FORCE (TF), TERRITORIAL ARMY (TA), SERVICE BATTALIONS

Medal	Bar	Seaforth Highlanders	The Queen's Own Cameron Highlanders
Queen's South Africa Medal 1899-1902	Cape Colony	3 Volunteer Companies served with 2nd Seaforth	Volunteer Company served with 1st Camerons
	Orange Free State	,,	,,
	Transvaal	,,	,,
	Wittebergen	,,	,,
	South Africa 1901	,,	,,
	South Africa 1902	,,	,,
Queen's Mediterranean Medal 1899-1902		3rd (Militia) Bn 1900-01	
1914 Star		4th Bn (TF)	1/10th Liverpool Scottish (TF)
1914-1915 Star		5th, 6th Bns (TF) 7th, 8th 9th Service Bns	4th Bn (TF), 5th, 6th, 7th Service Bns
British War Medal 1914-1920 and Victory Medal 1914-1918		3rd (Militia) Bn, 4th, 5th, 6th Bns (TF), 7th, 8th, 9th Service Bns, 10th (Reserve) Bn, 1st Garrison Bn	3rd (Militia) Bn, 4th, 10th (Lovat Scouts), 1/10th, 2/10th King's (Liverpool Scottish) Bns (TF), 5th, 6th, 7th, 8th, 9th, 11th Service Bns
1939-1945 Star		4th, 5th, 6th, 7th Bns (TA)	4th, 5th Bns, 4 Independent Coy Liverpool Scottish (TA)
Africa Star 1940-1942	8th Army	5th Bn (TA)	5th Bn (TA)
Italy Star 1943-1945		5th, 6th Bns (TA)	5th Bn (TA)
France & Germany Star 1944-1945		5th, 6th, 7th Bns (TA)	5th Bn (TA)
Defence Medal 1939-1945 and War Medal 1939-1945		4th, 5th, 6th, 7th Bns (TA), 8th, 9th Bns	4th, 5th Bns, 1st, 2nd Liverpool Scottish Bn (TA) 6th, 7th Bns

7.   *DESIGNATIONS OF THE REGIMENT*

The designations of the predecessors of the Queen's Own Highlanders varied over the years. The list given here shows the official designations as given in the Army List.

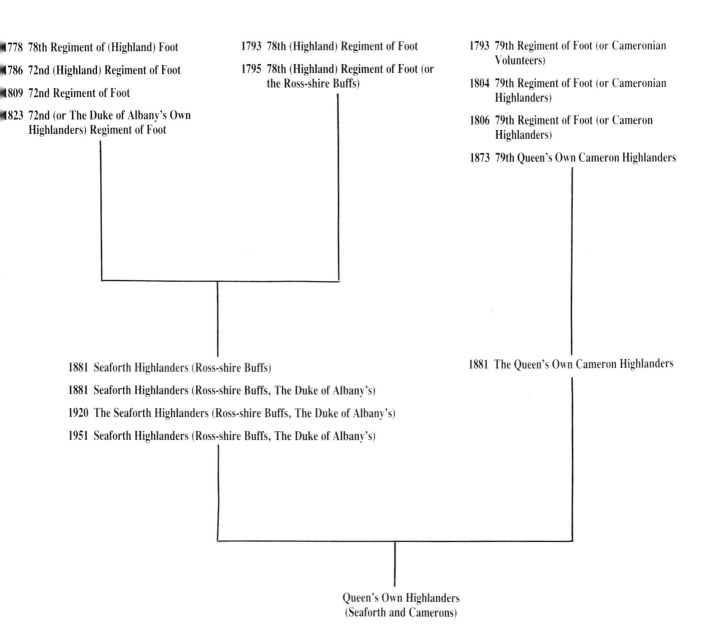

1778 78th Regiment of (Highland) Foot

1786 72nd (Highland) Regiment of Foot

1809 72nd Regiment of Foot

1823 72nd (or The Duke of Albany's Own Highlanders) Regiment of Foot

1793 78th (Highland) Regiment of Foot

1795 78th (Highland) Regiment of Foot (or the Ross-shire Buffs)

1793 79th Regiment of Foot (or Cameronian Volunteers)

1804 79th Regiment of Foot (or Cameronian Highlanders)

1806 79th Regiment of Foot (or Cameron Highlanders)

1873 79th Queen's Own Cameron Highlanders

1881 Seaforth Highlanders (Ross-shire Buffs)

1881 Seaforth Highlanders (Ross-shire Buffs, The Duke of Albany's)

1920 The Seaforth Highlanders (Ross-shire Buffs, The Duke of Albany's)

1951 Seaforth Highlanders (Ross-shire Buffs, The Duke of Albany's)

1881 The Queen's Own Cameron Highlanders

Queen's Own Highlanders
(Seaforth and Camerons)

v

8.   THE UNIFORM OF THE QUEEN'S OWN HIGHLANDERS

A selection of orders of dress in use by the Queen's Own Highlanders in 1976.

The Highland regiments, more than any other part of the British Army, have managed to preserve a distinctive form of uniform, and the Queen's Own Highlanders take particular pride in this inheritance. To anyone unfamiliar with the Scottish regiments, the variety of uniform badges and accoutrements is often bewildering. Yet the uniform, of the regiment, and the occasions on which it is worn, is methodically explained in Regimental Standing Orders, and they are only varied on the authority of the Colonel of the Regiment.

The notes in this book do not attempt to repeat Regimental Standing Orders: they are intended to explain something of the background to the uniform of the Queen's Own Highlanders and how it has evolved.

The story of the dress of the Highland regiments is one of over 200 years of gradual change, brought about by constant modifications and improvements in the dress and equipment of the army, and by the frequent retention of small features which are survivals of uniform long since obsolete and which, if recognized, are fascinating reminders of times past. In the story of the dress of the Queen's Own Highlanders there are two extra major upheavals: the amalgamation of the 72nd and the 78th in

1881 to form the Seaforth Highlanders; and the amalgamation of Seaforth and Camerons in 1961 to form the Queen's Own Highlanders. On each occasion the uniform went through radical change, but a surprising number of features managed to survive, albeit on a reduced scale.

These notes are therefore intended both to give a general idea of how each item of dress has developed, and also to attribute some of the distinctive features to their regimental ancestors.

For easy reference the notes on uniform have been arranged in the following order:

> Tartans
> Facings
> Badges and Insignia
> Kilt, trews, plaids
> Orders of dress
> Head-dress
> Belts
> Sporrans
> Legdress and Shoes
> Swords, dirks and accoutrements
> Pipe Banners

TARTANS OF THE REGIMENT

The Queen's Own Highlanders use two main tartans, the MacKenzie of Seaforth and the 79th or Cameron of Erracht. Both have been worn continuously, and without variation in design, since 1793. Because the dress of the Army has been closely controlled by the War Office Clothing Board, and in recent times by the Army Dress Committee, variations are only allowed when there are good reasons for them. And so, in contrast to the story of civilian tartans, which has become greatly distorted by romantic nonsense and by commercialisation, the history of military tartans is relatively easy to follow.

The MacKenzie of Seaforth Tartan

Evidence is scarce on the date when the Mackenzie of Seaforth tartan was introduced, because many of the records of the War Office Clothing Board have been lost, many being destroyed in a fire at the Tower of London in 1841. It is generally believed that the MacKenzie of Seaforth tartan was designed for the 78th Highlanders when they were raised by Lt Col Francis Humberston MacKenzie (later Lord Seaforth) in 1793. There is no firm evidence that it was used earlier, for example by the 72nd Highlanders when they were raised in 1778.

QUEEN'S OWN HIGHLANDERS
(SEAFORTH and CAMERONS)

Drummer
78th (Later 72nd) Highlanders
1778

Piper
79th or Cameronian Volunteers
1794

Officer
78th Highlanders
(Ross-shire Buffs)
1793

Officer
The Queen's Own
Cameron Highlanders
1900

Band Corporal
78th Highlanders (Ross-shire Buffs)
1859

Private
Seaforth Highlanders
1909

Sergeant
Queen's Own Highlanders
1978

Private
72nd Duke of Albany's
Own Highlanders
1825

Drum Major
79th Cameron Highlanders
1852

Officer
Queen's Own Highlanders
1978

Drummer
Queen's Own Highlanders
1978

Piper
Queen's Own Highlanders
1978

Douglas N. Anderson
78

When the Highland Regiments were first raised, the normal uniform was the Government or 42nd Black Watch tartan. But, as the Highland regiments proliferated, they sought to encourage their individual indentities by introducing differences into the Government tartan.

The MacKenzie tartan is a variation of the Government or Black Watch tartan, having two white stripes and one red stripe added to the sett. A similar tartan, but of a slightly different sett, was adopted at about the same period by the 71st Highlanders, who were also raised as a MacKenzie regiment. The reason for the choice of red and white stripes is not known, although it has been suggested that they may have come from the colours of the stockings which were made up of the traditional red and white hose tartan.

The MacKenzie of Seaforth tartan has been worn continuously in the regiment since 1793. It was also used by many of the Fencibles, Militia and Volunteer units raised in Ross-shire, and so it has been aptly termed the 'Ross-shire Military Tartan'. The civilian Clan MacKenzie tartan is derived from it.

The 79th or Cameron of Erracht Tartan

The 79th, or Cameron of Erracht tartan, is unique in being the only one of the old regimental tartans which is not derived from the Government or Black Watch tartan. It is generally believed that it was designed for the 79th by Mrs Marjory Cameron of Erracht, mother of Major Alan Cameron of Erracht who raised the regiment. She was born a MacLean of Drimnin, and there have been theories that she devised the 79th tartan by combining two or more clan tartans, such as the MacDonald, Cameron or MacLean. However it is generally accepted that there was no rigid system of clan tartans as such, in 1793, and that they evolved during the early 19th Century. It is therefore more likely that she used a design which was popular at the time in Lochaber, and which included the old pattern known as the 'MacDonald motif', a feature in common use among weavers in the West Highlands at the time but not confined to any clan or district. Indeed it is likely that the 79th tartan is many years older than the various Clan tartans of which it has been suggested to be a combination.

There are three Cameron tartans in civilian use: the Cameron of Lochiel tartan is used by Lochiel and his immediate family, and is known to date back to at least 1810; the Clan Cameron tartan, which is predominantly red, is of uncertain date of origin, and was not illustrated before 1842; and the Hunting Cameron was chosen in 1956, from an old sett illustrated in 1852, for use as a day or hunting tartan which would be less bright than the red Clan Cameron tartan.

The 79th tartan, which seems to be the oldest of all the Cameron tartans, has been worn continuously by the regiment since 1793, and still remains solely a regimental tartan.

OTHER TARTANS WHICH HAVE BEEN WORN BY THE REGIMENT

A number of other tartans have been used over the years by the Regular Army, Militia, Volunteer and Territorial elements of the Regiment, and so they too have their place in the regimental history.

The Government or 42nd Black Watch Tartan

When the Earl of Seaforth raised the 78th (later 72nd) Highlanders in 1778, the regiment was dressed in Government, 42nd or Black Watch Tartan. The Account books of the tartan manufacturers at the time refer to supplies of 'Black, blue and green tartan for the 72nd'. In 1809, together with six of the other Highland regiments, the 72nd was removed from the Highland establishment and ordered to adopt the uniform of a normal line regiment; and so it ceased then to wear the Highland dress and the Government tartan.

There is evidence that the drummers of the 72nd wore the Government tartan with a stripe of the regimental facing. If this was so, their tartan would have included a yellow stripe and would have been similar to the tartan of the 92nd Gordon Highlanders.

The Royal Stuart Tartan (Prince Charles Edward Sett)

In 1823 the 72nd were restored to the status of a Highland regiment as the 72nd Duke of Albany's Own Highlanders, and were authorised to wear the Highland dress, but with trews instead of the kilt. (Only the pipers wore the kilt). In deference to the Duke of York and Albany, brother of King George IV and Commander in Chief of HM Forces at the time, the 72nd was dressed in the Royal Stuart tartan. The sett used was the 'Prince Charles Edward' which, by tradition, was worn by Bonnie Prince Charlie at the Palace of Holyrood in Edinburgh during the Jacobite Rising of 1745. It is the same as the normal Royal Stuart, except that the red background is reduced in width.

The 72nd wore the trews of the Royal Stuart tartan from 1824 until 1881 when, under the Army Reforms, they were amalgamated with the 78th Highlanders and became a kilted regiment once again. Having originally been a MacKenzie regiment, it was natural that the amalgamated regiment should wear the kilt of MacKenzie of Seaforth tartan.

The Royal Stuart tartan of the old 72nd is still commemorated in the pipe ribbons carried by pipers of the Queen's Own Highlanders.

The Royal Stuart Tartan

The Royal Stuart tartan was in occasional use as a military tartan in the early days of the Highland regiments, and there is evidence that the 'band of music' of the 78th Highlanders wore it shortly after the regiment was raised in 1793.

The Royal Stuart tartan has come to be considered as the tartan of the Royal family, and the Sovereign has occasionally granted its use to a Scottish regiment as a personal honour. HM King George VI honoured The Queen's Own Cameron Highlanders in this way when, in 1943, he ordered that the pipers of the Camerons should be dressed in Royal Stuart tartan, to mark the 150th Anniversary of the raising of the 79th. The Royal Stuart tartan was discontinued in 1961 when, on the formation of the Queen's Own Highlanders, the pipers reverted to 79th tartan.

TARTANS OF THE MILITIA, FENCIBLES, VOLUNTEERS AND TERRITORIALS

Details of the uniform worn by the various militia, fencible, volunteer and territorial units of the regimental area are not complete, because many of the irregular regiments only existed for a few years. During the Napoleonic wars there were numerous fencible and local militia regiments, such as the Ross and Cromarty Rangers and the Glengarry Local Militia, raised for local defence or garrison duty.

There is evidence that in Ross-shire, the majority of the Militia and Volunteer regiments adopted the MacKenzie tartan if they were authorised to wear the kilt or trews, because it was considered the Ross-shire military tartan.

In Moray, the Carr Bridge Company of Volunteers wore the kilt of Grant tartan, but otherwise the Moray volunteers did not adopt Highland dress until after 1881 when they became part of the Seaforth Highlanders. They were authorised to wear MacKenzie trews in 1886.

In Inverness-shire the Volunteer companies wore a remarkable variety of uniforms, and their tartans included 79th or Cameron of Erracht, Black Watch, Celtic, MacPherson, Fraser, MacKintosh and MacDonald of the Isles. In 1880 they were all ordered to adopt Black Watch tartan, but because they became part of the Cameron Highlanders in 1881, they subsequently changed to 79th tartan.

The 76th Inverness (Highland Light Infantry) Militia wore the kilt of Hunting Fraser tartan from 1855 until the regiment became the 2nd (Militia) Bn of the Cameron Highlanders in 1881, when it adopted the 79th tartan.

In the recent history of the regiment two other tartans apart from the MacKenzie and the 79th, have been prominent: The Forbes and the Sutherland.

The Forbes Tartan
The first Commanding Officer appointed when the Liverpool Scottish were raised in 1900 was Lt Col Christopher Forbes-Bell. When Highland dress was authorised for the regiment on 16 April 1901, it adopted the kilt of Forbes tartan. It remains in use by 'V' (Liverpool Scottish) Company, 51st Highland Volunteers TA.

The Sutherland Tartan
The 5th (Caithness and Sutherland) Battalion Seaforth Highlanders, which originated in 1859 as the Sutherland Rifle Volunteers, retained the Sutherland tartan throughout its history until disbanded after World War II.

The Sutherland tartan is identical to the Government or Black Watch tartan, but the kilt is pleated to show the green, instead of the blue as in the Black Watch kilt.

FACINGS

The term 'facing' comes from the material used to 'face' or line a soldier's jacket. When the cuffs, lapels, shirts and collars of the jackets were turned back, the coloured facings would show. British infantry regiments all wore red jackets from the earliest days of the Standing Army in 1660, but each had its own colour of facing by which it could be identified.

As uniform and accoutrements developed, the facing colour came into wider use. It was used as the background for the Regimental Colour, for the Pipe banners, as a stripe in the sergeant's red sash, and sometimes in the dicing of the bonnets. The drummers normally wore jackets in the facing colour of the regiment.

The 78th (later 72nd) Highlanders had yellow facings from their raising in 1778. The buff facings of the 78th Highlanders led to the nickname from which they derived their secondary title of 'Ross-shire Buffs'. When the 72nd and the 78th were amalgamated in 1881 to form the Seaforth Highlanders, the new regiment took the yellow facings of the 72nd, as the senior partner. This conformed with the rule that, with the exception of Royal Regiments who were allowed blue facings, all Scottish regiments were

to have yellow facings. However, like all good rules, this was soon bent, and in 1899 the Seaforth Highlanders changed to the pre-1881 buff facings of the old 78th.

The 79th Cameron Highlanders had green facings from their raising in 1793 until they were granted the status of a Royal Regiment by Queen Victoria in 1873. Then, as the 79th Queen's Own Cameron Highlanders, they changed from green to blue facings.

On the amalgamation of Seaforth and Camerons in 1961 it was decided to perpetuate the facings and tartans of both regiments; and so the Queen's Own Highlanders are unique in the Army in having two tartans and two facing colours, Buff and Blue. Examples of present day uses of the facings colours of the Queen's Own Highlanders are the Regimental Colour which has a buff ground with blue fringe, the pipe banners which are buff on the obverse and blue on the reverse, the officers mess jackets which have buff lapels and blue collar and cuffs, the 'slashes' of the No 1 Dress jacket which are buff, the bugle cords of the drummers which are buff and blue, and the drums which are painted with a blue background.

BADGES AND INSIGNIA

The Badge of the Queen's Own Highlanders

The badge of the Queen's Own Highlanders is described as 'A Stag's Head caboshed, between the attires the Thistle ensigned with the Crown, with the motto Cuidich 'n Righ'.

The 'Thistle ensigned with the Imperial Crown' is the badge of Scotland as sanctioned by Queen Anne in 1707. It was granted to the 79th Cameron Highlanders on 10th July 1873 by Her Majesty Queen Victoria when she commanded that the 79th should in future be styled as the '79th Queen's Own Cameron Highlanders'.

The Stag's Head 'caboshed' (a heraldic term meaning cut off to show no part of the neck) comes from the Arms of MacKenzie of Seaforth. There are two possible explanations of the Arms and of the motto 'Cuidich 'n Righ'.

Tradition has it that King Alexander III of Scotland, while hunting in the Forest of Mar, was charged and unhorsed by an angry stag; and that Colin Fitzgerald, ancestor of the MacKenzies of Seaforth, saved the King's life by killing the stag, shouting as he did so 'Cuidich 'n Righ' (Help the King').

A more empiric, but possibly less romantic, explanation is that the arms and motto come from the annual reddendo, or Feudal tribute, of a stag, which the MacKenzies of Seaforth were required to deliver to the Sovereign each year as payment for their lands in Kintail; the motto, in this feudal sense, meaning 'Tribute to the King'.

Both the 72nd and the 78th were raised by the MacKenzies of Seaforth, and both used the 'Stag's Head caboshed' on their badges and appointments. In the 72nd the Stag's Head was used with the motto 'Caber Feidh' (Gaelic for 'Deers Antlers'), which is one of the historic Gaelic titles for the Chief of Clan MacKenzie. In the 78th Highlanders the motto 'Cuidich 'n Righ' was used on the Colours and appointments of the regiment from its formation in 1793. At the request of the 78th, the old spelling of 'Rhi' was officially altered to 'Righ' in April 1869 by an order issued from the War Office.

The Stag's Head and motto 'Cuidich 'n Righ' have been used by the Queen's Own Highlanders since the regiment was formed in 1961. The Queen's Own Highlanders are the only regiment to have a Gaelic motto.

Bonnet Badges

The regimental badge is worn in the Glengarry, the Balmoral bonnet and the feather bonnet. The badge is made in two forms: Officers, Warrant Officers and Sergeants wear a silver or silver plated, three dimensional badge, comprising three separate pieces, the Stag's Head, the Thistle ensigned with the Crown, and the motto 'Cuidich 'n Righ' on a scroll; Rank and File of the regiment wear a flat anodised badge.

Since the earliest days of the regiment, it has been a privilege of the sergeants mess to adopt certain variations of dress to distinguish them from the Rank and File. The privilege of wearing the same bonnet badge as that of the officers is an example of this tradition.

A woven version of the regimental badge, in black thread on a green background, was worn on the front of the jungle hat when the 1st Battalion served in the Far East in 1980-82.

The Queen's Own Highlanders, in common with other regiments, wore the Highland Brigade badge from 1961 until 1970 when regimental bonnet badges were reintroduced. The 51st Highland Volunteers TA continue to wear the Highland Brigade bonnet badge.

From 1961 to 1970 the pipers of the Queen's Own Highlanders wore a different bonnet badge. It was discontinued when the regimental bonnet badge was introduced in 1970.

Collar Badge

The Collar badge worn with No. 1 Dress, or with tropical No. 3 Dress, is the Elephant superscribed with the Battle Honour 'Assaye'. This badge commemorates the service of the 78th Highlanders (Ross-shire Buffs) at the battle of Assaye in 1803, when Major General The Hon Arthur Wellesley's force defeated the Mahratta Army. The same design of badge is worn by all ranks except the Pipe Major, who wears the brass badge worn by Pipe Majors of the Seaforth Highlanders before 1961.

Cross Belt Plate

The plate worn on the white buff cross belt (or shoulder belt) is of turned brass with the regimental badge in silver mounted on it. It is worn in No. 1 Dress or with tropical No. 3 Dress. It is worn by Officers and also by the Regimental Sergeant Major and the Bandmaster.

Shoulder Titles

The shoulder title is made of brass and has the inscription 'QO HIGHLANDERS'. In combat uniform a slip-on shoulder title with the same lettering is worn, the letters being woven in black thread on green cloth. The same pattern of shoulder title is worn by all ranks of the regiment.

Waistbelt Plate

The Waistbelt plate is the former bonnet badge of The Queen's Own Cameron Highlanders, introduced in 1841. The figure of St Andrew and his Cross comes from the badge of The Order of the Thistle. Instead of the word 'CAMERON', which was inscribed on the scroll of the bonnet badge of the Cameron Highlanders, the Battle Honour 'WATERLOO' is substituted, commemorating the service of the 79th Cameron Highlanders at the Battle of Waterloo in 1815.

The waistbelt plate has a white metal badge on a brass background. It can be worn with a white or green belt according to the order of dress.

Pipers wear a different pattern of waistbelt plate.

Sporran Badges

The badge worn on the leather sporran, and on the hair sporran worn by soldiers, is the Thistle ensigned with the Crown.

The hair sporran worn by officers, the RSM, Bandmaster, and the Drum Major, has a brass top engraved with thistles modelled on the officer's sporran of the Seaforth Highlanders. It is embellished with the regimental badge, and also the Cypher of HRH Prince Philip, Duke of Edinburgh, Colonel in Chief of the Queen's Own Highlanders.

Top Row: Sporran badge worn by all ranks Officers. Warrant Officers and Sergeants bonnet badge.Collar badges worn by all ranks. 2nd Row: Officers Cairngorm mess waistcoat button. Large and small Regimental buttons worn by all ranks. Brass shoulder title worn by all ranks. 3rd Row: Officers Dirk belt and No. 1 Dress waistbelt buckle. Rank and File bonnet badge. Waistbelt buckle worn by all ranks. 4th Row: Officers kilt pin. 5th Row: Officers shoulder (or cross) belt plate. Highland Brigade bonnet badge worn from 1961-1970. Plaid brooch worn by pipers and bandsmen.

Badges and Insignia worn by pipers of Queen's Own Highlanders since 1961. Top Row: Rank and File bonnet badge. Duke of Albany's Star worn on cross belt. Pipers bonnet badge worn 1961-1970. 2nd Row: Shoulder title. Pipers crossbelt buckle. Sporran badge. 3rd Row: Collar badges. Cameron badge worn on crossbelt. Large and small regimental buttons. 4th Row: Pipers Plaid brooch. Slide and tip of pipers crossbelt. Pipers waistbelt buckle (introduced 1974).

Pipers Cross Belt fittings

Pipers wear a black cross belt (or shoulder belt) with white metal fittings. At the top is the Duke of Albany's Star which was worn by the pipers of the 72nd Duke of Albany's Own Highlanders and their successors 1st Bn Seaforth Highlanders. Below the buckle is the badge of The Queen's Own Cameron Highlanders (less the Sphinx).

The Pipe Major of the 1st Battalion wears the fittings worn by the Pipe Major of 1st Bn The Queen's Own Cameron Highlanders, with the addition of a Seaforth Highlanders officer's plaid brooch on which the Cypher of Prince Leopold, Duke of Albany, has been replaced by the Thistle and Crown of Scotland.

Buttons

The buttons of the Queen's Own Highlanders have the Stag's Head and the Thistle and Crown of the Regimental badge, but the scroll is omitted. The reason for this is that, at the time of the amalgamation of Seaforth and Camerons, the process of producing buttons for the new regiment had to be started in time for them to be ready for the new regiment to wear on amalgamation day, 7th February 1961. The proposed design for the regimental badge did not at first include the scroll, and the decision to include the scroll was taken after the die for the buttons had been made.

Plaid Brooch

The plaid brooch is worn by Pipers and Bandsmen of the Queen's Own Highlanders. It has a brass background with white metal ornaments. At the top is the Cypher and Ducal Coronet of Prince Frederick, Duke of York and Albany from whom the 72nd Duke of Albany's Own Highlander took their title from 1823-1881. The 72nd became the 1st Battalion Seaforth Highlanders in 1881.

At the foot of the plaid brooch is the Sphinx which was the first (although not the earliest) battle honour to be granted to the 79th Cameron Highlanders, and commemorates their part in the defeat of Napoleon's Army in Egypt in 1801. The Sphinx formed part of the regimental badge of The Queen's Own Cameron Highlanders.

In the centre of the plaid brooch is a bar with the Battle Honour ALAMEIN, commemorating the part played by both regiments at the historic victory of El Alamein in 1942 where the 2nd and 5th Battalions Seaforth Highlanders and the 5th Battalion The Queen's Own Cameron Highlanders, fought side by side as 152 Highland Infantry Brigade in the 51st Highland Division.

The wreath of oak leaves comes from the badge of Clan Cameron, and was included in the designs of the pipe banners and various accoutrements worn by the Cameron Highlanders.

The Pipe Major of the 1st Battalion Queen's Own Highlanders wears an officers plaid brooch of the Seaforth Highlanders with the Thistle and Crown added to replace the Cypher of Prince Leopold Duke of Albany. The Drum Major wears an officers plaid brooch of The Queen's Own Cameron Highlanders.

Piper Majors Plaid brooch, Queen's Own Highlanders.

Piper Majors waistbelt plate, Queen's Own Highlanders.

KILT, TREWS, PLAID

The Kilt

Although the Highland regiments have worn the kilt since the days of their origin in the 18th Century, there has always been pressure from the War Office to abolish the kilt as being unsuitable for wear in battle, and also because tartan is considered difficult to supply.

The 78th (later 72nd) Highlanders were originally raised as a kilted regiment, but in 1809, together with the 71st, 73rd, 74th, 75th and 91st Highlanders, they were removed from the Highland establishment. They did not become kilted again until 1881 when they became the 1st Bn Seaforth Highlanders.

The 78th Highlanders (Ross-shire Buffs) and the 79th Cameron Highlanders, together with the 42nd, 92nd and 93rd Highlanders, were the only Highland regiments which retained the kilt throughout their history down to the 20th Century. Thus the Queen's Own Highlanders can claim to have worn the kilt since 1778, and continuously since 1793.

Officers and soldiers of the Queen's Own Highlanders wear the kilt of MacKenzie of Seaforth tartan, while Pipers, Drummers and Bandsmen wear the kilt of the 79th or Cameron of Erracht tartan.

Trews

Tartan trews (from the Gaelic 'triubhas') were first authorised for use in undress uniform (i.e. when not in Full Dress) by kilted regiments in 1830. Since then they have always been treated as a convenient and comfortable form of barrack dress, but never as a substitute for the principal dress of the regiment which is the kilt.

The Queen's Own Highlanders wear tartan trews for barrack duties, and in the evening after Retreat. Officers and soldiers wear trews of the 79th or Cameron of Erracht tartan, while Pipers, Drummers and Bandsmen wear trews of MacKenzie of Seaforth tartan; thus reversing the tartans worn as the kilt.

Plaids
The Belted Plaid

When the Highland regiments were first raised in the 18th Century, they wore the 'breacan-an-fheilidh' (Gaelic for 'belted plaid'), which combined kilt and plaid in one piece of tartan. By 1800 they had adopted the little kilt or philibeg (Gaelic — fheilidh beag) which was similar to the kilt as we know it today, although more roughly stitched together. The officers continued to wear the top of the old 'breacan-an-fheilidh' even when wearing breeches or trousers, and the soldiers wore a small 'fly' plaid fixed by a loop at the left shoulder. (The term 'fly' plaid is either a corrupted form of the Gaelic 'fheilidh' or refers to the way the small plaid flies loose at the lower end). The term 'belted plaid' thus acquired a new meaning: that of the plaid worn separately from the kilt.

The belted plaid is still worn as a fly plaid by the drummers of the Queen's Own Highlanders, and as an officer's belted plaid by the Bandmaster. They are of 79th or Cameron of Erracht tartan.

The Full Plaid (or Scarf, Big Plaid, Cross Plaid)

About 1830 the field officers (i.e. the Colonel, Majors, Adjutant) of Highland regiments started to wear a shoulder plaid or 'scarf'. It was worn over the left shoulder and across the chest, being fixed with a plaid brooch. By 1841 it was often worn by all officers instead of the belted plaid, and it later became part of Levee Dress.

Since the 1840s the pipers and bandsmen have also worn the full plaid. At first it was worn with the tartan folded on the cross, but later it was worn pleated as it is today. The Pipers and Bandsmen of the Queen's Own Highlanders wear the Full Plaid of 79th or Cameron of Erracht tartan.

JACKETS, JERSEYS, SHIRTS

Since the Highland regiments originated in the late 18th Century a wide variety of jackets have been worn. They have included coatees, doublets, waistcoats, frock coats, tunics, shell jackets, patrol jackets and many others. The variety still exists today, but it is in fact controlled, more rigidly than may at times be apparent, by the dress regulations of the regiment which define nine 'Orders of Dress', each governed by a particular type of jacket and shirt.

These orders of dress apply only to the regiment (Army Clothing Regulations, in fact, list fourteen 'Orders of Dress'), and so it should not be assumed that No. 8 Dress, for example, means tropical mess kit when worn by another regiment.

No. 1 Dress (Piper Green Jacket)

The custom of dressing the regimental pipers in green doublets was introduced by Lt Col The Hon Lauderdale Maule while commanding the 79th Cameron Highlanders in 1841. The colour came from the green facings of the 79th at the time. This distinctive uniform for pipers was soon adopted by most other Highland regiments; hence the term 'Piper Green'.

Piper Green jackets remained the exclusive wear of the pipers until in 1952 the Highland regiments were issued with the No. 1 Dress Coatee, of Piper Green, for ceremonial use by all ranks. The coatees were fitted with regimental buttons and 'slashes' in the regimental facing colour.

A modified pattern of the green No. 1 Dress doublet, for wear by Highland and Lowland regiments of the Scottish Division, was introduced in 1981. It is a compromise between the piper green coatee of the Highlander and the blue doublet of the Lowland regiments. It has the Inverness flaps of the old Highland Full Dress doublet, and its colour is termed, rather incongruously, 'Archer Green'.

The Queen's Own Highlanders wear the No. 1 Dress jacket with the regimental collar badge of the Elephant superscribed 'Assaye', with buff 'slashes', and with badges of rank in gold on a blue backing. Officers wear gold braid shoulder cords.

Captain N. G. Smith in No. 1 Dress, 1974.

Piper Major I. M. Morrison in No. 1 Dress, 1976.

Band Lance Corporal Burt in No. 1 Dress, 1976.

Cpl B. Christie in No. 1 Dress, 1979.

Pipe Lance Corporal P. Fraser in No. 2A Dress, 1976.

Lieutenant Lord Balgonie in No. 2B Dress, 1976.

Colour Sergeant R. Craib in No. 2A Dress, 1976.

Captain N. G. Smith in No. 2C Dress (Jersey), 1976.

X

Sgt A. Duffus, RSM D Duffus and CSM J. Duffus in No. 2C Dress, 1979.

No. 2 Dress (Khaki Service Dress)

Khaki (from the Hindustani word for 'dusty') was first used in India by the Corps of Guides in 1846. During the Indian Mutiny Campaign of 1857, most regiments were issued with white twill jackets which they stained or dyed to khaki, (although it is said that the 78th stuck firmly to their red woollen doublets). Khaki Drill jackets were worn by the Seaforth and Camerons during active service abroad in campaigns such as those in Chitral, Sudan and South Africa.

In 1902 Khaki Service Dress was introduced as the normal working dress of the British Army in peace and war. From after World War I it was used for both training and ceremonial, the red full dress having been discontinued in 1914. In 1938-39 Khaki Battle Dress replaced Service Dress as the fighting uniform of the Army, and after the Second World War it remained in use as the normal working dress of the Army. In 1961 the clock was turned back when khaki No. 2 Dress, modelled closely on the old Service Dress, was issued to replace Battle Dress. Unlike the 1902 design, it is worn with a shirt, collar and tie. The regiments of the Scottish Division wear a pattern cut away in front so that it can be worn either with kilt and sporran or with trews.

No. 2 Dress (Jersey)

The evolution of the Jersey is perhaps typical of the Army's insatiable instinct to modify and embellish its clothing. The Khaki Heavy Wool Jersey was introduced during the Korean War of 1951-53 for wear in the intense cold of the Korean winter. It was worn in combat dress. When battledress was replaced in the early 1960s by No. 2 or Khaki Service Dress for barrack and parade use, the jersey became a popular alternative uniform for normal barrack wear, being much more comfortable than a jacket. Inevitably regiments introduced their own distinctive patterns of jersey, and almost every colour imaginable was in use in the British Army by the 1970s.

The Queen's Own Highlanders wear a jersey in the facings colours of the regiment. It is dark blue and officers wear badges of rank on buff epaulettes. It can be worn with the kilt or trews as an alternative form of No. 2 Dress, and is worn with shirt, collar and tie.

No. 3 Dress (White Tropical Jacket)

When serving in tropical stations, the No. 1 Dress Green jacket is replaced by a white tropical jacket for ceremonial occasions. It can be worn with the kilt or trews.

The Queen's Own Highlanders have worn No. 3 Dress white tropical uniform while serving in Singapore and Hong Kong. It was also issued to Pipers, Drummers and Bandsmen when the battalion served in Sharjah and Belize.

Drum Corporal M. Monaghan in No. 3 Dress, 1980.

No. 4 Dress (Khaki Drill Jacket)

The khaki drill jacket was worn by the Seaforth and Camerons on active service during the Colonial Wars of the 19th Century, and was worn in overseas stations such as India, Sudan and North Africa while the British Army still served there. With the end of the overseas garrisons khaki drill is seldom used nowadays, but it remains an authorised order of dress which is occasionally worn, for example by individual officers serving as Military Attaches in hot climates. The jacket can be made of Gaberdine material.

Piper Major N. Gordon in No. 3 Dress, 1980.

Drum Major J. Finnie in No. 3 Dress, 1980.

L/Cpl A. Stewart, Pte K. Scott, Pte R. Henderson, Pte D. Wilson, L/Cpl G. Bonnyman, Pte K. Valentine, in No. 3 and No. 4 Dress in South Korea, 1980.

Lance Corporal Boyes in No. 5 Dress in Northern Ireland, 1979.

Sergeant D. MacLeod in No. 5 Dress in Hong Kong, 1980.

CSM J. Duffus in No. 6 Dress, 1980.

Lieutenant J. N. W. McHardy in No. 6 Dress 1980.

Captain N. F. M. Lamb in No. 7A Dress, 1976

Colour Sergeant G. Brown in No. 7B Dress, 1976.

Sergeant R. Towns in No. 7A Dress, 1976.

Sgt J. Peddie in No. 8 Dress, 1969.

No. 5 Dress (Combat Uniform)

Combat dress, the uniform which the Army uses for training and operations, is modified frequently as a result of research and development. It has to meet the often conflicting requirements of camouflage, comfort, climate, protection and other factors of modern warfare.

Although combat dress tends deliberately to obscure regimental identity, Esprit de Corps demands that an element of individuality is preserved under nearly all circumstances. The Queen's Own Highlanders are fortunate in that the distinctive badge and Royal Blue hackle, worn in the Balmoral bonnet, serve the purpose for which they were intended: to make a member of the Regiment in combat dress clearly recognisable as a Queen's Own Highlander from a distance.

No. 6 Dress (Tropical Shirt)

In tropical climates the standard army issue shirt, which varies according to the pattern in use at the time, is worn with the kilt, shorts or slacks and is termed No. 6 Dress. The 1st Battalion normally produce local dress regulations to define the details of dress and the occasions when it is worn.

No. 7 Dress (Scarlet Mess Jacket)

Since the establishment of the Standing Army in 1660 the traditional colour of the jackets of the British infantry has been red. Full Dress uniform, which for Highland regiments included the feather bonnet and red doublet, was abolished in 1914, but the traditional red still survive in the mess dress jackets worn by Officers, Warran Officers and Sergeants.

The Mess Dress jacket evolved from the red shell jacke which was introduced in about 1830 for wear with undres uniform. It had a high collar and was buttoned up the from to the neck. During the 1850s, to make a more comfortabl uniform to wear when dining in mess, it was worn with th collar turned down, with the front unbuttoned, and with waistcoat of tartan or of the regimental facings colour.

The officers mess jacket of the Queen's Ow Highlanders is scarlet, and has buff lapels, blue collar anc cuffs, white piping, and gold braid shoulder cords Miniature medals are worn with mess dress. The waistcoa is of the 79th or Cameron of Erracht tartan, and has three Cairngorm buttons which were worn by the Seaforth Highlanders on the mess waistcoat.

The Warrant officers and Sergeants pattern of mess jacket is similar, except that the lapels, collar and cuffs are all buff, and no white piping is worn. The waistcoat is of the 79th or Cameron of Erracht tartan with three brass regimental buttons. Warrant Officers and Sergeants of the Pipes, Drums and Regimental Band wear a waistcoat o MacKenzie tartan.

The mess jacket and waistcoat is worn with the kilt o trews.

No. 8 Dress (White Tropical Mess Jacket)

In tropical climates the red mess jacket is replaced by a white tropical mess jacket.

Private S. Griffiths in No. 9 Dress, 1980.

Pioneer Sgt K. Hunter in No. 9 Dress, 1980.

No. 9 Dress (Fatigue or Working dress)

No. 9 Dress tends to vary according to local conditions and may include Khaki flannel shirt, overalls, denims, or protective clothing used when working on vehicles. The special clothing worn by cooks and butchers comes under this order of dress.

Other Orders of Dress

A number of other types of dress are used which are not covered by the numbered Orders of Dress. Examples are:

Full Dress. Although Full dress is officially obsolete, the drummers of the regiment wear the red doublet on regimental occasions. The doublets are maintained at regimental expense. They have regimental buttons, blue collar and cuffs, and are worn with drummers 'wings' on the shoulders.

Mess Orderlies Uniform. The officers mess steward wears a green tail coat with buff and blue striped waistcoat on formal occasions. Orderlies in the officers and sergeant's messes normally wear a green coatee and cummerbund, with trews. The style varies from time to time.

Officers Mess Orderly, 1976.

HEAD DRESS

The Glengarry

The Glengarry takes its name from the shape of bonnet worn by Alasdair MacDonell of Glengarry and his 'tail' of clansmen, who attended King George IV on his visit to Edinburgh in 1822. The normal bonnet of the Highlander was the flat blue bonnet, and Glengarry, to make his men more distinctive, dressed them in bonnets of an upright shape.

It is believed that the Glengarry bonnet was first introduced to the British Army by Lt Col The Hon Lauderdale Maule while acting as Commanding Officer of the 79th Cameron Highlanders in 1840, and so the Queen's Own Highlanders can claim to have worn the Glengarry longer than any other regiment. It was a practical and popular form of bonnet which soon replaced the round bonnet for undress wear in the Highland regiments, and by the 1870s was even worn by all the Lowland, English and Welsh line regiments. A wide variety of dicing and ribbon was used to mark individual regimental patterns.

The Queen's Own Highlanders wear the plain blue Glengarry with black ribbons worn by the Cameron Highlanders since 1840. It has the black silk rosette which was worn on the diced pattern of Glengarry worn by the Seaforth Highlanders. The regimental badge and the Royal Blue hackle are worn with the Glengarry. Pipers wear a Golden Eagle's feather in ceremonial dress.

The Feather Bonnet

The feather bonnet is by far the oldest form of hat worn by the Queen's Own Highlanders. It is worn in No 1 dress by Drummers and Bandsmen. The feather bonnet has red, white and blue dicing, black ribbons, a black cockade behind the badge, a white hackle and five foxtails of ostrich feathers.

The feather bonnet originated as the flat blue bonnet of the Highlands, which was then 'cocked', or shaped to make the sides stand up in a more military style. It had a strip of ribbon woven in and out for tightening it. The term 'Hummel' or humble bonnet, as it was known, derives from the word for a stag without antlers; hence the bonnet without feathers.

By the end of the 18th Century the ribbon for tightening had become purely decorative, but was retained as an ornament in the form of the dicing round the bonnet. The bonnet could still be tightened by the black tapes at the 'V' shaped slit in the rim.

It soon became the custom to embellish the bonnet with fur, cloth, or ostrich feathers fitted behind the cockade. This was partly the result of the military instinct for decorative uniforms, but it also helped to make the British soldier look taller and more impressive in the eyes of the enemy. The bonnet was issued flat and unadorned, and each company had its own 'bonnet cocker' who set up the feathered bonnet at the soldier's expense. This transformed the 'Hummel' bonnet to a 'feathered' bonnet.

The bonnet was worn cocked to the right, with a regimental button on a black silk cockade. (The black cockade was worn by the Hanoverian Army as a distinguishing mark from the white cockade of the Jacobites).

After the Napoleonic wars the bonnet was given even more and bigger feathers, until it became the unwieldy object which it is today. It presented a magnificent spectacle on a ceremonial parade, but was wholly impractical for wear on active service, even by the standards of the mid 19th Century. The Full Dress of scarlet doublet and feather bonnet was worn in Review

Order until 1914, but after the Great War it was only worn by drummers and bandsmen.

During the 20th Century, the enormous spread of pipe bands, beyond the Scottish regiments where they originated, has resulted in the feather bonnet becoming a most popular Scottish national headdress, rather than just the bonnet of the Highland infantry soldier.

The Balmoral Bonnet (or 'Tam O' Shanter')

When the Highland regiments went to war in 1914 they wore the Glengarry, but it was found to be so impractical for trench warfare that the Highlanders generally took to wearing a Balaclava or a cap comforter instead. In 1915 a flat Highland bonnet was introduced to replace the Glengarry. At first there was a wide variety of styles: there were dark green, blue, and khaki bonnets; some had ribbons, some had toories and some did not; some were even worn with a cloth cover. The term 'Tam O' Shanter' seems to have been a War Office misnomer for the older term 'Balmoral', and the two are synonymous. The Balmoral was generally worn with a regimental badge and sometimes with a tartan patch.

In its early form the Balmoral was a wide-brimmed, practical, hat, which kept sun and rain out of the eyes when firing a rifle. But over the years it has suffered the inevitable changes of style that are an inherent part of military usage, and its width has been reduced to about half its original size.

The Queen's Own Highlanders wear the khaki Balmoral bonnet with a square of 79th or Cameron of Erracht tartan, the regimental badge and the Royal Blue hackle. The badge and hackle can be removed on training or operations, if demanded by camouflage or anonymity of regiment.

Hackles

The hackle (or 'Vulture's feather' as it was termed) worn in the feather bonnet, was originally an aid to identification in battle. When the regiment was drawn up in line, the Grenadier Company on the right of the line could be identified by their plain white hackles. On the left of the line was the Light Infantry Company, the scouts of the regiment, whose hackles were green, the colour derived from the green camouflaged uniforms worn by the Light Infantry in the wars in North America. The eight battalion companies in the centre of the line wore hackles of red and white. In 1860-63 the light companies were abolished, and all companies were ordered to wear the white hackle.

True to form there were regimental variations of these rules. In the 72nd the pipers wore a red hackle from 1823, although a War Office letter of 1822 had specifically ordered that the red Vulture's feather was only to be worn by the 42nd Highlanders. They were worn until the pipers took to wearing the Glengarry in 1855. In the 78th the pipers wore the feather bonnet with a green hackle until 1871, when the Glengarry was adopted.

Tropical helmets were introduced for wear in hot climates in the 1870s, and a small version of the hackle was often worn with them. In the Seaforth Highlanders the pipers wore green hackles in their tropical helmets until World War II, and the drummers and bandsmen wore red hackles until 1951.

The Royal Blue Hackle

After the British Expeditionary Force had gone to France in 1939, the War Office ordered that 'the active service dress of Highland regiments would be the universal battle dress'. This order, which was in effect to abolish the kilt as the uniform of the Highland soldier in battle, caused much resentment in the Highland regiments. A similar order in 1914 had been successfully rescinded the same year, after a storm of Highland protest.

The Commanding Officer of the 1st Battalion The Queen's Own Cameron Highlanders, Lt Col D. N. Wimberley MC, (later Major General D. N. Wimberley Colonel of the Regiment) appealed against the order in the strongest terms but, knowing that it takes time to alter War Office decisions, was determined that, kilted or not, the Cameron Highlanders should be distinctively dressed. He had patches of 79th tartan sewn on the sleeves of the battledress jackets, and considered that the white hackle as worn in the tropical helmet, would make the Balmoral bonnet more distinctive.

On 5th December 1939 HM King George VI visited the British Expeditionary Force in the field, and the 1st Camerons paraded for their Colonel in Chief on the Belgian border. The battalion, still dressed in Service Dress and the kilt, earned the congratulations of the Corps Commander as the best turned out unit of the Army Corps and the King, as he was escorted round the ranks by Colonel Wimberley, was notably impressed. The Commanding Officer seized his opportunity to suggest to His Majesty that, if the regiment was not to be allowed to retain the kilt, it should at least be allowed to wear a hackle behind the badge in the Balmoral bonnet. The King agreed to the idea, and also to the suggestion that Royal Blue would be the most appropriate colour. 800 Royal Blue hackles were quickly made, and were first worn at Arras on 11th February 1940.

After the 1st Camerons had withdrawn through Dunkirk (still dressed in the kilt: they were the last battalion to wear it in action), the Royal Blue hackle had to be discontinued until it could be officially approved by the War Office. It was resumed again in 1951 for use with the Balmoral bonnet.

The Queen's Own Highlanders wear the Royal Blue hackle in the Glengarry and the Balmoral bonnet. It is slightly smaller than the Camerons hackle because it has to fit the Glengarry. It is a proud reminder of the last regiment to wear the kilt in action against the enemy.

Eagle's Feather

The Golden Eagle's feather was introduced for wear by the pipers of the regiment by Lt Col The Hon Lauderdale Maule in about 1841, while he was in command of the 79th Cameron Highlanders. Contemporary paintings show the pipers wearing two eagle feathers.

The pipers of the Queen's Own Highlanders wear the eagle's feather in the Glengarry in ceremonial dress. The feather comes from the right wing of the Golden Eagle. On some occasions it has been the practice to allow the Pipe Major, when playing in Mess, to follow the original custom of wearing two eagle feathers in his Glengarry.

BELTS

The Cross Belt (or Sword belt, Shoulder belt)

In the early days of the regiment the sword was carried in a variety of ways. Field officers used a sabre carried on a waistbelt with slings; flank company officers carried the broadsword on a shoulder belt with slings; and battalion company officers, sergeants, pipers, drummers and bandsmen the broadsword in a buff shoulder belt which had a sword frog at the back.

All three patterns still survive in the No. 1 Dress of the Queen's Own Highlanders. Officers, the RSM, and the Bandmaster carry the broadsword with the white buff crossbelt (or shoulder belt) with two slings. The Drum Major carries the broadsword from a waistbelt with two slings. The black cross belts of the pipers still have the sword frog at the side (although the pipers no longer carry the broadsword).

The 'Sam Browne' Belt

The 'Sam Browne' belt takes its name from its inventor General Sir Sam Browne VC (1824-1901). While serving as an officer of the Indian Cavalry in the Indian Mutiny campaign in 1858 he won the Victoria Cross for his gallantry in charging and capturing a nine pounder rebel cannon, accompanied only by his orderly. He captured the cannon but lost his left arm, severed at the shoulder by one of the rebel gunners.

He recovered to take part in further active service on the frontier and found that, while he could still handle his sword and revolver effectively, it was difficult to secure them when not in use. (The sword was carried suspended from sword slings at the time). In about 1860 he invented the leather belt with shoulder brace, sword frog and holster, to carry sword and revolver more conveniently.

The belt soon became popular for use on active service, and officers had them made by saddlers. There were many variations in style at first, with pouches, holsters, braces, whistles and buckles arranged to suit individual taste. The officers of the 72nd and 78th first wore the 'Sam Browne' with khaki drill jackets in the Afghanistan campaign 1878-80. The officers of the 1st Camerons first had Sam Browne belts made by the saddler in Gibraltar in 1882 before leaving for the Egyptian campaign.

Although a standard pattern of Sam Browne belt was authorised for officers in Army Dress Regulations of 1900, regiments tended to wear their own patterns. The 'Sam Browne' belt is not well suited for carrying the Highland broadsword and so the basket hilt of the sword was often replaced by the cross hilt. The Seaforth Highlanders generally preferred a pattern of Sam Browne with a slightly wider cross strap and heavier sword frog, because it was better suited to the broadsword. The same pattern is worn by the Household Cavalry.

The officers of the Queen's Own Highlanders wear the 'Household Cavalry' pattern of Sam Browne when in No. 2 Service Dress, with the broadsword carried in a leather scabbard.

White Waistbelt

A white waistbelt, with regimental belt plate, is worn with No. 1 or No. 2 Dress when on parade, or as ordered.

Green Waistbelt

A green waistbelt, with regimental belt plate, is used for daily wear in barracks with No. 2 Service Dress jacket, or as ordered.

Tartan Waistbelt

Tartan waistbelts, made under regimental arrangements, are worn with shorts or slacks in some orders of dress at home and in tropical stations. The tartan corresponds to the kilt, and so pipers, drummers and bandsmen wear 79th or Cameron of Erracht tartan belts, while the remainder of the regiment wear MacKenzie of Seaforth tartan.

Black Waistbelt

The black waistbelt was originally part of the distinctive uniform worn by the regimental bandsmen. It was intended to contrast with the white jacket which became universal wear for bandsmen in about 1830. From the early 1840s the pipers were also given distinctive uniform and they too wore black waistbelts.

The pipers and bandsmen of the Queen's Own Highlanders still wear the black waistbelt today. The Pipers have worn a square, ornate belt plate since 1973, and the bandsmen wear the normal regimental waistbelt plate.

SPORRANS

Sporrans

In the early days of the Highland regiments, the sporran was a simple and useful purse ('sporan' is Gaelic for purse) made of goatskin or leather. It was not worn on active service. After the Napoleonic Wars the sporran became more elaborate, with metal top and decorative tassels.

The black hair sporran with two white tassels worn by the Queen's Own Highlanders comes from the undress sporran introduced to the 79th Cameron Highlanders in 1856. It is believed to have been modelled originally on a civilian sporran owned by Captain W. H. Campbell of the 79th.

Sporrans — Left: Rank and File hair sporran introduced 1970. Centre: Officers hair sporran. Right: Pipers hair sporran.

The Officers Hair Sporran

The pattern of sporran worn by officers of the Queen's Own Highlanders has a brass top and bells, engraved with thistles, and modelled on the officers sporran worn by the 78th and the Seaforth Highlanders. The badge of the Queen's Own Highlanders is added, flanked by the Cypher of HRH Prince Philip, Duke of Edinburgh, Colonel in Chief of the Regiment.

The Soldiers Hair Sporran

The present pattern of soldiers sporran, with a white metal top, was introduced in 1970 for use by all the Highland regiments; each regiment having its own badge on the sporran top and its own arrangement of tassels. The sporran badge of the Queen's Own Highlanders is the Thistle ensigned with the Crown.

The Pipers Hair Sporran

The pipers wear a distinctive pattern of hair sporran. It has two black tassels on a grey background, the pattern worn by pipers of the 78th Highlanders until 1881, and then by pipers of 2nd Bn Seaforth Highlanders. The tops of the sporrans have a silver edge with three knobs, and are the old 79th Cameron Highlanders pattern of Pipe Fund sporran introduced in 1873. The sporran badge is the Thistle ensigned with the Crown as worn on the soldiers pattern of sporran.

The Leather Sporran

Until World War II the kilt was either worn with the hair sporran or covered with the khaki kilt apron. During the early stages of the war the kilt was worn without a sporran, but soon officers took to wearing the leather sporran, sometimes with leather tassels. (Some battalions had worn them in World War I). After the war a larger leather sporran on a chain was issued to soldiers, but it was soon discontinued.

Officers and sergeants of the Queen's Own Highlanders wear the small leather sporran, with the sporran badge of the Thistle ensigned with the Crown.

LEGDRESS AND SHOES

Diced Hose

The red and white diced hose have been worn by Highland regiments since their earliest days. For many years they were made of red and white cloth, referred to as 'hose tartan', which was cut to shape and sewn up the back of the leg. In 1848 the cloth hose were replaced by knitted woollen hose.

The red and white hose were worn by the 78th (later 72nd) Highlanders from 1778 until they were ordered to give up the Highland dress in 1809, and also by the 78th and 79th Highlanders from the time they were raised in 1793.

The 79th Cameron Highlanders changed from the red and white hose in about 1843 when the Commanding Officer of the 79th, Lt Col The Hon Lauderdale Maule, introduced red and green hose which incorporated the green facings of the regiment. Other regiments followed this idea, the 42nd and the 92nd both changing to red and black hose. The 78th, and their successors the Seaforth Highlanders, did not vary from their red and white hose except for the pipers of the 78th and the 2nd Seaforth who wore MacKenzie hose.

The Queen's Own Highlanders wear the traditional red and white hose, with the exception of the pipers who wear the red and green hose of the 79th Cameron Highlanders.

Lovat Hose

In the First World War khaki hose tops were introduced to replace the diced hose which were difficult to supply and to keep clean in the trenches. The khaki hose were worn until after the second World War when the Highland regiments adopted hose of Lovat green for wear with the kilt in non-ceremonial dress.

Garters

From the earliest days of the Highland regiments, the red and white hose were held up by red garters worn round the top of the hose without a turnover. After the Napoleonic Wars the uniform became more and more ornamental, and the garters were tied in elaborate garter knots, often with rosettes, loops, bows and tails added.

During the Crimean war the conditions of active service in mud and snow resulted in the garters becoming simpler again: the tape was worn under the turnover of the hose, with only the ends, or flashes, showing.

The Queen's Own Highlanders wear the red garter flashes worn by The Queen's Own Cameron Highlanders, except for the pipers who wear the MacKenzie garter flashes worn by pipers of the Seaforth Highlanders.

Highland Shoes

In the early days of the regiment the British Army wore black shoes with buckles, but in 1823 all but the Highland regiments changed to half boots. Highlanders continued to wear buckled shoes until the 1860s, although the shoes were normally worn with spats to keep dirt and stones out of them.

Shoes remained the normal issue to Highland regiments until 1914, although they were often found to be so unsatisfactory for wear on active service that boots were issued instead. In the early days of World War I the Highland regiments replaced their shoes and spats with ankle boots and short puttees. The issue of the present pattern of Highland shoe or brogue (Gaelic for shoe is 'brog') dates from after World War I.

The old style of buckled shoe, which survived as pumps worn in levee dress, has vanished, but brogues with a strap and a toe buckle are still worn by officers and sergeants in mess dress, and by pipers when wearing long hose.

Spats

Gaiters or 'Spatterdashes' were worn by the infantry of the line from the 17th Century, and were designed to protect the soldier's hose and to prevent stones and mud getting into the shoes. The Highland regiments took to wearing grey canvas half-gaiters during the Napoleonic Wars. After about 1818 white linen spats were issued and have changed little in design since then.

The Queen's Own Highlanders wear spats with eight buttons and rounded at the toe, with a white leather strap under the shoe.

Puttees

Puttees (Hindustani for 'bandages') came into use by the army in India in the 1870s. The officers of the 72nd Highlanders wore long puttees of Prince Charles Edward Stuart tartan with their tartan riding breeches in the Afghanistan campaign of 1878-80.

The Highland regiments wore spats with the kilt until 1914, the spats being khaki for field training and whitened for peace time duty in barracks. But, soon after the start of World War I, they took to wearing short puttees with khaki hose tops and boots, because they were more comfortable and practical than spats.

During World War II, and until the 1960s, the web anklet or gaiter was worn with battledress trousers; but these were given up and the more comfortable puttees were reintroduced.

In the Queen's Own Highlanders officers wear Fox's Pale puttees and soldiers wear dark khaki puttees. They can be worn with either kilt, boots and hose tops, or with long trousers.

SWORDS, DIRKS AND ACCOUTREMENTS

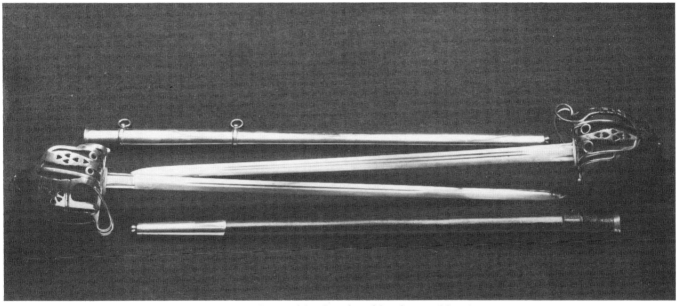

Broadswords — with plated and leather scabbards.

The Broadsword

In the early days of the regiment, the basket-hilted broadsword (often incorrectly termed the 'Claymore') was carried by officers, sergeants, pipers, drummers and bandsmen. It was carried with the shoulder belt or cross belt.

Sergeants carried swords until 1852 and the staff sergeants carried them until the First World War; and the RSM, Bandmaster and Drum Major still carry a sword in ceremonial dress today. The drummers carried swords until 1872, when the Valise equipment was introduced with which the broadsword could not be worn. Pipers carried swords until the late 1870s, the pipers of the 72nd being armed with them in the Afghanistan campaign of 1878-80. The pipers of the Queen's Own Highlanders still wear the black sword belt today. When the Seaforth and Camerons went to war in 1914, officers were at first armed with the broadsword, but it was soon discarded as unsuitable for use in the trenches.

In No. 2 Dress, the normal ceremonial uniform worn by the Queen's Own Highlanders today, the broadsword is worn with a leather scabbard and carried in the sword frog suspended from the Sam Browne belt. In No. 1 Dress it is worn with a plated scabbard and carried on sword slings from the white buff shoulder belt or cross belt. The Drum Major carries the sword slung from the waistbelt with slings.

The broadsword basket hilt has a white buff leather lining covered with red material and edged in Royal blue silk. It has a red fringe. The blade of the broadsword is normally etched with insignia, Royal on one side and regimental on the other.

The Dirk

The dirk is a weapon of great antiquity which was used in the Highlands from about the 15th Century. As an item of regimental dress, however, although it has been carried by officers since the early days of the regiment, it has never been anything but ornamental.

The dirk was carried by pipers, drummers and bandsmen from the 1840s. They were supplied at regimental expense, but since 1881 Ordnance dirks have been available. However the regimental pattern has generally been preferred to the rather plain, heavy pattern of the issue dirk.

In the Queen's Own Highlanders the dirk is worn by field officers in mess dress. Seaforth, Cameron or Queen's Own Highlanders patterns of dirk may be worn. Officers dirks are of ornate gilt, with carved wooden handles, and with a knife and fork in the black leather scabbard; they are mounted with Cairngorms. The blade of the dirk is usually etched with various insignia. The Bandmaster and Pipe Major also wear officers pattern dirks.

The pipers wear the old Cameron pattern of piper's dirk, which are silver mounted but have no knife and fork on the scabbard. The drummers wear Ordnance pattern issue dirks.

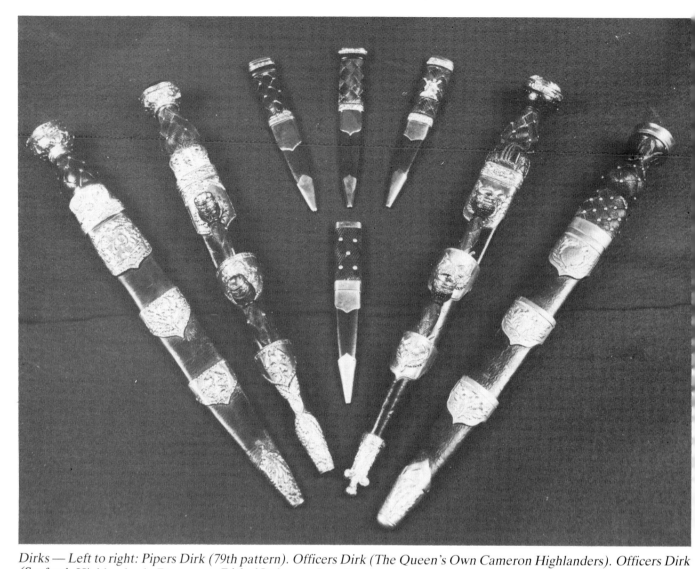

Dirks — Left to right: Pipers Dirk (79th pattern). Officers Dirk (The Queen's Own Cameron Highlanders). Officers Dirk (Seaforth Highlanders). Drummers Dirk (Ordnance Issue).
Sgian Dubh — Top left to right: Officers Sgian Dubh (The Queen's Own Cameron Highlanders). Officers Sgian Dubh (Queen's Own Highlanders). Officers Sgian Dubh (Seaforth Highlanders). Lower: Pipers Sgian Dubh.

The Sgian Dubh

The sgian dubh (Gaelic — Black knife) is not a weapon of any great history. It seems to have come into fashion with civilian Highland dress in about 1822, very probably being a product of the enthusiasm generated by the appearance of King George IV in full Highland dress when he visited Edinburgh. Officers and pipers of the Highland regiments started wearing the sgian dubh from about 1840, when uniforms were becoming increasingly ornamental. It is still worn by officers and pipers of the Queen's Own Highlanders, and by the RSM, Bandmaster and Drum Major.

The pattern of sgian dubh worn by the 78th Highlanders, and after 1881 by the Seaforth Highlanders, had a Cairngorm top and a brass St Andrew and Cross on the handle. The pattern worn from 1840 by the 79th and The Queen's Own Cameron Highlanders had a Cairngorm top, a studded handle, and a brass Sphinx from the 79th battle honour for Egypt 1801.

The present pattern worn by the Queen's Own

Highlanders has a plain studded handle with thistles round the top and bottom of the handle. Officers who have inherited Seaforth or Cameron sgian dubhs are allowed to wear them.

The Kilt Pin

A silver kilt pin of the pattern worn by the Seaforth Highlanders is worn by Officers, the Regimental Sergeant Major, the Bandmaster and the Pipe Major.

The Sash

The red sash which distinguishes the uniform of the officers and sergeants dates back to the 17th Century. In its early days its purpose was to carry a wounded Officer off the battlefield, and a rather doubtful tradition asserts that its red colour was intended to minimise the discolouration caused by blood stains.

In the early days of the regiment, officers and sergeants wore the sash over the left shoulder. The sergeant's sash was red with a stripe of the regimental facing colour; yellow for the 72nd, buff for the 78th and green for the 79th. However these colours tended to fade and to run together when the sash got wet, and so were discontinued in 1845.

In 1856 the War Office ordered that sergeants should wear the sash over the right shoulder. However the Pipe Major and Pipe Sergeant have always continued to wear the sash over the left shoulder, and the reason for this seems to be that the sash was intended to cross diagonally under the sword belt which is still worn by the pipers.

In the Queen's Own Highlanders the red silk sash is worn by officers in No. 1 Dress, over the left shoulder. It is also worn by the RSM, the Bandmaster and the Pipe Major, all over the left shoulder because they wear the cross belt. Sergeants wear the red sash in worsted material over the right shoulder.

The Cromag

It is traditional for the Highland Chief, as symbolic 'shepherd' of his flock, to carry a cromag (Gaelic for a shepherd's crook); and the officer of the Highland regiment has the same symbolic responsibility for his men.

The custom originated in the South African war of 1899-1902 when officers distinctions of dress and arms were discouraged because they presented obvious targets to Boer sharpshooters. Officers discarded their swords and Sam Browne belts and took to carrying walking sticks or cromags instead.

In the Queen's Own Highlanders officers may carry a cromag, thumb stick or ash plant, when on the range or on training out of barracks.

PIPE BANNERS

Piper Banner — Queen's Own Highlanders.

Pipe banners are carried by the pipers on ceremonial occasions. They are attached to the brass drone of the pipes by ribbons.

The banners are buff on the obverse side and blue on the reverse, from the facings colours of the regiment. The regimental badge is embroidered on each side, and the fringe is of buff and blue.

It is the custom for an officer appointed to command a company to have his own banner made. It is carried on parade or in mess by his company piper. The banner remains the property of the officer, and he is allowed to have his personal crest embroidered in the top corner of the reverse side. If he is appointed to command a battalion of the Regiment, or to be Colonel of the Regiment, he is allowed to add the Union flag to his banner, in the top corner of the obverse side.

9. REGIMENTAL PIPE MUSIC

The Pipes and Drums of the 1st Bn Queen's Own Highlanders at Edinburgh 1969, Pipe Major John Allan and Drum Majo[r] Walter Grant.

Although the pipers and the pipe music have been part of the everyday life of the Highland regiments since their origins in the 18th Century there is little evidence about what tunes were played in the early days. Some historians claim that the pipe music played for daily regimental calls was the Ceol Mor (Gaelic — Great music) or piobaireachd as we know it today. By the mid 19th Century the pipers were certainly playing the Ceol Beag (Gaelic — Small music), the marches, strathspeys and reels which were popular with the soldiers. Many of the regimental routine pipe tunes which are played today date from this period.

The 72nd and 78th Highlanders had their own separate lists of regimental pipe tunes. In 1901 an attempt was made to standardise the tunes and settings used when a book of

pipe music 'Duty Calls and Favourite Tunes of the Seafort[h] Highlanders' was published for regimental use, but i[t] contained only the 2nd Battalion tunes. It was the firs[t] book of purely regimental pipe music ever published. I[n] 1911 the two regular battalions agreed on a common list o[f] duty tunes which were embodied in regimental standin[g] orders. The music was subsequently published in 1936 i[n] 'Standard Settings of Pipe Music of The Seafort[h] Highlanders'. It became a standard work for pipe bands.

The Queen's Own Cameron Highlanders also had thei[r] own list of duty tunes and it was published in the Historica[l] Records of the Cameron Highlanders in 1909.

When the Seaforth and Camerons were amalgamated i[n] 1961 to form the Queen's Own Highlanders, a pipe musi[c] committee was formed to decide on the list of pipe tunes to be used in the new regiment. They were selected from the tunes played by the Seaforth and Camerons. The committee also produced a book of bagpipe music 'Queen's Own Highlanders, Standard Settings of Pipe Music' which incorporated the music of both regiments. It too has become a standard work and has been reprinted many times. A second volume of regimental music, 'The Cabar Feidh Collection', which includes many tunes written by members of the regiment since 1961, as well as a large number of tunes which were unpublished or long out of print, complements the 'Standard Settings'.

The Pipes and Drums

When the Highland regiments were raised in the 18th Century, their establishments normally allowed for two drummers per company and also two pipers to the Grenadier company. The pipers were intended to be the equivalent of the two fifers allowed in the line regiments.

The drummers had the important task of giving signals in battle or on the march, by beat of drum or by bugle call. They were, in effect, the equivalent of the regimental signallers of today. When music was required on parade or on the line of march, it was provided by the fifers accompanied by the drum, or by the musicians of the regimental band.

The status of the pipers was largely unofficial, but such was the importance of the bagpipe music to the Highlander, and in particular to the encouragement of the Highland soldiers in battle, that the Highland regiments normally had at least one or two pipers per company. Their duties were to complement the drummers in sounding the calls of daily routine, to encourage the regiment in battle, and to play for soldiers off duty the music which is such an inherent part of Highland life and tradition.

The regimental pipers were given every support by the Colonels and officers of the Highland regiments, with the result that the Highland regiments played a significant part in the revival of bagpipe music after it had been almost extinguished after the Jacobite Rising of 1745-46.

The drummers' key role in the regiment earned them higher pay than the private soldier, and they were normally distinctively dressed in jackets made of cloth of the regimental facings colour. The drummers of the 72nd, for instance, had yellow jackets, the 78th buff, and the 79th Cameron Highlanders green.

The unofficial status of the pipers caused some difficulties. Their bagpipes and dress distinctions had to be paid for by the Colonel and Officers; and variations in dress regularly used to incur adverse comment by inspecting officers. However in 1854, as a result of years of pressure from the Highland regiments, the War Office authorised an establishment of a Pipe Major and five pipers for each Highland regiment.

The official recognition of the pipes coincided with an enormous increase in the popularity of the Ceol beag (Gaelic — small music). Many new quicksteps, strathspeys, reels and jigs were being published and were popular with the regimental pipers. The pipes soon superceded the fifes for playing on the march. It is believed that the technique of combining pipes with drums dates from this period and was the result of the pipes replacing the fifes, and of the new marches and quick steps proving ideal material for pipes and drums to play together for parade and ceremonial music.

However, the pipers and drummers were to remain separately organized for many years to come. The Drum Major and drummers came under the Adjutant for discipline and training. The drum beat was indispensable to route marching but, since World War II, with the decline of the traditional route march as the main form of fitness training, the drummers have lost one of their most important roles: that of beating step on the route march. But, as the military requirements for drumming has dwindled, the popularity of civilian pipe bands has grown, and the art of drumming has developed accordingly. The flamboyant drumming of today, being no longer subject to the constraint of having to give a good steady beat on the march, bears little resemblance to the traditional military style. But it has led to new musical fields for the drummers to develop.

The Pipe Major and pipers were managed by a committee under the Pipe President, and their pipes and distinctive uniforms were paid for by the Pipe Fund to which all officers subscribed. The system still largely applies today. The standard of piping in the regiment has always been a matter of pride, and the regiment boasts an unrivalled list of gold medallists in the field of competitive piping, dating back to the earliest days of the regiments from which Queen's Own Highlanders are descended.

The Pipe Major of every Scottish regiment has to qualify for his Pipe Major's certificate at the Army School of Piping in Edinburgh Castle. The course was first started at Cameron Barracks Inverness in 1910 as the Military Pipers School, under the instruction of Pipe Major John MacDonald, famous as a player and Gold Medallist, and Pipe Major of the 1st Volunteer Bn and 4th Territorial Bn of the Cameron Highlanders for 24 years.

Since World War II, the Pipes and Drums have been combined as a single platoon. On parade they are commanded by the Drum Major, but for musical instruction the pipers and drummers are taught by the Pipe Major and Drum Major respectively. Pipers and drummers have always been fully trained as fighting soldiers, and the Pipes and Drums become a normal infantry platoon on active service. In recent years it has operated as a platoon in Ireland whenever the 1st Battalion has served there. It is traditionally a matter of pride to the pipers and drummers that they maintain equally high standards in their ceremonial and operational roles.

REGIMENTAL TUNES

March Past in quick time — PIBROCH OF DONUIL DUBH

March Past in slow time — THE GARB OF OLD GAUL

The Charge — THE STANDARD ON THE BRAES OF MAR

THE COMPANY MARCHES

A Company — THE DORNOCH LINKS

B Company — THE HIGHLAND BRIGADE AT TEL-EL-KEBIR

C Company — THE BROWN HAIRED MAIDEN

D Company — THE BUGLE HORN

S Company — THE 51st HIGHLAND DIVISION AT WADI AKARIT

HQ Company — FAREWELL TO THE CREEKS

DAILY ROUTINE

Reveille — JOHNNIE COPE

Breakfast — BROSE AND BUTTER

Marching off the Guard — MACDONALD'S AWA TAE THE WAR

Dinner — OVER THE WATER TO CHARLIE

Tea — JENNY'S BAWBEE

Retreat — DARK LOWERS THE NIGHT

Staff Parade — HIGHLAND LADDIE

First Post — 72nd HIGHLANDERS

Last Post — LOCHABER NO MORE

Lights out — SLEEP DEARIE SLEEP

PARADE MUSIC

Half hour to parade — UP AND WAUR THEM ALL WULLIE

Quarter hour to parade — BUNDLE AND GO

Assembly — THE BLUE BONNETS

Fall in — LADS WITH THE KILT

Officers fall in — MACKENZIE HIGHLANDERS

Marching the Colours on and off parade — SCOTLAND THE BRAVE

General Salute — THE POINT OF WAR

Royal Salute — ST ANDREWS CROSS

Inspection tunes — I LOVE THE HIGHLANDS, ISLE OF HEATHER, MIST COVERED MOUNTAINS, MY HOME

March Past in slow time — THE BADGE OF SCOTLAND

March Past in quick time — PIBROCH OF DONUIL DUBH.

Advance in Review Order — THE BLUE BONNETS (3rd Part)

Dispersal from parade — 25th NOVEMBER 1960

TROOPING THE COLOUR

(Additional and alternative tunes are listed under Regimental Band Music)

Keepers of the Ground march on — 72nd HIGHLANDERS

Guards march on — THE INVERNESS GATHERING, THE BLUE BONNETS

WOs and NCOs to the front — THE CAMERON MEN

Officers fall in — MACKENZIE HIGHLANDERS

Officers, WOs and NCOs take post — THE SKYE GATHERING.

General Salute — THE POINT OF WAR

Slow Troop — LOCH DUICH

Quick Troop — CABAR FEIDH

Escort for the Colour marches forward — SCOTLAND THE BRAVE

Trooping the Colour along the line of Guards — ST ANDREW'S CROSS

March Past in slow time — BADGE OF SCOTLAND

March Past in quick time — 79th HIGHLANDERS, PIBROCH OF DONUIL DUBH

Advance in Review order — THE BLUE BONNETS (3rd Part)

Dispersal from parade — THE HIGHLAND BRIGADE AT TEL-EL-KEBIR, 25th NOVEMBER 1960.

CEREMONIAL MUSIC

The Long Reveille

Reveille (Bugles), THE POINT OF WAR, JOHNNIE COPE, UP IN THE MORNING EARLY (Alternatively).

The Crimean Reveille — THE SODGERS RETURN, GRANNY DUNCAN, SAE WILL WE YET, MISS GIRDLE, CHISHOLM CASTLE, HEY JOHNNIE COPE.

Retreat

THE CAMERON MEN, Retreat Call (Bugles), THE POINT OF WAR, The Drummers Call (Drums).

— Retreat Marches — DARK LOWERS THE NIGHT Other Retreat marches as selected

Selection — Slow March, March (Tunes as selected)

Selection — March, Strathspey, Reel, March (Tunes as selected)

March off — CABER FEIDH

Tattoo

March on — March as selected.

First Post — First Post (Bugles), THE POINT OF WAR 72nd HIGHLANDERS

Selection (one or two sets may be played) — Slow March (optional), March, Strathspey, Reel, March (Tunes as selected), THE CAMERON MEN (last march of final set)

Last Post — Last Post (Bugles)

March off — March off without music

MESS DINNER NIGHT

1st Pipes, half an hour before dinner — Officer's Mess — THE RED COAT, Sergeants Mess — CUIDICH 'N RIGH (followed by Retreat air, March, Strathspey and reel set)

2nd Pipes, as dinner is announced — Officers Mess — BANNOCKS OF BARLEYMEAL, Sergeants Mess — CORN RIGS

1st Set — CABAR FEIDH, THE CAMERON MEN. March, Strathspey, Reel, March, (As selected)

Piobaireachd — Piobaireachd as selected.

2nd Set — Slow March, March, Strathspey, (Reel as selected), PIBROCH OF DONUIL DUBH

ENTERING AND LEAVING BARRACKS AND STATIONS

Entering Barracks — CABAR FEIDH, 79th HIGH-LANDERS (Alternately)

Leaving Barracks — WE WILL TAKE THE GOOD OLD WAY

Leaving a station — BUNDLE AND GO, THE 79th's FAREWELL TO GIBRALTAR

PLAYING A DRAFT IN AND OUT OF BARRACKS

Playing in a draft — OH BUT YE'VE BEEN LONG A' COMING

Playing out a draft — THE 79th's FAREWELL TO GIBRALTAR, HAPPY WE'VE BEEN ALL TOGETHER

FUNERALS

Marching to the cemetery — FLOWERS OF THE FOREST, WE WILL RETURN HOME TO KINTAIL, MACGREGOR OF RORO

At the Graveside — LOCHABER NO MORE

The Pipes and Drums and the Regimental Band of 1st Bn Queen's Own Highlanders at Edinburgh Castle 1970.

10.   THE REGIMENTAL BAND MUSIC

Bandman L. Doherty, Lance Corporal D. E. Loftus, Bandsman T. Mayer in Hong Kong 1980.

10. The Regimental Band

The Regimental (or Military) Bands of the British Army originated in the 18th Century as groups of musicians employed by the Colonel and the Officers both for entertainment and to provide music on parade. The band consisted of a group of six or eight musicians, and used the hautbois (a rudimentary form of oboe), French horn, clarinet, bassoon and drum. They were paid, dressed and equipped at the expense of the Colonel and officers. Because the bandsmen were often civilian musicians, and not attested into the Army, they could not be compelled to accompany the regiment on active service and so, unlike Pipers, Drummers and Fifers, they were not expected to fight. Many of them were foreigners, and the band was commonly referred to as 'The German Band'. The bandsmen were dressed in a distinctive uniform, normally white jackets, and from 1830 this became the official dress for bandsmen throughout the Army.

The standard of music in the regimental bands was variable and, until about 1860, depended on the employment of a professional civilian conductor. However in 1857 the Royal Military School of Music was established to train bandmasters and regimental bandsmen, and the British Army has enjoyed an enviably high standard of music in its regimental bands ever since.

The bandsman today is an accomplished and versatile musician. The range of the regimental band's repertoire extends from ceremonial parade music to the latest 'pop' songs and dance tunes. Their music, both on and off parade, is a popular and inherent part of regimental life. In addition to their role as musicians, the bandsmen are trained as medical orderlies and so have an important part to play in wartime.

REGIMENTAL MARCH

The Regimental March of the Queen's Own Highlanders is an arrangement of 'Scotland the Brave' the march of the Seaforth Highlanders, and 'The March of the Cameron Men', the march of The Queen's Own Cameron Highlanders.

PARADE MUSIC

Royal Salute — THE NATIONAL ANTHEM
General Salute — SCOTLAND THE BRAVE
March past in slow time — GARB OF OLD GAUL
March past in quick time — THE REGIMENTAL MARCH
Advance in Review Order — HIGHLAND LADDIE

TROOPING THE COLOUR
(In addition to the tunes for parade)
The Troop-Slow time — LOGIE OF BUCHAN
Escort moving for the Colour — BRITISH GRENADIERS
Escort and Colour move to place in line — THE GRENADIERS MARCH

MESS DINNER NIGHT

Royal Toast — THE NATIONAL ANTHEM
After the programme — MARCH OF THE CAMERON MEN (Sung by bandsmen), Marches of the Guests, RULE BRITANNIA, GARB OF OLD GAUL

ENTERING BARRACKS

Entering Barracks — THE REGIMENTAL MARCH

PLAYING A DRAFT OUT OF BARRACKS

Leaving Barracks — THE GIRL I LEFT BEHIND ME
As the train moves off — AULD LANG SYNE

CHURCH PARADE

Fall in — THE CHRISTCHURCH BELLS, THE OLD 100th PSALM, NOW THANK WE ALL OUR GOD

11. REGIMENTAL TOAST AND SONGS

PIBROCH OF DONUIL DUBH

Piobaireachd Dhomhnuill Duibh, as a pipe tune and Gaelic song, is probably over 500 years old. It has a place in both Clan Cameron and Clan Donald tradition. In Clan Cameron history it is believed to refer to Donald Dubh, traditionally the 11th Chief, who led the clan from about 1400 to 1460.

The well known song was written by Sir Walter Scott in 1816 for Alexander Campbell's 'Albyn's Anthology'. The music was transposed from canntaireachd to staff notation by Alexander Campbell, as a basis for Sir Walter Scott's words, and the well known 6/8 pipe march has evolved from it.

The tune, being particularly good for marching, became popular throughout the Scottish regiments. In the mid 19th Century it was adopted as the March Past of both the 78th Highlanders (Ross-shire Buffs) and the 79th Cameron Highlanders. For the 79th, it had obvious historical associations, but the reason for its use by the 78th has been forgotten; it may simply be that it is such a good marching tune. It later became the March Past of the Seaforth Highlanders.

On the amalgamation of Seaforth and Camerons in 1961 it was selected as the March Past of the Queen's Own Highlanders.

Pibroch o' Donuil Dubh, Pibroch o' Donuil.
Wake thy wild voice anew, summon Clan Conuil.
Come away, come away, hark to the summons! Come in your war array.
  Gentles and Commons!

Come from deep glen, and from mountain so rocky,
The war pipe and pennon are at Inverlochy;
Come ev'ry hill plaid and true heart that wears one.
Come ev'ry steel blade and strong hand that bears one!

Leave untended the herd, the flock without shelter;
Leave the corpse uninterr'd, the bride at the altar;
Leave the deer, leave the steer, leave nets and barges,
Come with your fighting gear, broadswords and targes!

Come as the winds come when forests are rended;
Come as the waves come when navies are stranded;
Faster come, faster come, faster and faster;
Chief, vassal, page and groom, tenant and master!

Fast they come, fast they come, see how they gather!
Wide waves the eagle plume, blended with heather.
Cast your plaids, draw your blades, forward each man set!
Pibroch o' Donuil Dubh, knell for the onset!

THE REGIMENTAL TOAST OF THE QUEEN'S OWN HIGHLANDERS

The Regimental Gaelic toast is believed to have been used from the earliest days of the 78th or Earl of Seaforth's Highland Regiment, and to have been used by the Clan Mackenzie before that. It is used on occasions such as the regimental ceremony to welcome the New Year, and an abbreviated form is given by the Pipe Major when he has played the pibroch at a mess dinner.

"Tir nam Beann, nan Gleann, 's nan Gaisgeach;
  Far am faighear an t-eun fionn,
  'S far am faigh am fiadh fasgadh.
  Cho fada 's chitear ceo mu bheann
  'S a ruitheas uisge le gleann.
  Mairidh cuimhne air cuchd nan treun.
  Slàinte agus buaidh gu bràth
  Le Gillean Chabar Fēidh!
      Cabar Fēidh gu Bràth!"

"The Land of Hills, Glens and Heroes;
Where the Ptarmigan thrives
And where the red deer finds shelter.
As long as mist hangs o'er the Mountains
And water runs in the glens,
The Deeds of the Brave will be remembered.
Health and Success for ever
To the lads of 'Cabar Fēidh'."
      CABAR FEIDH GU BRATH!
      (The Deer's Horns for Ever!)

THE MARCH OF THE CAMERON MEN

The song 'The March of the Cameron Men' was written by Miss Mary Maxwell Campbell in about 1829. It has been translated into Gaelic. The song is sung by the Regimental Band as part of the programme of music after dinner, when playing in mess.

The tune is also set as a 6/8 march for the pipes, and is used as a Regimental pipe tune.

There's many a man of the Cameron Clan
That has followed his chief to the field;
He has sworn to support him or die by his side,
For a Cameron never can yield.

  I hear the pibroch sounding, sounding,
  Deep o'er the mountain and glen,
    While light-springing footsteps are trampling the heath,
    'Tis the march of the "Cameron Men."

Oh! proudly they walk; but each Cameron knows
He may tread on the heather no more;
But boldly he follows his chief to the field,
Where his laurels were gather'd before.

  I hear the pibroch, &c.

The moon has arisen, it shines o'er the path
Now trod by the gallant and true;
High, high are their hopes, for their chieftain hath said,
That whatever men dare they can do.

  I hear the pibroch, &c.

12. REFERENCES

SEAFORTH HIGHLANDERS

Title	Author	Publisher	Date
Historical Record of the 72nd Regiment	Richard Cannon	Parker, Furnival & Parker	1848
Historical Records of the 72nd Highlanders	(Manuscript Records of the Regiment printed privately)	William Blackwood & Sons	1886
Historical Records of the 78th Highlanders	James MacVeigh	J. Maxwell & Sons	1887
Rules and Records of the Officers Mess, 72nd Regiment	(Printed for private circulation)	William Blackwood & Sons	1896
History and Services of the 78th Highlanders (2 volumes)	Major H. Davidson	W. & A. K. Johnston	1901
The Seaforth Highlanders in South Africa 1899-1902	Edited by Major H. Davidson	W. & A. K. Johnston	1904
History of the 3rd Volunteer Bn, Seaforth Highlanders 1860-1906	AJCC and AMS	Northern Scot, Elgin	1906
With the Seaforth Highlanders in the Sudan Campaign	Maj Gen Granville Egerton	Eden Fisher & Co. Ltd.	1909
Betting Book of the Officers Mess 78th Highlanders 1822-1908	(Printed for private circulation)	St. Catherine Press Ltd.	1909
A Short History of the Seaforth Highlanders	Col G. MacKintosh and Capt W. M. Thomson	St. Catherine Press Ltd.	1909
Great Deeds of the Seaforth Highlanders	F. W. Walker	J. M. Dent & Sons Ltd.	1915
War Diary of the 5th Seaforth Highlanders	Capt D. Sutherland	John Lane	1920
Seaforth Highlanders of Canada	Bernard McEvoy and Capt A. H. Findlay	Cowan and Brookhouse	1920
6th Seaforth Highlanders, Campaign Reminiscences	Capt R. T. Peel and Capt A. H. Macdonald	W. R. Walker & Co.	1923
Pipers and Pipe Music in a Highland Regiment	Maj I. H. MacKay Scobie	Ross-shire Printing and Publishing Co. Ltd.	1924
A History of the 4th Bn Seaforth Highlanders	Lt Col M. M. Haldane	H. T. & G. Witherby	1927
10th Bn Seaforth Highlanders in the Great War	Lt Col C. L. Addison-Smith	J. Bain & Sons	1927
A Short History of the Seaforth Highlanders	Col C. S. Nairne	Ross-shire Printing and Publishing Co. Ltd.	1928
Sans Peur (History of the 5th Seaforth Highlanders in World War II)	Alastair Borthwick	Eneas MacKay	1946
Seaforth Highlanders	Col John Sym	Gale & Polden	1962
The Seaforth Highlanders of Canada 1919-1965	R. H. Roy	Evergreen Press, Vancouver	1969

THE QUEEN'S OWN CAMERON HIGHLANDERS

Title	Author	Publisher	Date
Alphabetical List of Officers of the 79th, 1800-1851	H. Stooks-Smith	Simpkin, Marshall & Co.	1852
Historical Records of the 79th Regiment or Cameron Highlanders	Capt R. Jameson	William Blackwood & Sons	1863
Narrative of the part taken by the 79th Queen's Own Cameron Highlanders in the Egyptian Campaign 1882	Capt K. S. Baynes	Printed Privately	1883
Historical Records of the 79th Queen's Own Cameron Highlanders	Capt T. A. MacKenzie, Lt J. S. Ewart, Lt C. Finlay	Hamilton Adams & Co.	1887
Historical Records of the 79th Highlanders, 1793-1888	James MacVeigh	Maxwell & Sons, Dumfries	1888
79th Highlanders in the Indian Mutiny	Capt Douglas Wimberley	Highland Monthly Magazine, Inverness	1891

Title	Author	Publisher	Date
Illustrated Histories of the Scottish Regiments — No. 3. The Queen's Own Cameron Highlanders	Lt Col Percy Groves	W. & A. K. Johnston	1893
South African War Record of the 1st Bn Queen's Own Cameron Highlanders	Maj N. J. G. Cameron	Northern Counties Printing Co.	1903
A Short Regimental History	Lt A. H. MacKintosh		C.1906
Historical Records of the Cameron Highlanders 1793-1908 (Vols I & II)	Historical Records Committee	William Blackwood & Sons	1909
Cameron Highlanders. Officers Present at Campaigns, Battles etc.	Maj S. S. Clarke	William Blackwood & Sons	1913
The Sixth Cameron Highlanders Souvenir Book	WDR	Spottiswoode & Co. Ltd.	1916
History of the 7th (S) Bn Queen's Own Cameron Highlanders	Col J. W. Sandilands & Lt Col N. MacLeod	Eneas MacKay	1922
Queen's Own Cameron Highlanders. A Short Regimental History	Lt Gen Sir Spencer Ewart	Northern Counties Printing Co.	1927
History of the Liverpool Scottish (TA)	Lt Col A. M. McGilchrist	Henry Young & Sons	1930
Historical Records of the Cameron Highlanders (Vols III & IV) 1908-1931	Historical Records Committee	William Blackwood & Sons	1931
War History of the 6th (S) Bn Queen's Own Cameron Highlanders	Lt Col N. MacLeod	William Blackwood & Sons	1934
The Queen's Own Cameron Highlanders of Canada	Lt Col J. D. Sinclair	Winnipeg	1935
The 5th (S) Bn Camerons	Capt J. H. F. McEwen, MP	David Macdonald Ltd.	1938
4th Bn Queen's Own Cameron Highlanders TA. A Short History		Inverness Chronicle	C.1947
History of the 1st Bn Cameron Highlanders of Ottawa (MG)	Lt Col R. M. Ross	Runge Press, Ottawa	C.1947
Queen's Own Cameron Highlanders. A Short History	Re-edited by Col R. D. M. C. Miers	Northern Counties Printing Co.	1948
Historical Records of the Cameron Highlanders (Vols V & VI) 1932-1948	Historical Records Committee	William Blackwood & Sons	1952
The Heart is Highland	Maj A. F. MacGillivray (editor)	Morecambe Bay Printers	1954
Whatever Men Dare. A History of The Queen's Own Cameron Highlanders of Canada 1935-1960	R. W. Queen-Hughes	Bulman Bros., Winnipeg	1960
Biographical List of Officers (other than Regular, Militia and Territorial) of The Queen's Own Cameron Highlanders	Col M. J. H. Wilson	Highland Printers Ltd.	1960
Historical Records of the Cameron Highlanders (Vol VII) 1949-1961	Historical Records Committee	William Blackwood & Sons	1962
Historical Records of the Cameron Highlanders (Vol VII) (Addenda and Corrigenda)	Historical Records Committee	—	1975
Charlie Company — In service with C Company 2nd Queen's Own Cameron Highlanders 1940-44	Maj J. A. Cochrane	Chatto & Windus	1977
The Raising of the 79th Highlanders	Mrs D. A. L. MacLean of Dochgarroch	Society of West Highland and Island Historical Research	1980

QUEEN'S OWN HIGHLANDERS (SEAFORTH AND CAMERONS)

Queen's Own Highlanders. A Short History	Regimental Headquarters	Highland Printers, Inverness	1961
Queen's Own Highlanders. A Short History (2nd Edition)	Regimental Headquarters	John Eccles, Inverness	1973
Queen's Own Highlanders 1961-1971	Regimental Headquarters	A. Learmonth & Son	1971
An Introduction to the Queen's Own Highlanders	Regimental Headquarters	Pilgrim Press Ltd.	1975
Queen's Own Highlanders (Bicentenary Booklet)	Regimental Headquarters	John Eccles, Inverness	1978

REGIMENTAL JOURNALS

'*Cabar Feidh*' The Regimental Magazine of the Seaforth Highlanders (109 Issues) — January 1922 to October 1960

'*The 79th News*' The Journal of The Queen's Own Cameron Highlanders (288 Issues) — April 1891 to September 1960

'*The Queen's Own Highlander*' The Regimental Journal of the Queen's Own Highlanders — Since May 1961

WAR DIARIES — WORLD WAR I AND WORLD WAR II

World War I		World War II	
1st Seaforth	1st Camerons	1st Seaforth	1st Camerons
2nd Seaforth	2nd Camerons	2nd Seaforth	2nd Camerons
1/4th Seaforth	1/4th Camerons	4th Seaforth	4th Camerons
1/5th Seaforth	5th Camerons	5th Seaforth	5th Camerons
1/6th Seaforth	6th Camerons	6th Seaforth	
7th Seaforth	7th Camerons	7th Seaforth	
8th Seaforth	9th Camerons		
9th Seaforth	10th Camerons		
1st Garrison Bn Seaforth	11th Camerons		
	1/10th Liverpool Scottish		
	2/10th Liverpool Scottish		

13. SOURCES OF INFORMATION

The main sources of the references given are listed below. Researchers or enquirers are advised to make appointments by letter beforehand.

Regimental Headquarters,
Queen's Own Highlanders
Cameron Barracks
Inverness IV2 3XD

The Scottish United Services Museum
The Castle
Edinburgh EH1 2YT

The Imperial War Museum
Lambeth Road
London SE1

The Ministry of Defence (Army) Library
Old War Office Building
Whitehall
London SW1

The National Army Museum
Royal Hospital Road
Chelsea
London SW3 4HT